M000027504

Knowledge

Knowledge

Ian Evans
and
Nicholas D. Smith

polity

The right of Ian Evans and Nicholas D. Smith to be identified as Author of this Work has been asserted in accordance with the UK Copyright, Designs and Patents Act 1988.

First published in 2012 by Polity Press

Polity Press
65 Bridge Street
Cambridge CB2 1UR, UK

Polity Press
350 Main Street
Malden, MA 02148, USA

ISBN-13: 978-0-7456-5052-4
ISBN-13: 978-0-7456-5053-1(pb)

A catalogue record for this book is available from the British Library.

Typeset in 10.5 on 12 pt Sabon by Toppan Best-set Premedia Limited

Printed and bound in Great Britain by MPG Books Group Limited, Bodmin, Cornwall

The publisher has used its best endeavours to ensure that the URLs for external websites referred to in this book are correct and active at the time of going to press. However, the publisher has no responsibility for the websites and can make no guarantee that a site will remain live or that the content is or will remain appropriate.

Every effort has been made to trace all copyright holders, but if any have been inadvertently overlooked the publisher will be pleased to include any necessary credits in any subsequent reprint or edition.

For further information on Polity, visit our website: www.politybooks.com

Contents

check

1

Introduction to the Theory of Knowledge

Philosophy, from its earliest times, has made greater claims,
and achieved fewer results, than any other branch of learning.

Russell 1929: 3

1.1 The Theory of Knowledge: Some Disclaimers

Our project in this book belongs to epistemology, which is
the philosophical study of cognition (including belief, knowledge, perception, and other cognitions). More specifically,
our project is to provide an up-to-date introduction to the
theory of knowledge. But our target is a moving one: epistemology continues to be one of the most active areas in contemporary philosophy, and so as we write this book it becomes
obsolete, as new arguments and proposals in the area we seek
to cover are published by epistemologists even as we try to
report them as accurately and currently as we can. Accordingly, there is a kind of irony in what we provide here: we
seek to explain knowledge, but in the end we cannot claim
to know that what we say in this book is correct. So what
we shall offer herein is a *theory* – a theory of knowledge. But
it is only a theory, and theorizing in this field continues in

such a way as almost certainly to reveal shortcomings in the theory we eventually come to offer.

Even so, we can promise more than just what, sooner or later, will probably be revealed as a faulty theory. For we will survey many of the arguments and theories other epistemologists have offered about knowledge, and we will offer to our readers arguments for why our own theory should be preferred to others. When epistemologists offer arguments for their theories, they also allow and invite other epistemologists to detect and critique what may have gone wrong – or what may be inadequate – in that theory. So, the way in which epistemology advances and makes progress is mostly through the critical assessment of preceding arguments and theories. The result is that epistemologists can become quite good at figuring out what is wrong with other arguments and theories – without necessarily becoming expert in articulating completely correct or final arguments and theories in this subject matter. It is a kind of backing into the future, as it were. We don't necessarily see where we are going, but we can have a very good idea of where we have been and why we need to keep going.

Now, one of the most important instruments epistemologists use in order to test arguments and theories is called the "thought-experiment." Thought-experiments rely on our intuitions about the subjects they treat, and insofar as we have clear and strong shared intuitions about the subject of knowledge, our intuitions can be very helpful as we try to formulate our arguments and theories. But appeals to intuitions have important drawbacks, and these have become matters of increasing significance as the field of epistemology has developed. We will have several occasions in this book to use appeals to intuitions as we criticize certain arguments and theories and make our own arguments, but we will also occasionally pause to reflect on the question of whether or not appeals to intuitions are perhaps causing more problems than they are solving, and consider what our alternatives at that point might be.

To help to see how and why appeals to intuitions can sometimes cause serious problems in the process of philosophizing about knowledge, consider the famous paradox of the preface. The way this paradox works is to show how our intuitions lead us into an inconsistent set of judgments. The paradox begins by imagining an author who is writing the preface to a book she has now completed. The book, to which she has dedicated years of hard work and careful thought, represents her own best judgments on a subject in which she is an expert. But just as we have already done in this introduction, the author in the paradox finds herself reflective about how the field in which her book will make its contribution continues to grow and develop. So, our author decides to make a certain disclaimer in her preface. She writes:

> As I sit here now thinking about all that I have written in this book, I sincerely believe that **each sentence I have written is the truth, the whole truth, and nothing but the truth.** Indeed, I have gone back through the claims I have made in this book over and over and over again to ascertain that none of them is false. And yet, as hard as I have tried, surely at least once – and probably more than once – *I have failed to achieve my goal and have said something herein that is false.*

Our author's claim here seems appropriately modest and thoroughly reasonable. But look more closely at what we have put into boldface and compare it to what we have put into italics. She has asserted both that:

(a)   Each sentence in the book is true,

and

(b)   At least one sentence in the book is false.

Intuitively, it seems quite reasonable for our author to believe (a), given how hard she has worked on her book. It is also quite reasonable for her to believe (b) – after all, she is only human, and her field is an active and progressing one. However, (a) and (b) are inconsistent: it can't be the case that both (a) and (b) are true. And, we think, inconsistent beliefs are unreasonable: we could challenge the author by asking her how she can reasonably believe both (a) and (b) while recognizing that they cannot both be true. So here we have three intuitions that can't all be correct:

1. The author is reasonable to believe that (**a**).
2. The author is reasonable to believe that (**b**).
3. It is unreasonable to hold obviously inconsistent beliefs.

This is the *paradox* of the preface. It seems that one of our intuitions must be incorrect – but which one? Well, if confronted with the paradox she has created, our author would probably disavow (**a**) in favor of (**b**). So maybe it's not so intuitive that the author is reasonable to believe (**a**), maybe such epistemic immodesty is unreasonable – that is, maybe we should deny intuition **1**. Unfortunately, this will not resolve the paradox. Suppose we go through her book and ask her about each sentence. We'll find that, for all *n* sentences of the book, she believes that:

(**a₁**) Sentence 1 is true.
(**a₂**) Sentence 2 is true.
(**a₃**) Sentence 3 is true.
. . .
(**aₙ**) Sentence n is true.

Intuitively, each of these beliefs is reasonable: each sentence is the result of meticulous research on the author's part. But, once again, (**a₁**) through (**aₙ**) and (**b**) cannot all be true: after all, (**b**) *says* that one of (**a₁**) through (**aₙ**) is false! So we still have three inconsistent intuitions:

1*. The author is reasonable to believe each of (**a₁**) through (**aₙ**).
 2. The author is reasonable to believe that (**b**).
 3. It is unreasonable to have obviously inconsistent beliefs.

This is not the place to resolve the paradox of the preface. The lesson to draw for now is that in this case (and many other cases we will consider in this book), if we *only* appeal to intuitions to derive our conclusions as we theorize about knowledge, we run the risk of error and inconsistency, as our intuitions themselves may contain errors and inconsistencies. This, then, is one risk our methodology faces, and we will do well to be aware of this risk as we proceed.

1.2 A Preliminary Theory

One way to begin to theorize about knowledge is to begin with a kind of preliminary theory and then consider the various ways in which that theory seems to need modification or further clarification. It is fairly standard practice, accordingly, to begin with a theory which had its first expression in Plato's dialogue, the *Meno*. This theory, call it the *true belief theory* ("TB," for short), is as follows:

TB. *S* knows that *p* just in case:
1. ⌜*p*⌝ is true.[1]
   and
2. *S* believes that *p*.

TB has this much going for it: 1 and 2 both appear to be *necessary* for *S* to know that *p*. How could you know that your mother's birthday is July 9 if it's *not true* that your mother's birthday is July 9? If you thought your mother's birthday was July 9 when it in fact was July 15, we would say that you don't know your own mother's birthday. Further, supposing your mother's birthday is July 9, how could you know this if you didn't at least *believe* it? If you believed that her birthday was not July 9 (or simply had no belief at all about her birthday), then you surely would not *know* that her birthday is July 9. But even if 1 and 2 are necessary for knowledge, we still need to ask whether they are *sufficient* – is a true belief that *p* *all there is* to knowing that *p*? If not, TB is at best an incomplete theory of knowledge.

As Socrates notes in the *Meno*, true belief is good enough to get one from one place to another (in Plato's example, from Athens to Larissa, in Greece). One who *knew* the way to Larissa would not give better advice about how to get there than one who simply had a true belief about how to get there. But there is still a difference, Socrates says, between one who knows and one who merely has true belief.

> True beliefs, so long as they remain with us, are good to have and what they produce is good, but they're not willing to remain for long and they run away from the person's soul, so

that they're not worth much until one ties them down with an explanation of why. (Plato, *Meno* 97e–98a; trans. N. D. Smith)

Socrates' objection seems to be that true beliefs can too easily turn into false beliefs unless something else – something that can explain the belief in some way – can be added to secure the belief. Contemporary epistemologists make a similar point by saying that it might only be a bit of good luck that a belief is true. For example, suppose Tom really hopes that he has enough money in his wallet for lunch, but has no reason to think so and doesn't bother to check. Still, Tom is prone to wishful thinking and believes that he has $10 in his wallet – more than enough for lunch. It just so happens that Tom *does* have $10 in his wallet; but does he *know* that he has $10 in his wallet? It seems that he doesn't. Suppose we asked him, "Tom, how do you know you have $10 in your wallet?" What could he say? He has no reason to believe as he does and, given the unreliability of wishful thinking, most times he comes to have beliefs in this way, his beliefs will be false. Tom does not know; he made a lucky guess. Beliefs that are true by luck are not knowledge.[2] So something else is needed to turn true belief into knowledge. This "something else" has come to be known in epistemology as "warrant."[3] A precise (but uninformative) definition of "warrant" may now be given:

- **Warrant** = whatever it is that differentiates knowledge from other forms of true belief

Given this definition, we can now also provide an obviously uninformative definition of knowledge:

- **Knowledge** = Warranted true belief

This definition preserves what seemed correct in **TB**, by retaining true belief as necessary for knowledge, but now adds an additional condition. As we have acknowledged, this definition is not terribly informative – something must be said about what warrant is. In fact, we will try to show that this definition is not only incomplete, but is also misleading in several ways. But it is a start. We may as well accept this definition as a working hypothesis and begin to look more closely at its features, which are three. Let us break the definition down into distinct conditions and include reference to a knower (*S*) and thing known (*p*). This gets us the *warranted true belief* account of knowledge ("**WTB**," for short):

> **WTB.** *S* knows that *p* just in case:
> (1) ⌜*p*⌝ is true,
> (2) *S* believes that *p*,
>   and
> (3) *S* is warranted in believing that *p*.

1.3   What Kind of Knowledge is This?

Before we inspect the individual conditions of **WTB**, it is worth noting that the analysis only concerns a *certain kind of knowledge*. The analysis says what it is for *S* to know that *p*. This is knowledge that a proposition is true. Philosophers accordingly call this kind of knowledge *propositional knowledge*. But there may well be other kinds of knowledge. **WTB** may not tell us, for example, what it is for *S* to know how to *F* (*know-how*), or what it is for *S* to know *T* (*knowledge by acquaintaince*; where *T* stands for a person, place, or thing), or what it is for *S* to *know what X* is, where *X* is a thing of a certain sort, such that *S* knows what sort of thing *X* is, or what it is for *S* to *know where Z* is (*know-where*). It also may not tell us about *contrastive* or *discriminatory* knowledge – for example, the kind of knowledge that allows us to know that something is a swallow, rather than a chicken.[4] Perhaps there is some relation between propositional knowledge and these other kinds of knowledge, and perhaps not.[5] At any rate, we make no attempt here to explain what such connections might be. Some of these different kinds of knowledge seem to us to fall outside the scope of the analysis we propose to give in this book – for example, knowledge by acquaintance. But others, such as *knowing where*, *knowing what*, and *discriminatory knowledge* seem to us to be directly and obviously pertinent to the general question we try to answer in this book, which is, "what is knowledge"?

WTB tells us about propositional knowledge – knowledge that *p*, where *p* stands for some proposition. But what are propositions? An unhelpful answer is that they're the things of which we have (or lack!) propositional knowledge. A more helpful answer begins by telling us what propositions are *not*: they're not sentences. To see why, suppose our variable "*p*" stood for sentences. Now consider Tom, a speaker of English but not Spanish, who knows that the cat is in the kitchen. Suppose Angel, a speaker of Spanish but not English, also knows that the cat is in the kitchen. There are two sentences, one in English and one in Spanish, that tell us that the cat is in the kitchen:

1. The cat is in the kitchen.
2. El gato esta en la cocina.

Plainly, 1 and 2 are different sentences: they have different arrangements of letters, they sound different, they look different, *they're in different languages*, and so on. Tom understands 1 but not 2 while Angel understands 2 but not 1. So, if what they know are sentences, Tom knows 1 but not 2 while Angel knows 2 but not 1. This, however, is absurd. Intuitively, Tom and Angel know the same thing: that the cat is in the kitchen! So it cannot be sentences that are the objects of knowledge. (Note that we are here already relying on intuitions!)

But notice that sentences 1 and 2 *say the same thing* or *express the same thought* or *are true in the same circumstances*. So there is some *thing* that both sentences say or some *thought* that they both express or some *circumstances* in which they're both true. This thing (or thought or set of circumstances) is a proposition: the proposition that the cat is in the kitchen. Sentences *express* propositions and different sentences (even in different languages) can express the same thing. Though Tom and Angel would express their knowledge in different ways, what they both know is that the cat is in the kitchen; so, "that the cat is in the kitchen" refers to a *proposition* and not a sentence in some particular language.

But the whole idea of propositions has troubled some philosophers. Just what *are* these shadowy creatures that aren't the ordinary sentences we're familiar with but are somehow "expressed" by them? And is it really true that "the cat is in the kitchen" says exactly the same thing as "el gato esta en la cocina" – perhaps "gato" has connotations in Spanish that "cat" does not have in English? Setting such metaphysical and linguistic worries aside, we will soon give a different reason for thinking that our analysis should not refer to propositions. Instead, we think knowledge should be conceived strictly in terms of *information*. But first we need to take a detour through the concept of *truth*.

1.4   The Truth Condition – What is Truth?

Our preliminary analysis posits that knowledge has a truth condition. In other words, what is known must be true and not false. (Note that this does not mean that we cannot know that something is false. Perhaps we know that "The moon is made of green cheese" is false. But if we do know this, it does not violate our first condition, because what we know is *not* that the "moon is made of green cheese" is true, but rather that "'the moon is made of green cheese' is false" is true.)

Of course, people sometimes make knowledge claims that violate the truth condition, and we all understand them perfectly well even when they do. This is actually an important point, and it will help to clarify better what we are trying to do in this book. Consider the coach whose team lost after blowing a big lead in the final minutes of an important game. He might tell the press afterwards, "I knew we were going to win," as part of his explanation of why he failed to make the kinds of adjustments in the closing minutes that might have made the winning difference. We understand what he is saying, and so we might conclude that the coach has used a perfectly acceptable use of the English verb "to know."

Our purpose in this book is not to adjudicate what is or what is not a proper use of the English verb "to know," and so cases such as the coach actually make no difference to us, because such cases do not really show that knowledge doesn't have truth as a necessary condition. To be clear: our purpose in this book is to provide a *conceptual analysis* of knowledge; our purpose is not to provide a survey of all of the ways people might use the word "knowledge." So we concede from the outset that there may be some ways in which people use the relevant words that will fall outside of our analysis. But their doing so is of no consequence to our analysis.

To see why this is, return to the case of the coach. Does what he said to the press show that knowledge does not require truth? It would do so only if such assertions are literally true; but we say plenty of things that are acceptable though literally false, for example:

> F. "I'm not *hungry* – I'm *famished!*"

Of course, if someone is famished, then they are hungry; *very* hungry, in fact. So the sentence is literally false (imagine if someone said "I'm famished, but I'm not very hungry" – we wouldn't know what they meant!). But it can be acceptable to say F because it's an emphatic way of saying something else:

> F*. "I'm not *merely* hungry – I'm so hungry that I'm famished!"

When someone says something like F, we know that they mean something like F*, which could very well be true. So perhaps what the coach said is literally false, but he means something else, something like, "I was very confident we were going to win – so confident that I didn't even consider the possibility that we might not."

But why *shouldn't* we take the coach's assertion as the literal truth? Again, we resort to an appeal to intuitions: it seems extremely counterintuitive to judge that the coach knew his team would win *even though they lost*. And if someone challenged our verdict, asking us, "Well, why do you think he didn't know?," we would simply point to the fact that he was *mistaken* – his team lost; they didn't win. Maybe he *thought* he knew; but he didn't know. The coach, then, poses no threat to the truth condition. Whether or not he has misused the verb "to know," however, is another matter – one for linguists, and not epistemologists, to determine.

But an appeal to the truth condition faces another concern. In this book, we attempt to provide an analysis of knowledge. In the preliminary version of such an analysis, we have proposed a truth condition. What if someone now challenges us to provide an analysis of truth, lest we be charged with providing an incomplete analysis? It is easy enough to see the underlying worry here. If someone claims to provide an analysis of X in terms of Y, but leaves the concept of Y unanalyzed, it's tempting to think they haven't finished the job: the analysis won't help anyone who doesn't know what Y is!

But this challenge isn't entirely fair. Within any analysis, some concepts must be left unanalyzed. After all, if absolutely every concept within an analysis must itself be analyzed then either the analysis will go in circles, or else it can never be concluded.

Circles:
1. x is G_1 just in case x is G_2
2. x is G_2 just in case x is G_3
3. x is G_3 just in case x is G_1

Never concluding:
1. x is G_1 just in case x is G_2
2. x is G_2 just in case x is G_3
3. x is G_3 just in case x is G_4 . . . and so on

Clearly, an analysis that goes in circles is of little value, even though it leaves no term unanalyzed. A never-concluding analysis – a so-called *infinite regress* – is equally unsatisfactory: even if such an analysis were correct, no human could ever comprehend the whole thing, because the whole is infinite in scope.

So any useful, human-readable analysis must leave some concepts unanalyzed. The fact that we do not offer an analysis of truth, then, is not in itself an objection. We must, however, be careful about the concepts we choose to leave unanalyzed: if a concept we leave unanalyzed is very obscure or problematic, it won't help to use it in our analysis. Is the notion of truth very obscure or problematic?

The notion of truth we have in mind is, on its face, straight-forward: it is the notion of something's being the case. It is the concept we use when we ask a friend whether she was telling the truth or when a newspaper reports that recent statements by the government are false. While there may often be great uncertainty and disagreement about which things are true, at least we all seem to understand what we mean when we ask whether something is true.

1.5   Truth, Propositions, and Information

But there is a second problem with truth, and this one leads us to a special worry about analyzing knowledge in terms of propositions. To begin to see what this other problem is, consider the question, what sorts of things are *true*? One answer to this question, as we have seen, is "propositions." Propositions, recall, are the thoughts expressed by (or the statements made by) sentences, and purport to represent states of affairs: the proposition expressed by "the cat is in the kitchen" represents the state of affairs of the cat's being in the kitchen. The proposition is true if this state of affairs obtains – if the cat is, in fact, in the kitchen – and false oth-erwise. But there are other ways to represent this state of affairs: we could make a drawing of the cat in the kitchen, for example. Does it make sense to ask whether the drawing is true? Not really; we might ask whether the drawing is *accurate*, but a drawing just isn't the sort of thing that can be true or false.

This rather obvious observation becomes critically impor-tant, however, when we ask a question to which we will return many times in this book, namely, "can (non-human) animals know anything?" Consider the cat again, sitting in the sunlight in the kitchen. Let us name him Wooj. Wooj feels the familiar urge, and trots down the hall to his litter box. He digs and scratches at the litter in the box, does his busi-ness, then buries it and returns to his favorite napping place in the kitchen. Question: does Wooj know where his litter box is? Now, of course, we cannot simply "go into Wooj's head," as it were, to see what exactly is going on as he finds his way to his litter box. What we can do is observe his behavior, and find that Wooj is remarkably good at finding and using his litter box. One vivid expression of the conclusion that non-human animals can and do know things has been made by Fred Dretske:

> Cats can see. Dogs know things. Fido remembers where he buried his bone. That is why he is digging near the bush. Kitty knows where the mouse ran. That is why she waits patiently in front of the hole. [..] (Dretske 1991: 15)

Dretske's view seems to be that the most obviously correct explanation of *why* the dog is digging near the bush, and of *why* the cat waits near the mouse hole, is that these animals know something. Similarly, we might suppose that it is perfectly obvious *why* Wooj is so good at finding his litter box when he needs it, namely, it is because he knows where it is. Wooj knows that his litter box is in the laundry room.

But Wooj probably does not possess the concept of a laundry room, in which case he can't think the thought "My litter box is in the laundry room." Perhaps Wooj doesn't even think in propositions at all – perhaps Wooj's thoughts are more like drawings or a map. Certainly, many philosophers have doubted that animals have thoughts with propositional structure. This creates problems for our preliminary analysis of knowledge. Our analysis requires believing a true proposition. If Wooj doesn't "do" propositions, our analysis says that he doesn't know. If we want to leave open the question of whether or not animals like cats can know things, our preliminary analysis (**WTB**) is not such a good start, after all.

Whether or not Wooj believes the proposition that his litter box is in the laundry room, it is clear that Wooj's cognitive system *in some way* represents the fact that his litter box is in the laundry room. If his cognitive representation is not propositional, then it is not capable of being true or false. This is not to say that Wooj can't make an error – he can: for example, he is always given some canned food at noon, but since Wooj can't tell time very well, he sometimes begins to cry for food an hour or so before noon. When he does this, he is mistaken about whether it is time for his canned food. But the mistake he makes is not one of believing a false sentence or proposition. His mistake is an *inaccurate representation*. Whatever form Wooj's representations take, they are capable of being accurate or innacurate.

When Wooj represents his litter box as being in the laundry room, things are the way he represents them as being; that's why we are inclined to say that he knows. It is not truth per se, but accuracy that matters for knowledge. It is best, then, to regard our target not as an analysis of *propositional* knowledge, but as an analysis of *informational* knowledge, because non-linguistic animals certainly process information, even if they do not engage in processing such information via language or propositions. This means that we already need to modify the truth condition in **WTB**, our preliminary theory.

One step we might take is to replace the truth condition with an accuracy condition:

- S knows that p only if S's representation of the information that p is accurate.

A problem with this solution is that accuracy comes in degrees – one drawing can be more accurate than another. But it might be thought that knowledge is not a matter of degree. We might think that one person can't know that cats are animals more than another person: you either know it or you don't. So maybe we could try to "tame" the problem of degrees of accuracy in our account of knowledge by specifying a minimum degree of accuracy:

- S knows that p only if S's representation of p is at least n% accurate.

Anything above n% would count as knowledge, while anything below wouldn't. But what's the right degree of accuracy? How do we measure degrees of accuracy? These questions are difficult and it would be best to avoid them. Fortunately, this is easy. We don't need to appeal to truth at all, if we understand the requirement this way:

NT. S knows that p only if p.

Notice that **NT** says nothing at all about truth or even accuracy. For Wooj to know that his litter box is in the laundry room, his litter box must be in the laundry room. This is enough to account for what was intuitive about the truth condition, but notice there's no need for explicit mention of truth or degrees of accuracy. This bit of conceptual economy allows us to sidestep difficult issues about truth and accuracy and it highlights the fact that S might not represent the world via propositions.

Our modified version of **WTB** now looks like this:

WTB*. *S* knows that *p* just in case
1. *p*.
2. *S* believes that *p*.
3. *S* is warranted in believing that *p*.

1.6   The Belief Condition

Another feature of the preliminary analysis of knowledge we provided was the belief condition. Although this condition has been challenged in the past (Radford 1966), most epistemologists have accepted some form of the belief condition. But let us try to be a bit more precise here. What exactly is belief? To begin with, we should notice that belief is a form of mental representation – a way of recognizing and understanding our world and whatever else we think about. But not all representation of the world is *mental*. Security devices, for example, can detect aspects of the world (think, for example, of a motion detector), and will perform functions that represent the information they detect (for example, electronically). But we do not generally believe that motion detectors, say, are *conscious* or *have minds* – so their forms of representation do not qualify as *mental representation*. Accordingly, we do not normally think of such things as *knowing* anything, because whatever knowledge might be, it seems that it must be something *mental* in nature. Of course, it is important not to beg any questions here, and we do not intend to make the claim that machines could never know anything. Maybe they could; science fiction, for example, is full of cases in which machines come to have consciousness, and such beings would seem to us good candidates for knowledge. But they would be good candidates precisely because they proved to be capable of engaging in mental representation.

Here, again, however, the problem of animal knowledge may seem to create a problem. WTB* treats knowledge as a species of belief. It is the warranted belief that p with p as a necessary condition. But many philosophers regard belief as an example of a propositional attitude – that is, as a cognitive relation to a proposition. As we have already said, however, it is likely that animals like Wooj do not represent the world in terms of propositions. If so, and if beliefs are *propositional* attitudes, then it will follow that Wooj does not have beliefs. But then, if knowledge is a species of belief and Wooj does not have beliefs, it will follow trivially that Wooj does not know anything. Once again, this seems to have closed the door against non-human animals knowing anything far too quickly and without adequate consideration.

Here is the argument in schematic form:

1. Beliefs are propositional attitudes.
2. Knowledge is a species of belief. (Nothing can be a case of knowledge that is not a case of belief).
3. (From 1 and 2) If something does not have propositional attitudes, it does not have knowledge.
4. Wooj does not have propositional attitudes.
5. Hence (from 3 and 4), Wooj does not have knowledge.

If we wish to deny the conclusion (5), then we either have to show that the inferences are invalid (but they're not), or else we have to deny one of the premises. The one we wish to deny is the first one, and to see why, it might help to offer our counter-argument in the same form, working the above argument, as it were, backwards:

6. Wooj knows some things.
7. But Wooj could not know anything if knowledge is always a propositional attitude.

8. (From **6** and **7**) Hence, knowledge is not always a propositional attitude.
9. (=2) Knowledge is a species of belief. (Nothing can be a case of knowledge that is not a case of belief)
10. Hence (from **8** and **9**), belief is not always a propositional attitude.

Both arguments accept (2) that knowledge is a species of belief – as we said at the start of this section, epistemologists now generally accept that belief is a condition of knowledge. If our own analysis is to allow for animal knowledge, then, we must give up on the idea that all beliefs are in the form of propositional attitudes. Wooj's knowledge about where his litter box is will also be a case of a *belief* that Wooj has. If his knowledge is not propositional in content, then neither will his belief be. Hence, we reject premise **1** of the first argument. At least *not all* beliefs are propositional attitudes.

1.7 Preface to the Warrant Condition: Internalism and Externalism

We have not yet examined the warrant condition. By the definition of "warrant," our warrant condition is necessary for knowledge. But we still want an informative account of *what warrant is* – one that doesn't explain warrant in terms of knowledge (we don't want a circular analysis!). Epistemologists have generally been inclined to one of two general approaches to the question of warrant. One of these general approaches has conceived of warrant in terms of the knower's *justification*. Now, as we will see when we more carefully consider conceptions of warrant of this kind, there have been quite a few very different accounts of what justification is and how it would work as warrant. But notice that one requirement for something to qualify as justification is that the knower be in a position to recognize whatever does the actual work of justification *as doing so*. This, very roughly speaking, is why (with one notable exception, which we will note when the time comes[6]) those who think of warrant in terms of justification have been called "internalists." An epistemologist is an internalist if he or she thinks that warrant consists in something that is *internal* to the epistemic agent, but also at least in principle internal to the agent's consciousness. For an internalist, warrant consists in something of which the epistemic agent can be aware. Hence, in order to answer the justificatory challenge, "How do you know?," one must be able to consider and recognize what it is that justifies one, so as to report that justification in such a way as to meet the justificatory challenge.

An externalist, by contrast, does not believe that warrant consists in states or processes internal to the epistemic agent's awareness. So, for example, some externalists think that knowledge is achieved via the reliability of our perceptual capacities. An epistemic agent may have some idea how these capacities work, but such conscious understanding of them is not required, in an externalist account – it is enough that the capacities are working properly and in the appropriate environment. We do not need to be aware of what warrants our knowledge, in order to be warranted, for an externalist.

Before we look more carefully at the different accounts of warrant, however, we will first visit what many have regarded as the most important problem in the field of epistemology, namely, the challenge of skepticism. The different accounts of warrant will certainly provide different kinds of responses to the challenge of skepticism. But before we are in a good position to assess such responses, we will do well to pay very close attention to the problem posed by skepticism, and to consider exactly how this threat works. It is to this issue, then, that we turn next.

Current Trends

A methodological assumption of this book is that the concept of knowledge can be analyzed – that non-trivial necessary and sufficient conditions can be stated. The general idea is that knowledge can be analyzed into more fundamental mental, environmental, and epistemic concepts (namely, belief, truth, and warrant).

One of the most widely influential epistemological programs of the last decade – that found in Timothy Williamson's *Knowledge and Its Limits* (2000) – rejects this approach. According to Williamson, *knowledge* is the most basic epistemic concept and, as such, is unanalyzable. Further, Williamson argues that knowledge is a mental state in its own right – it is not constituted by mental and non-mental conditions (though as a factive state it does entail that p is the case). For excellent discussions of these aspects of the Williamsonian approach to epistemology, see Sosa (2009) and Cassam (2009), both in Greenbough's and Pritchard's *Williamson on Knowledge* (2009). Indeed, the entire volume is indispensable.

For an excellent overview of recent trends in epistemology, the reader is encouraged to consult Pryor (2001).

In a way, it is no longer possible to do epistemology without responding to Williamson. But that doesn't mean that the best way to *introduce* epistemology is by responding to Williamson. For that reason, we set aside his fascinating views and proceed with more traditional assumptions. The interested student would do well to work her way through Williamson *after* working through our more traditional introduction.

2

The Challenge of Skepticism

A man that disbelieves his own existence, is surely as unfit to be reasoned with, as a man that believes he is made of glass. There may be disorders in the human frame that may produce such extravagances, but they will never be cured by means of reasoning. . . . [W]ould not every sober man form the same opinion of the man who seriously doubted [his own existence] . . . [a]nd if he were his friend, would he not hope for his cure from physic and good regimen, rather than from metaphysic and logic?

Thomas Reid, *An Inquiry Into the Human Mind on the Principles of Common Sense:* 16.31–17.23

2.1 The Basic Challenge

In the first of his *Meditations on First Philosophy*, René Descartes considers how many things he has long taken for granted have turned out to be false. Any beliefs based on these false foundations were then rendered doubtful. Who knows, then, what other beliefs might turn out to be false and, hence, which bits of knowledge are certain and which doubtful? Descartes finds this situation – in which he can't tell certain knowledge from doubtful opinion – unacceptable and seeks a remedy. His ultimate goal is to find something about which he can be certain, to serve as a firm foundation for knowledge. With a firm foundation in place, Descartes can rebuild a body of knowledge that is free from doubt. To achieve this end, he proposes to abandon *all* of his former beliefs that can be so much as doubted. Descartes' ingenious method is to find very general grounds that call into doubt as many of his former beliefs as possible. We can call the grounds for doubt that Descartes considers *skeptical scenarios*: they are possible scenarios in which you don't know what you think you know. These skeptical scenarios give rise to doubts. Descartes' hope is that he will be able to find something that is immune from this barrage of skeptical doubt – something that survives even the most powerful of skeptical scenarios.

One skeptical scenario Descartes considers is the perceptual illusion scenario: consider that what looks like water in the distance might be nothing more than the distorting effects of heat waves; or that a straight stick can appear bent when half-submerged in water; or that the person who looks just like your friend from this distance is in fact a complete stranger; and so on. Many of your perceptual beliefs could be founded on ordinary illusions. This renders them, to some small degree at least, doubtful. But, of course, many of your beliefs are not rendered doubtful by this scenario: your mathematical beliefs, your beliefs about who you are, and your beliefs based on very clear perceptual evidence – that you are, for example, holding a book in your hand – no ordinary perceptual illusion could cause such beliefs.

A more far-reaching skeptical scenario is that you are currently asleep and having a very vivid dream. Very much of what you believe could be the false imaginings of your sleeping mind. Most of us have had elaborate dreams in which our entire life histories are fabricated. Perhaps you aren't who you think you are, where you think you are, or doing what you think you are doing – perhaps this is all a dream. The *dreaming scenario*, then, makes room for doubting much of what you believe.[1] Still, it seems that some of what you believe isn't rendered doubtful by the possibility that you are dreaming. Even in dreams, $2 + 2 = 4$, triangles have three sides, red is a color, and so forth.

Descartes soon finds a much more powerful skeptical scenario, which seems at first to threaten absolutely everything

Descartes used to think he knew. He reports that he is used to believing in an all-powerful God, whose actions Descartes himself could hardly oppose or prevent. But what if there were some similar being – an evil demon – who had similar divine powers, but whose interest consisted in deceiving human beings into endless cognitive error, even on what seemed to be the issues of the greatest clarity.[2] Consider such a scenario for a moment. Obviously, the evil demon scenario raises doubts about all the beliefs that the dreaming scenario calls into question. But it goes farther. You think triangles have three sides – couldn't an all-powerful demon be deceiving you here? "But having three sides is part of the *definition* of a triangle," you say. Well, couldn't the demon deceive you about *that*? Maybe triangles are really defined as being 15-sided closed figures. The evil demon scenario thus makes room for doubt about even very basic mathematical and logical issues.

Having found a ground for doubt that seems to threaten everything he once believed, Descartes resolves to abandon all of his beliefs. His next task is then to seek something about which even an evil demon could not deceive him. It is here that we part company with Descartes, for our project is not his. Our aim is only to understand what knowledge is, what is required to know something. And for reasons we will explain as we go along, we do not think that knowledge requires what we know to be so certain that even an evil demon could not deceive us about it.

At this point we will introduce a character called the *skeptic*. The skeptic draws a lesson from the evil demon scenario: that we know nothing or, at least, *almost nothing*. The skeptic thinks that we cannot know that *p* if there is a possibility that we are being deceived about *p*. Further, he thinks that just about everything we believe could be the deceptions of an evil demon. The claim here is not that one is actually being deceived by an evil demon (to claim that would be insane). Nor is the claim that it is at all *likely* that one is being deceived by an evil demon. The claim is just that this evil demon scenario is *possible* and that this possibility threatens most of what we think we know. The skeptic thus has a view about what knowledge requires that has surprising implications about what we can know.

There are two ways of responding to skepticism:[3]

- *Ambitious anti-skepticism*: The ambitious anti-skeptical project is to rescue knowledge by showing that there are some things about which we cannot be deceived. From this foundation of indubitable knowledge, the ambitious anti-skeptic tries then to derive the rest of what we ordinarily think we know. This was Descartes' project.
- *Modest anti-skepticism:* The modest anti-skeptical project is to show how we can know things *in spite of* the possibility that we might be deceived. The modest anti-skeptic refuses to grant the skeptic the assumptions that lead to skepticism.

Basically, the ambitious anti-skeptic wants to convince the *skeptic*, on the *skeptic's* terms, that substantial knowledge about the world is possible. The modest anti-skeptic wants to convince *himself*, on *his own* terms, that substantial knowledge about the world is possible. To understand how this strategy works, you might compare it to ambitious anti-delusionary projects and modest anti-delusionary projects. Suppose you know a man who is clinically delusional – he thinks he is capable of telekinesis. The ambitious anti-delusionary project is to convince him, on his own terms, that he is not really capable of telekinesis. If you have any experience with delusional people, you know this project may be doomed to failure. The deluded may need *medication*, and reasoned argument may simply have no effect on them. The modest anti-delusionary project, on the other hand, is to convince *yourself* that the man is not capable of telekinesis. That's not too hard to do (just ask him to show you!) and it's a good idea if you're considering sending the man to a psychiatrist.

In this chapter, we will consider the most famous ambitious anti-skeptical approach – by Descartes himself – and show why we think it fails. We will then turn to the approach we will follow for the remainder of this book, a version of modest anti-skepticism, for, like most epistemologists since Descartes, we think ambitious anti-skepticism is a pipe-dream. To carry out the modest anti-skeptical project, we must first examine *how* the skeptic thinks the possibility of deception threatens our knowledge. We will, accordingly, examine *skeptical arguments* that move from the possibility of deception about *p* to the conclusion that we don't know that *p*. Once we have understood the skeptic's arguments, we can explain why resisting them is not unreasonable.

2.2   A Closer Look at the Challenge

Of course, Descartes doesn't actually *believe* that there is an evil demon. The problem seems to be that there *could be* such a being, and if there were and it deceived us, we would be unaware of the deception. Even if there is just the *slightest chance* that such a thing is happening, it seems we can generate a skeptical argument:

1. If there is any chance that *p* is false, however small, then you do not know that *p*.
2. There is a chance I am being deceived by an evil demon.
3. If there is a chance I am being deceived by an evil demon, then there is a chance that most of what I believe is false.
4. There is a chance that most of what I believe is false.

Therefore,

5. I don't know most of what I believe (e.g., I don't know that I have hands, that I am reading a book, etc.)

This is a powerful skeptical argument: it is valid, its premises have some degree of intuitive plausibility, and it threatens a lot of what we ordinarily think we know. However, as we will see in the next section, Descartes' evil demon scenario is even more powerful.

2.3   Necessity, *a priori* Truths, and the Chances of Error

If the previous argument were the best that the skeptic could offer, we might take some solace in considering some of the things we ordinarily claim to know are not at all matters of probability. Consider your belief that 2 + 2 = 4 or that red is a color. These are not contingent truths that might have been false. If they are true at all, they are necessarily true: you could have been born with a different hair color and Hitler might have won World War II, but 2 + 2 could not have equaled 5; nor could red have been a number. We might have used the *word* "red" to refer to a number, but red isn't a word; it's a color, and colors are not (could not be) numbers!

Notice that necessary truths like "2 + 2 = 4" and "red is a color" are in some sense *conceptual*: it is part of the concepts of 2 and addition that 2 + 2 = 4, and part of the concept of red that it is a color. You don't need to carry out any scientific investigation to know that 2 + 2 = 4 or that red is a color: you can sit in your chair with your eyes closed and just *think about it*. Necessary truths like these, so-called *necessary a priori* truths, are not matters of empirical or scientific investigation.[4]

Some philosophers think that there are necessary truths that are matters of empirical or scientific investigation (*necessary a posteriori truths*). Many think, for example, that "water is H_2O" is a necessary truth, but one that we discovered through chemical analysis. Now our beliefs in necessary *a posteriori* truths have the following feature: they are based on beliefs in contingent truths (for example, beliefs about how some chemical experiment turned out). This feature means that, though there is no chance that such beliefs are false (if, in fact, they're true), the skeptical argument of the previous section still threatens our knowledge of them. For the skeptical argument will show that we don't know the things that these beliefs are based on (since there is a chance that a demon is deceiving us about them – for example, deceives us every time we try to do a chemical analysis of water). Now, it seems that if your belief that *p* is based on your belief that *q*, and you don't know that *q*, then you don't know that *p*. So, since the skeptical argument of the previous section affects the bases of our beliefs in *a posteriori* truths generally, it thereby threatens our knowledge of necessary *a posteriori* truths.[5]

Our beliefs in necessary *a priori* truths, however, are not like this. They are not based on anything contingent. Suppose, then, that 2 + 2 = 4 and that red is a color. Then there is no chance that 2 + 2 ≠ 4 or that red is not a color. Nor are beliefs that 2 + 2 = 4 or that red is a color based on anything that has any chance of being false. The skeptical argument of the previous section, then, does not touch our purported knowledge that 2 + 2 = 4 or that red is a color. As far as that argument is concerned, we do know such things. Can we not say, then, that at least our knowledge of *a priori*, necessary truths are demon-proof?

Unfortunately, we cannot, as anyone who has made errors in balancing her checkbook knows, perhaps painfully well. In other words, it may well be that it is necessarily true that "2 + 2 = 4." But it is not necessarily true that when Smith adds 2 and 2, Smith gets 4. A distinction is in order here: on one hand, there is *metaphysical* possibility and *objective* chance; on the other hand, there is *epistemic* possibility and probability. Consider, for example, the following mathematical statement:

R. The square root of 2.73472369 is 1.6537

Metaphysically, it is either necessary that 1.6537 is the square root of 2.73472369 or it is impossible that 1.6537 is the square root of 2.73472369. But, *as far as you know*, it's possible that R is true and possible that it is false (assuming, of course, that you haven't already done the calculations to verify R). That is to say, that 1.6537 is the square root of 2.73472369 is for you neither epistemically necessary nor epistemically impossible. Further, even after you have done the calculation to verify R, it is tempting to think that there is some epistemic possibility that you are in error: you know that you sometimes enter numbers into the calculator incorrectly and that calculators have been incorrectly programmed before. That is, even after you have done the calculation, it might seem that there is some small epistemic chance that 1.6537 is not the square root of 2.73472369.

So even though there is no *metaphysical* possibility of our true beliefs in necessary *a priori* truths being false, the demon scenario purports to show there is an *epistemic* possibility that they are false. This suggests a revised version of our skeptical argument:

1*. If there is an epistemic chance that *p* is false, however small, then you do not know that *p*.
2*. There is an epistemic chance I am being deceived by an evil demon.
3. If there is an epistemic chance I am being deceived by an evil demon, then there is an epistemic chance that most of what I believe is false.
4. There is an epistemic chance that most of what I believe is false – *including beliefs in propositions that are metaphysically necessary.*

Therefore,

5. I don't know most of what I believe (e.g., I don't know that I have hands, that I am reading a book, *that 2 + 2 = 4, that triangles have 3 sides,* etc.)

To evaluate this argument, we need a better understanding of epistemic possibility: We might very well wonder whether the key skeptical premises 1* and 2* are really true. Here is one plausible way of defining epistemic possibility:

p is epistemically possible for *S* = df. not-*p* is not entailed by anything *S* knows.[6]

This definition has consequences that are relevant to the skeptic's argument. For one thing, it follows that if you know that *p*, then not-*p* is not an epistemic possibility for you – it is an epistemic *impossibility*. Conversely, if not-*p* is an epistemic possibility for you, then you don't know that *p*. This supports the skeptic's premise 1*.

But the definition undermines premise 2*. According to this definition, to say that it is possible (for you) that you are being deceived by a demon *just means* that nothing you know entails that you are not being deceived by a demon. But there are lots of things you think you know that entail you are not being deceived by an evil demon: if you have hands, then you are not being deceived by an evil demon into thinking that you have hands! The situation, then, is as follows. We think we know many things: that we have hands, that we live on planet Earth, that there are other people, that 2 + 2 = 4, and so on. The skeptic wants to show us that we don't know these things (or much, if anything, else). In order to do this, he needs to provide us with an argument whose premises do not *assume* that we don't have knowledge – for why should we accept such a premise? Premise 1* fails in this task. It asks us to accept that it is epistemically possible that we are deceived by a demon. That, however, just amounts to asking us to accept that we don't know that we have hands, which is precisely what the skeptic is supposed to be *proving*. This version of the skeptical argument, then, is question-begging.

We don't think this is the best the skeptic can do. The demon scenario we have been considering is one in which we are systematically in error. But we can imagine a different scenario. Suppose that we are being systematically manipulated in what we believe by a mad scientist. He constantly implants into our minds a stream of experiences and beliefs. You believe that you are sitting in a chair reading this book (and not, e.g., a disembodied brain floating in a tank of synthetic cerebrospinal fluid) because he is implanting the relevant perceptual experiences in your mind. You believe that you ate Cheerios for breakfast because he implanted a memory of eating Cheerios. And so on. The mad scientist might be manipulating us so that we have systematically false beliefs. He might just as easily be manipulating us so that we have systematically true beliefs. Or maybe he splits the difference. It doesn't matter. If you claim to know that you have hands (you can see them, can't you?!), the skeptic can forcefully respond: but it's possible that you're being manipulated by an evil scientist! This is a new skeptical premise (to replace the various versions of premise 2 we have already considered):

2**. It is epistemically possible (for you) that you are being manipulated by an evil scientist.

From the fact that you have hands, it follows that you are not being *deceived* into thinking that you have hands. It does *not* follow, however, that you are not being *manipulated* into believing that you have hands. So the skeptic may think that he can relaunch the argument we have been considering using his new premise:

1*. If there is an epistemic chance that *p* is false, however small, then you do not know that *p*.

2**. It is possible (for me) that I am being manipulated by a mad scientist.

3. If there is an epistemic possibility that I am being manipulated by a mad scientist, then there is an epistemic possibility that most of what I believe is false.

4. There is an epistemic possibility that most of what I believe is false.
   Therefore,

5. I don't know most of what I believe.

But now it's not clear why we should accept premise 3. Being deceived by an evil demon *obviously* entails that most of what one believes is false – that's what it is to be deceived. So if it is possible that one is deceived, it *must* also be possible that most of what one believes is false. As we have seen, however, being manipulated by a mad scientist does not entail that most of what one believes is false. So it's at best unclear whether we should accept the third premise.

Instead of worrying about the epistemic possibility of false belief, the skeptic should have us worry about the epistemic possibility of *defeated belief*. Let us say that a scenario defeats the belief that *p* just in case were we in that scenario, we would not know that *p*. Clearly, the evil demon scenario defeats most of what we ordinarily believe: for were we in that scenario, most of what we believe would be false, and if most of what we believe were false, most of what we believe would not be knowledge. This scenario is one in which we fail to satisfy the accuracy condition for knowledge. Interestingly, the mad scientist scenario also defeats most of what we ordinarily believe: if you only believe that you have hands because a mad scientist manipulated you into thinking you have hands, it seems that you don't know that you have hands; at best, you are just lucky to have the right belief. This scenario is one in which we fail to satisfy the warrant condition on knowledge.

All the skeptic needs, then, is that in order to come to know that *p*, you must first know that you are not in a scenario that defeats the belief that *p* – the skeptic demands reason for thinking you're in a situation in which you know that *p* rather than a defeated situation in which you don't know that *p*.

>   D. In order to come to know that *p*, you must first know that you are not in a scenario that defeats the belief that *p*.

Principle D has some plausibility. Suppose you're on a diet and decide to buy a kitchen scale so that you can weigh out your portions. You happen to find a scale of unknown origin and reliability. You plop down your piece of steak and the scale registers 3 ounces. "Perfect," you think. "Not so fast," cautions your girlfriend, "suppose that scale is off. You'd better check to make sure it's accurate." Until you know that the scale is not off, you don't know that the steak weighs 3 ounces. So we are now in a position to consider a very powerful skeptical argument.[7]

>   D. In order to come to know that *p*, you must first know that you are not in a scenario that defeats the belief that *p*.
>   2. The mad scientist scenario defeats most of your beliefs.
>   3. So, in order to come to know most of what you believe, you must first know that you are not in the mad scientist scenario.
>   4. You have no way of knowing that you are not in the mad scientist scenario.
>   5. So most of what you believe you cannot know.

This argument is valid; if there is a flaw, it will be that one of the premises is false. Premise 2, of course, is true given the definition of a defeating scenario and the assumption that lucky true belief is not knowledge. Premise 3 follows obviously from 2 and D.

Premise 4 deserves some comment. Why should we grant this premise to the skeptic? Well, consider some of the ways you might try to show that you are not being manipulated by a mad scientist. You might point out the fact that the technology does not yet exist to carry out such a manipulation, that scientists would never be allowed to perform such manipulations due to ethical considerations, and so on. But, according to premise **D**, in order to come to know these things you must first show *that you are not being manipulated by a mad scientist*. The skeptic has you in a difficult position: any reason *p* you might have for thinking that you are not being manipulated is such that you could only know *p* if you *already* knew you were not being manipulated. Plausibly, you can't know *r* on the basis of *s* if, in order to know *s*, you must *already know r*. (The only assumption here that might be questionable is that in order to know *r* on the basis of *s*, you must know that *s*. But it certainly is a plausible assumption.) So it does seem that, once **D** is in place, you have no way of knowing that you are not being manipulated.

The meat of the argument is premise **D**. Now, perhaps it is possible to find something about which you cannot be manipulated. If you cannot be manipulated about *p*, then the mad scientist scenario does not defeat the belief that *p*. If there were some such *p*, then, you could know that *p* even assuming premise **D**. It might then be possible, using your indubitable *p* as a premise, to construct a philosophical argument that you are not being manipulated about anything else. This would allow you to grant the skeptic his assumption about what knowledge requires – as represented in **D** – but argue nonetheless that we are not deceived and so do know many things. Attempting to prove that we are not deceived given the constraints of premise **D** is a very *ambitious anti-skeptical project*. We frankly think that such a project is not likely to succeed, but for what it is worth, let us review the most famous attempt to defeat the skeptic in such a way.

2.4 Descartes' "Cogito" as an Answer to Skepticism

Descartes' own response to his demon scenario was to look for something that he might know, such that he could not be mistaken about it. If he really could find something of this sort, the fact that he could not be mistaken about it would certainly recommend it as adequate evidential support for whatever he might be able to derive from it. As we have now said, this ambitious approach is one that most epistemologists have now abandoned, but it is worthwhile giving it a closer look, to see why the idea has lost its appeal. Recalling the demon scenario from his first *Meditation*, Descartes realizes something:

> I was persuaded that there was nothing in the world, that there was no heaven, no earth, that there were no minds, nor any bodies: was I not then persuaded that I did not exist? Not at all; of a surety I myself did exist since I persuaded myself of something [or merely because I thought of something]. But there is some deceiver or other, very powerful and very cunning, who ever employs his ingenuity in deceiving me. Then without doubt I exist also if he deceives me, and let him deceive me as much as he will, he can never cause me to be nothing so long as I think that I am something. So that after having reflected well and carefully examined all things, we must come to the definite conclusion that this proposition: I am, I exist, is necessarily true each time that I pronounce it, or that I mentally conceive it. (Descartes, *Meditation II*, trans. Haldane and Ross 1931: 150)

Descartes' argument is extremely clever. The idea is that a deceiver couldn't deceive someone, if that someone didn't exist. So, even if all of Descartes' experiences are deceptive, the very fact that he *has* those experiences proves that he exists. That would seem to be a start, and perhaps from this start, we can build the rest of a whole edifice of knowledge.

Unfortunately, there are problems here. For one thing, notice how very limited this first step turns out to be. Each of us, using Descartes' method, can reassure ourselves of our existence each time we consider it. But exactly what does this win us? For example, can a person know that he is the *same* person each time he thinks about his existence? Using his method, perhaps he can establish his own existence, but it is existence *at that time*. How does one establish one's existence *through time*, and have the same certainty of that continuing existence? Could the demon not supply a thinker with a false set of memories, convincing the thinker that he has thought these same thoughts before, when, in fact, he did not actually exist until just a moment ago? Given the possibility of false memories, how can we know that we have existed for more than just a moment?

Moreover, Descartes seems to make an inference that we might need to consider a bit more carefully before we accept it. The inference seems to go from "Thinking exists," which his self-reflective thought *may* establish (though more about this in a moment), to "That which thinks [Descartes himself] exists." But could the demon be clever enough to make this inference seem obvious, when, in fact, it is not actually necessary for a *thinker* to exist, in order for *a thought* to exist. It *seems* as if there must be a thinker in order for there to be thought. But given a Cartesian demon, can we be indubitably certain of this metaphysical principle?

We might even wonder about another question: how do we know, about a thought, *that it is a thought*? Presumably, we have to be able to tell the difference between what are thoughts and what are, for example, tickling sensations. So now we might wonder how it is, or by what *infallible* method, we are able to tell wholly accurately when we are thinking from when we are feeling a tickling sensation – even if the demon would like to trick us about this very discrimination? In other words, given a sufficiently powerful demon, why couldn't our very concepts of *what thoughts are* and *what tickling sensations are* be corrupted? If even our most basic concepts, by which we distinguish one sort of thing from some other sort of thing, can be open to distortion and deception, then it seems Descartes cannot even affirm that the relevant experience is that of thought. The more we think about Descartes' example, the less and less certain the whole business starts to seem.

These considerations, we hope, are sufficient to show why few epistemologists continue to pursue aggressive anti-skeptical strategies. At any rate, we are interested in modest anti-skepticism. What we must do, then, is find a compelling (to us) reason for denying premise **D** (again, the premise that in order to come to know that *p*, you must first know that you are not in a scenario that defeats the belief that *p*). It's OK if the skeptic sticks to his guns about **D**. If *we* can find a plausible reason for rejecting **D**, that's good enough to persuade *ourselves* that knowledge is possible.

2.5   The Skeptical Challenge and Knowing that One Knows

You look at your hands and think, "I have two hands." The skeptic now asks you to consider the possibility that you are being manipulated into thinking this by a mad scientist. He points out that if you are being so manipulated, then you do not know that you have two hands – at best you have a luckily true belief. So as you are looking at your hands and thinking "I have two hands," there are two salient possibilities:

(i)   It appears to me that I have two hands. The entire reason it seems that way is because of the mad scientist making me think so.

(ii) It appears to me that I have two hands. The entire reason it seems that way is because I do have two hands and my perceptual capacities are working correctly. There is no mad scientist involved here at all – just me and my two hands.

Now, if (i) obtains, you don't know that you have two hands because your belief has nothing to do with your actually having two hands. It doesn't matter whether you actually do have two hands in this circumstance: either (a) you don't and so have a false belief, or (b) you do and so have a lucky true belief. Either way, you don't know that you have two hands. If case (ii) obtains, however, it seems that you do know that you have hands. In this case you have a true belief that seems properly connected to the truth – a paradigm case of knowledge if ever there was one.

The skeptic's suggestion, however, is that you cannot distinguish between (i) and (ii). But it now looks like the skeptical challenge doesn't actually prove we can't know anything – it seems that we *do* know something if and when our situation is like (ii). To *be* in situation (ii) is to know that you have hands. To *know* that you are in situation (ii) is to know that you know that you have hands. In arguing that you can't know that you're in situation (ii) rather than (i), the skeptic has only argued that you can't know that you know that you have hands. But since he's given you no reason to think that you're *not* in situation (ii), he has not argued that you don't know that you have hands.

This suggests that the skeptical premise **D** is false. When you are in situation (ii), you know that you have hands, *even though you can't rule out the mad scientist scenario.* Knowing that you're not being manipulated – being able to tell whether you're in situation (i) or (ii) – is, at best, only relevant to knowing whether you know. The only principle that's still plausible is the following:

> **D*.** In order to know that you know that *p*, you must first know that you are not in a scenario that defeats the belief that *p*.

The only skeptical conclusion that will follow from **D*** is that, for most things you know, you cannot know that you know them. Now whether **D*** is true and whether we can ever know that we know is a topic to which we will return soon. At this point, it is enough to note that skepticism is not as threatening as it might first have seemed. For the most part, we can go about our business knowing many things. We only get into trouble when we become reflective and wonder, not whether or not we can know that we have hands, but whether we know that we know that we have hands.

2.6 The KK-Regress

In the last section, we argued that the skeptical challenge really attacks the possibility of knowing that one knows and does not attack the possibility of knowing. But the skeptic might respond by advocating the following principle:

> **KK thesis.** If *S* knows that *p*, then *S* knows that *S* knows that *p*.

If the **KK thesis** is true, and the skeptic has established that we can't know that we know, then she has established that we don't know. The **KK thesis**, however, is one we have very obvious reasons to resist. First of all, the lesson we should draw from the preceding discussion is that knowing that *p* does *not* require knowing that one knows that *p*. After all, the intuitive thing to say about situation (ii) is that it is a situation in which you know that you have hands – even if the skeptic is right that you can't know that you're in situation (ii) – that you can't know that you know.

Second, notice that if we make knowing that we know a condition of knowing anything at all, then we will quickly face an infinite regress. In order to know that we know that *p*, we will have to know that we know that we know that *p*, and in order to know *that*, we will have to know that we know that we know that we know that *p*. And so on. (Are you following this? It *will* be on the test!) This will now iterate into an infinite regress, which is called the KK-regress. According to the **KK thesis**, then, in order to know anything at all, one must know an infinite number of other claims about what one knows. It is plainly impossible that finite beings such as ourselves could possess such an infinite store of knowledge. So, with the **KK thesis**, the skeptic doesn't need evil demons or the subtle argument we considered above. He can argue as follows:

1. You cannot possess an infinite amount of knowledge.
2. If you know that *p*, then you know that you know that *p*.
3. If you know that *p*, then you do possess an infinite amount of knowledge.

Therefore,

4. You don't know that *p*.

This argument is, to say the least, unimpressive. The claim that we know things is intuitively compelling. The **KK thesis** is *much* less intuitively compelling. When we see that it leads very directly to skepticism, we should reject it.

The problem is not just that finite beings cannot possess an infinite amount of knowledge, however. The **KK thesis** imposes a constraint on knowledge that requires that the knower be able to perform meta-cognition – that is, be able to form cognitions that are about their own cognitions. Now, perhaps we should not be too quick to dismiss the idea that non-human animals can actually perform meta-cognition. A recent study of rats (Foote and Crystal 2007), for example, indicates that they actually are capable of assessing their own cognitive condition, relative to different problems confronting them. Rats were given a certain kind of test, but could also decline to take the test. These rats were trained to expect a large reward for accurate performance on the test, no reward for inaccurate performance, and a small but guaranteed reward for declining to take the test. The study showed that rats were much more likely to decline to take the test if the test was difficult, a result that indicated to those who created the study that rats are able to assess their own cognitive condition, relative to the tests presented to them.

It is not as clear to us as it seemed to be to those who studied the rats that what the rats proved in this test is that they can actually perform meta-cognition. Their assessment of their own cognitive condition may not, after all, be a *cognitive* assessment, so much as a kind of *feeling* about their own state of cognition – such as a feeling of uncertainty. But whether or not rats can perform meta-cognition, it is plain enough that this is a fairly sophisticated cognitive process – one that requires quite complex forms of cognitive processing. And if one level of meta-cognition already seems to involve considerable sophistication, just think how each new level of meta-cognition adds to the degree of sophistication and complexity required! Perhaps rats do share our ability to engage in meta-cognition. But can a rat also know that it knows that it knows? (In other words, can rats also perform meta-meta-cognition?) Perhaps human beings can do even this. How far can even human beings continue to meta-cognize about additional levels of meta-cognition? What would it be like even to get clear in our minds what it would mean to entertain the question, "Can we know that we know that we know that we know that p?" At a certain point – and not very far up the ladder of meta-levels – we find that even we cannot engage in further meta-cognition. Each species that has knowledge, accordingly, will therefore have to be able to have knowledge (at some level) that does *not* require meta-knowledge, or meta-cognition beyond that level. We rather suspect that some animals know things without being able to meta-cognize even one level up. But even if we are wrong about that, we don't have to go very far up in levels before even fully functional human beings will not be able to perform further meta-cognition. Accordingly, we should reject the **KK thesis**, because its requirements are impossible to achieve. So we maintain our conclusion from the previous section: the skeptic has at best given us grounds for doubting our ability to know that we know. Our ability to know remains unthreatened by skepticism.

2.7   Fallibilism

The modest response to skepticism we have sketched in this chapter is a version of what has come to be known as "fallibilism." It is called that because it rejects the Cartesian requirement that we must be invulnerable to manipulation, in order to know anything. In other words, we are *fallible*, even when we are doing our best, epistemically; but just because we are fallible, as we have shown, we needn't think we always actually fail, and just because we are in principle vulnerable to manipulation does not mean that we do not know anything. We have provided a modestly anti-skeptical argument for thinking that we actually do know many things. And we have also forecast the analysis of knowledge that we will eventually come to give later in the book: roughly, whenever we really do manage to do things in the right way, epistemically, given the cognitive equipment that we have, we will know.

2.8   The Epistemology of Disagreement

Before concluding this chapter, we'd like to turn briefly to a new sort of skeptical threat, one to which epistemologists have only recently begun to attend. You may have found Descartes' skeptical arguments unpersuasive: why should we care about strange and remote possibilities like the evil demon scenario? If so, get ready: the skeptical threat we are about to consider relies not on a remote possibility, but a common occurrence in daily life – disagreement.

Let's begin with a simple example (which we take from Christensen 2007). Suppose you and four friends go out to dinner. After the meal, you begin dividing up the bill to see how much everyone owes. Rex begins doing this too. The task falls to the two of you as it always does when you go out because the two of you are quick and very reliable at this sort of calculation. Since you both almost always get it right, you both almost always agree. Of the rare occasions when one of you got it wrong, it was just as often you who made the mistake as Rex. So: you finish your calculation and determine that everyone owes $10.50. You tell your friends to get out $10.50. But then Rex finishes his calculation and tells everyone to wait: according to him, everyone owes $12.50.

To facilitate discussion, let's introduce some terminology. Let us say that *A* and *B* are *epistemic peers* about *p* ("peers" for short) just in case *A* and *B* have access to all the same evidence relevant to *p* and are equally reliable at evaluating this sort of evidence.[8] Absent some special information, peers about *p* are equally likely to be right about *p*. Now, let us say that something is a case of *peer disagreement* just in case *A* and *B* (i) disagree about *p*, (ii) know that they disagree about *p*, and (iii) know that they are peers about *p*.

In our restaurant example, then, you and Rex are peers (with respect to how much everyone owes). Once the two of you found out you disagreed, you were in a case of peer disagreement. Before hearing from Rex, you reasonably believed that everyone owed $10.50 for dinner. If you were right, this is something we might naturally say you *knew*. But what happens after you find out that Rex, who is your peer, disagrees with you? Can you still reasonably believe – and just as confidently – that the total is $10.50?

We can begin to answer this question by thinking of the peer disagreement as a surprising phenomenon that needs to be explained. Why is it surprising? Well, the two of you are reliable calculators and reliable calculators rarely disagree. To explain the disagreement, we are forced to conclude that (at least) one of you has made a mistake – but who? It seems that you can't tell: given that you're both equally reliable, you're both equally likely to have made a mistake (you can remember just as many instances in the past where you were wrong and Rex was right as you can instances where you were right and Rex was wrong). So, it seems that you should conclude that one of you made a mistake but you don't know who. But then, it seems, you should no longer be confident that the answer is $10.50: you should think it just as likely that the answer is $12.50. The same applies to Rex. This line of thinking suggests, then, that you and Rex should both give up your beliefs and suspend judgment about how much everyone owes (at least until the two of you have time to doublecheck your calculation; but bear in mind that the disagreement could easily persist after doublechecking). The restaurant case, then, quite naturally leads one to the equal weight view:

> **Equal Weight.** In cases of peer disagreement, one should give equal weight to the opinion of a peer and to one's own.[9]

Giving a disagreeing peer's opinion equal weight to your own results in suspending judgment on the matter in question.[10] Many philosophers who have thought about disagreement have come to hold something like the equal weight view: Richard Feldman (2006), David Christensen (2007), and Adam Elga (2007) are three prominent examples. This view of the restaurant case is, we think, quite plausible. However, if we adopt the equal weight view, it seems that we are led into a surprisingly broad form of skepticism.

Consider some of the more interesting (and controversial!) things you might believe: that, say, colleges and universities pay too much to promote intercollegiate sports programs, that an all-powerful and benevolent deity created the world, that the Yankees will win the next World Series, that killing animals for meat is immoral, that Thomas Jefferson fathered a son with his slave Sally Hemings, or that the best way to lose weight is to decrease carbohydrate intake and increase protein intake. What all these beliefs have in common is that they are highly controversial: there are people who disagree with you but who have access to the same evidence as you have and are generally just as intellectually virtuous as you are.

If you doubt this, just consider the debate over the historical claim that Thomas Jefferson and his slave Sally Hemings had children together:

> [T]he Thomas Jefferson Foundation formed a research committee consisting of nine members of the foundation staff, including four with Ph.D.s. In January 2000, the committee reported its finding that the weight of all known evidence - from the DNA study, original documents, written and oral historical accounts, and statistical data - indicated a high probability that Thomas Jefferson was the father of Eston Hemings, and that he was perhaps the father of all six of Sally Hemings' children listed in Monticello records . . .
>
> Since then, a committee commissioned by the Thomas Jefferson Heritage Society, after reviewing essentially the same material, reached different conclusions, namely that Sally Hemings was only a minor figure in Thomas Jefferson's life and that it is very unlikely he fathered any of her children. This committee also suggested in its report, issued in April 2001, that Jefferson's younger brother Randolph (1755–1815) was more likely the father of at least some of Sally Hemings' children. (<http://www.monticello.org/site/plantation-and-slavery/thomas-jefferson-and-sally-hemings-brief-account>)

Here we have two groups of researchers – who we may assume are equally credible, honest, and capable historians and scientists – that have reached very different conclusions upon evaluating the same body of evidence.

If expert historians and scientists can reach such different conclusions while examining the same evidence, then surely someone just as smart as you, and with access to the same evidence as you, might disagree about (for example) the morality of abortion. Indeed, you've probably met such a person. And if you haven't, a quick Google search will reveal them. We can conclude, then, the following about your many controversial beliefs: for each of them you have peers who disagree with you.[11] But that means that for a great many of your controversial beliefs, you are in a case of peer disagreement. And if the equal weight view is right, that means you ought to give up those beliefs – you must suspend judgment about these controversial matters.

There is good reason to think, then, that the equal weight view entails that we are irrational to maintain a great many of our firmly held beliefs. So the equal weight view has startling skeptical implications. The point is especially pressing when we reflect on the fact that this skepticism seems to threaten many of our most important beliefs: in a way, beliefs about politics, religion, morality – even philosophy! – form an important part of our identity. It would be surprising if rationality required that we give them all up!

The natural way to avoid this skeptical result is to deny the reasoning behind the equal weight view. We will consider two ways this sort of denial might go.

One way of denying the equal weight view begins by noticing that our argument for the view itself relied on a controversial assumption. Recall the reasoning behind the equal weight view. The thought was that when two peers disagree, at least one of them is wrong, but since (in the relevant sort of case) they can't tell which, they cannot rationally continue believing as they do. But what do we mean when we say that one of them must be "mistaken"? If we just mean that one of them holds a false belief, then it is hard to see how they are both required to give up their beliefs – false beliefs can sometimes be reasonable, for example, when they are based on good reasoning. If both parties base their beliefs on good evidence, couldn't they both have reasonable beliefs, even though one of them believes falsely? For the argument to support the equal weight view, we need to mean something stronger by "mistaken": mistaken about what conclusion the evidence supports. In this case, even if two people know that one of them has misjudged the force of the evidence, but cannot tell who, then neither would be irrational to continue to believe that the evidence supports their favored conclusion. But to assume that in cases of disagreement, one of the parties must have made a mistake about what the evidence supports is to endorse the following thesis:

Uniqueness. A body of evidence *E*, supports a unique attitude towards any proposition *p* (either belief, disbelief, or suspension of judgment).

We can contrast uniqueness with a different attitude that Roger White (2005) has called:

✗ **Extreme Permissiveness.** There are possible cases in which you rationally believe *p*; yet it is consistent with your being fully rational and possessing your current evidence that you believe not-*p* instead.

Extreme permissiveness is not implausible, at first glance anyway. Return to the historical research on Jefferson's alleged affair with Hemings. The two groups of researchers reached startlingly different conclusions about what conclusion the historical evidence supports. How can this happen? One way different people can reach different conclusions from the same evidence is by discovering different *arguments* that appeal to the same evidence. We can imagine Watson looking at some evidence and reasonably concluding that it does not suffice to establish the accused's guilt. Holmes, however, might discover a subtle and inobvious argument, appealing to the same evidence, that proves the man's guilt. Both reached reasonable, though incompatible, conclusions from the same evidence. We can imagine that one group of Jefferson researchers discovered an argument that supports the claim that Jefferson fathered many sons by Hemings, while the other groups discovered an argument that supports the claim that Jefferson fathered *no* sons by Hemings.

The above reflections seem to favor permissiveness rather than uniqueness. But we must admit that we're unsure about this. Fortunately, it seems to us that the equal weight view can be supported even if extreme permissiveness is true. It may be true that from a given body of evidence, one can reasonably argue to different conclusions. If one *A* notices one of the arguments, but not the other, and *B* notices the other argument but not *A*'s, then *A* and *B* could reasonably reach different conclusions from the same evidence. But cases of peer disagreement are not simply cases where people reach different, but reasonable, conclusions. They are cases in which two people, who each believe the other to be just as reliable as the other, *know* that they have reached different conclusions from the same evidence. Since they're peers, they should judge that they each reached reasonable conclusions given their evidence. But then they can conclude that their evidence can support *p* just as well as not-*p*, and if they know *that*, then it seems that they are no longer rational to maintain their conclusions. For consider the following thesis:

Revealed Uniqueness. If *S* knows that from *E* one can reasonably argue to both *p* and not-*p*, and *S* has no reason to prefer one argument over the other, the only rational attitude to take towards *p* is suspension of judgment.

Revealed uniqueness is extremely plausible. If you know that the same body of evidence can reasonably support either *p* or not-*p*, then believing one rather than the other seems epistemically *arbitrary*.[12] If the evidence equally reasonably supports both *p* and not-*p*, then the evidence is *inconclusive*. Plausibly enough, one might not know that a body of evidence is inconclusive, and so reasonably draw a conclusion from it. But if one *knows* that the evidence is inconclusive, then one cannot reasonably draw a conclusion from it. So even if permissivism is right in general, it has no significance for the problem of peer disagreement. Revealed uniqueness is compatible with permissivism and can be used to support the equal weight view.

Thomas Kelly (2005) rejects the equal weight view while *accepting* uniqueness – indeed, he thinks uniqueness itself is part of the reason that the equal weight view is false. He claims that if uniqueness is right, then in cases of disagreement, one of the parties has formed a reasonable belief and the other has not. That means that one of us has a good reason for her conclusion and the other does not. Return to the restaurant case. You believe everyone owes $10.50 and Rex believes everyone owes $12.50. Let us suppose that it is you who is right and Rex has made a mistake. Kelly claims that it then follows that you have a good reason for thinking Rex is mistaken: everyone owes $10.50, but Rex thinks everyone owes $12.50. You reasonably believe that $10.50 is the right amount and from that you reasonably infer that Rex is mistaken. So, even in the face of disagreement, you are reasonable to maintain your position. Rex might, of course, reason in the same way and decide to maintain his position. The difference, though, is that Rex does not have a good reason for his belief that everyone owes $12.50 (even if he thinks he does), and so he does not have a good reason for his belief that you made a mistake. Rex, then, is not reasonable to maintain his belief. Kelly's view, then, can be summed up as follows:

The Total Evidence View. In cases of peer disagreement, the peer who has made a mistake should revise her belief while the peer who was correct should maintain her belief (unless both peers made a mistake, in which case they should both revise).

This is just to say that evidence of peer disagreement is of no special significance. When you find out a peer disagrees with you, your belief is just as rational as it was before: if you correctly judged the force of the evidence, then your belief is still rational, and if you didn't it is still irrational.

While Kelly's argument is exceedingly clever, we discern a flaw. Let us grant Kelly's claim that the correct peer has a reason for thinking the other has made a mistake. This is not sufficient to establish that she is rational to maintain her belief. For that to be rational, it must also be the case that she lacks a reason to think that she has made a mistake. Unfortunately, the fact that a peer disagrees with you seems to provide just such a reason: the fact that your equally reliable peer thinks the answer is $12.50 is a reason to think that you're wrong that $10.50 is the answer. And that *you* believe the answer is $10.50 is a reason to think that your peer is wrong that the answer is $12.50. The reasons seem to cancel each other out: neither of you can tell who is mistaken. So both of you need to revise.[13]

Even so, we are still not inclined to think that accepting equal weight can only lead to skepticism. The skeptical argument seems to go like this:

 1. (**Equal Weight**) In cases of peer disagreement, one should give equal weight to the opinion of a peer and to one's own.
2. With respect to most of our controversial beliefs, we are aware that there are peers who disagree with us.
3. Hence, we should give equal weight to our peers' opposing opinions.
4. Hence, it is not rational for us to hold most of our controversial beliefs.

Now, before we raise our own skeptical doubts about this skeptical argument, it is worth noting that this is a rather different argument from the other kinds of skepticism we have considered in this chapter, for it is both more powerful and also less powerful than the other arguments. It is more powerful, because it leads to the conclusion that we cannot even rationally *believe* many of the things we think we can believe rationally. It is less powerful in the sense that it appears to deny rationality only to the beliefs we recognize as *controversial*. Most of the beliefs we are inclined to count *as knowledge* (as per the main focus of this book) are not in this category.

But it also seems to us that premise 2 in the above argument may assume more than we really have good reason to believe. While it is true that we have reason to believe that even smart and thoughtful people disagree with us about our controversial beliefs, it is not so clear that we have reason to believe that these smart and thoughtful people really are our epistemic *peers* when it comes to these beliefs. From the fact that you respect someone's intelligence and thoughtfulness *in general*, it obviously does not follow that you must automatically assume thay they are your epistemic peer *with respect to any given topic*. Recall that a true epistemic peer will be someone with access to *all of the same evidence* that you have. But is this really true when it comes to disagreements about controversial issues? Note that even in those very idealized cases in which we might think this is true, there can still be differences in how two people *weight* the evidence presented to them. But in that case, they really are *not* working from the same (weighted) evidence after all; they will not really be *peers*, in such a case, strictly speaking. And this concern becomes even more important as the cases get further away from the very idealized sorts of cases (such as the restaurant example).

Now the skeptic wielding the equal weight view would probably respond as follows. True, in many cases of disagreement, you and your would-be peer weight the evidence differently. So perhaps you are not peers in the technical sense with which we began. However, this just pushes the issue back. For now we want to know who weighted the evidence correctly. Unless you have independent reason for thinking that you weighted the evidence right, then you should suspend judgment about who has the right weighting. But that leads to suspending judgment on what conclusion the evidence supports. So it may be that the skeptical threat survives in some less idealized cases.

But we think that there is a way to mitigate the skeptical threat posed by the equal weight view. In many real-life disagreements, we don't know much about the reasoning used by those who disagree with us. You might know, for example, that some very smart and informed people have concluded, contrary to your own view, that raising the debt ceiling will not improve the Federal deficit. But you might very well *not* know how they reached that conclusion. You might, at the same time, know that your own view was reached by reasoning processes that you have independent reason to think are quite reliable. But then the very existence of disagreement would seem to suggest that the one who disagrees with you *is not* a peer, strictly speaking. When you have reason to think you've used a pretty reliable reasoning method to form the belief that *p*, and you find out that someone disagrees with you about *p*, but you don't know much about how they reasoned their way into this position, then you can reasonably infer that they didn't use a reliable reasoning method and so aren't your peers with respect to *p* (on the grounds that it's unlikely that two reliable methods would disagree). But that means that in this sort of real-life disagreement, there is no reason to suppose that it is *peer* disagreement going on. If not, then premise 2 of the skeptical argument is lost, and the equal weight principle will not lead to skepticism on the present topic. So it may not be the case that acceptance of equal weight leads to skepticism in the way some have supposed.[14]

No doubt, the equal weight view will recommend that we give up some of our controversial beliefs. The difficult – and interesting – question that remains is just how many beliefs this amounts to. We have suggested that the equal weight view doesn't threaten your controversial beliefs when (*a*) you have good reason to suppose you used a reliable method to form the belief and (*b*) you don't know much about the methods of those who disagree with you. Of course, if you *do* have reason to believe that those who disagree with you used an equally reliable method, then the equal weight view would seem to recommend suspending judgment. So perhaps we should end this chapter with a question for the reader: which of your own controversial beliefs can you rationally maintain if the equal weight view turns out to be correct?

Current Trends

The interpretation of the skeptical argument presented in this chapter has been greatly influenced by the account found in Pryor (2000), which is an excellent source for beginning to explore some of the contemporary literature on skepticism. Another topic that has received a great deal of attention in recent years is G. E. Moore's anti-skeptical argument:

1. I know that I have hands.
2. If I know that I have hands, then I know that I am not being deceived by Descartes' evil demon.
3. I know that I am not being deceived by Descartes' evil demon.

Is this a good argument? For excellent discussion and survey of the relevant literature, see Pryor (2004).

Many contemporary epistemologists view the problem of skepticism as a sort of paradox: we have a set of claims each of which is highly plausible, but which are mutually inconsistent (e.g., (i) If I know that I have hands, then I know that I am not being deceived by an evil demon; (ii) I know that I have hands; (iii) I don't know that I am not being deceived by an evil demon). They think the challenge skepticism presents is one of explaining why skeptical arguments seem so compelling even though they are mistaken. Hawthorne's *Knowledge and Lotteries* (2004) is an excellent overview of this hotly debated topic.

The epistemology of disagreement is a new topic – the inaugural article is Kelly's (2005) paper, "The Epistemic Significance of Disagreement." The brief survey we've given here, then, already captures the "current trends." But we will offer a prediction about what will become an important issue: is the equal weight view self-defeating? Notice, after all, that equally competent philosophers disagree about whether the equal weight view is correct. But then adherents of the equal weight view should, by their own lights, suspend judgment about the equal weight view. For one recent discussion of how a proponent of the equal weight view might handle this problem, see Elga (2010). Those interested in reading more on the topic will enjoy Feldman and Warfield's (2010) anthology on the epistemology of disagreement. Another excellent resource is a 2009 issue of the journal *Episteme* (issue 3 of volume 6) devoted to the topic.

3
Contextualism

There is, after all, a sense in which we can properly enquire and even say "what it really means to say so and so." . . . And I am for the present inclined to believe that . . . this is the sole and whole function of philosophy . . . But, as confession is good for the soul, I must admit that I do not very much relish the conclusions towards which these conclusions point. I would rather allot to philosophy a sublimer task than the detection of the sources in linguistic idioms of recurrent misconstructions and absurd theories. But that it is at least this I cannot feel any serious doubt.

Ryle 1932: 169–70

3.1 The Skeptical Paradox

In the last chapter, we examined the challenge of skepticism, but before we get onto the business of the rest of this book – which is to try to obtain an adequate conception of warrant that will complete our analysis of knowledge – we should perhaps now pause and consider a problem that is closely connected to the skeptical challenge. Perhaps the best way to get a view of this problem is to consider what has come to be known as "the skeptical paradox," which consists in the following trilemma:

1. I know that I have two hands.
2. Since my knowing that I have two hands entails that I am not deceived about that (a brain in a vat or deceived by Descartes' demon, etc.), and I also know *this* entailment, then if I know that I have two hands, then I also know I am not being deceived.
3. I don't know that I am not being deceived.

These three statements form a paradox because each of them seems extremely plausible, but at least one of them has to be false; we must, it seems, figure out which one to give up. At the same time, we must explain why the one we give up seems so plausible. And *that* is a real problem, because it does not immediately seem that giving any one of these statements up is going to be very plausible.

Skeptics, of course, reject **1**. But they have no good explanation of why it's so plausible to assume, as most of us do all the time, that we actually do have knowledge. Everyday discourse is filled with claims that so-and-so knows such-and-such. If the skeptic is right, all of these everyday claims are false. How could competent speakers of English be so bad at using the word "knows"?

Traditional fallibilists reject **3**. This is the position we defended in the last chapter, and maybe our argument there was right, but consider the following claims:

- I know that my lottery ticket will lose;
- I know that no one broke into my house while I was in the library today;
- I know that I won't get hit by a car on my walk home.

Most people find it extremely implausible to say that I can know such things, but each is the basis for a skeptical paradox. For example:

A. I don't know that my lottery ticket will lose.
B. If I know that I'm teaching two classes in the spring, then I know my lottery ticket will lose (if it won, I'd quit my teaching job).
C. I know that I'm teaching two classes in the spring.

The traditional fallibilist, then, is committed to accepting what look like all sorts of implausible knowledge claims. What's worse, she doesn't seem to have any explanation of *why* such claims are so implausible.

But if skeptics and traditional fallibilists cannot adequately defend the plausibility of denying 1 or 3, it seems our only *other* option is to deny 2, which is known as the "**closure principle**" (or more completely, it expresses the principle that knowledge is closed under known logical entailment: if one knows that *p*, and also knows that *p* entails *q*, then one knows that *q*). There have been epistemologists who have challenged this principle, as well, and perhaps we can now see why: if we do not deny this principle, it seems we have to deny one of the *other* statements in the skeptical paradox! We will consider the topic of closure much more carefully when we get to chapter 6, but for now, let us simply note that, whatever the advantages of denying 2 may be for avoiding the paradox, the denial of closure is *not* obviously more plausible than the denials of either 1 or 3. An example of a failure of closure might help here. Consider the case of someone who knows the story of Oedipus:

> Sam knows that Jocasta is Oedipus' mother.
> Sam knows that being Oedipus' mother entails that Jocasta is older that Oedipus.
> Sam does not know that Jocasta is older than Oedipus.

If, as those who deny closure insist, knowledge is not closed under known logical entailment, then there can be a case like this one in which all three of statements **i–iii** are true. It's not clear, however, what such a case would actually look like.

Perhaps we would do better to go back and see if there is some *other* option than trying to explain why the denials of 1, 2, or 3 of the paradox are plausible. While it might seem that there is simply no way out of the paradox, it turns out that a strategy that actually accepts the plausibility (and, indeed, the *truth*!) of all three statements in the paradox has been offered. According to this strategy, called "**Contextualism**," there is reason to think that the verb "to know" is being used in different ways in the inconsistent triad. And that is because, according to the contextualist, the verb: "to know" is *context sensitive*. So let us take a closer look at this way out of the skeptical paradox.

3.2 Context Sensitivity: A Brief Foray into the Philosophy of Language

We should begin by making very clear that the view we are about to explore is very different from the other theories we will consider in this book, because it is about the verb "to know," rather than about knowledge. Our aim, in this book, is to give an account of *knowledge* – what it is; it is *not* to give an account of the word, "knowledge" (in the way that Jones could write a book about the meaning of the word "myself" without writing anything about Jones). Because it is a theory about how the verb, "to know" works, therefore, we should recognize from the outset that, at best, even if contextualism may give us some insight into how the skeptical paradox works, it will not and cannot answer our questions about what knowledge is or what warrant is. Even so, and because it offers a unique way out of the skeptical paradox, it is worth looking at further here, before we return to our main topics of knowledge and warrant.

So let's briefly familiarize ourselves with some facts about language. What concerns us here is a phenomenon called *context sensitivity*. Some words mean different things on different occasions or *contexts*. In the philosophy of language, a context is a set of facts about the utterance of a sentence – who said it, when they said it, where they said, what had been said before, the goal of the conversation, the interests of the speakers, and so on. Different words are sensitive to different features of the context. "I," for example, is sensitive to the speaker of the context, while "now" is sensitive to the time of the context. As we saw, "I am in Tucson" can be true in one context but false in another. If we wanted to give an account of the meaning of "I am in Tucson," then, we will have to make explicit reference to the context in which that sentence is uttered:

- "I am in Tucson" is true in a context C iff the speaker of C is in Tucson.

There are many different categories of words that are context-sensitive. Below, we discuss two important kinds: quantifiers and gradable adjectives.

3.3   Quantifier Domains

One important source of context-sensitivity in ordinary language is in our quantifiers. Suppose you visit Tucson's well-liked seafood restaurant, Kingfisher, on a busy Friday night. You order a plate of oysters and the waiter says, "I'm sorry, but there are no oysters left. Perhaps you'd like some baked clams?" The waiter, of course, is not reporting an ecological disaster: there are still billions of oysters left in the world. What he means is that there are no oysters left *in the restaurant*. There was, however, no need for him to make this explicit, for the context determined this. Whether there are oysters in other parts of the world, or in other restaurants, is not relevant to your order. All that matters is that Kingfisher has no more oysters in the kitchen for you.

In general, our quantifiers (e.g., "all," "every," "some," "none") have restricted domains: the domain might be a restaurant, the utilities drawer in your kitchen, the first five pages of this book, the city of Tucson, the western hemisphere, the Milky Way, etc. Sometimes we make the restriction explicit, as when we say that there is a lot of good pizza in Tucson. But just as often, perhaps more often, the restriction is implicit – we let our conversational partners work out the relevant restriction from context. The result is that a sentence of the form "There are no oysters left" might express truth in one context (a restaurant on a busy Friday night) but express a falsehood in another context (a debate about the impact of global warming on Northern Atlantic oyster populations).

3.4   Gradable Adjectives

Another important source of context-sensitivity lies in our so-called *gradable adjectives*. These adjectives refer to properties that come in degrees. Some examples include "smart," "tall," "flat," and "fast." One person can be smarter than another. Some buildings are taller than others. Tucson is flatter than Boulder. Evans is not a very fast runner. These sorts of considerations led Unger (1979) to argue that nothing is flat (or smart, tall, fast, etc.):

1. If something really is flat, then nothing could possibly be flatter – to be flat is to be *absolutely* flat.
2. Nothing is absolutely flat (everything has bumps to some degree).
3. Nothing is flat.

What's the motivation for Unger's first premise? You might, for example, be looking for a place to set your coffee down and think, "This table is flat – a good place for my coffee." What you say sounds plausible. But imagine a physicist were to come into the room looking for a surface on which he could place an expensive high-powered microscope – the height of the four legs can only differ by a few microns. Would you be right to tell the physicist that the table was flat? No. Your table is somewhat flat, but it ain't *that* flat. But, the thinking goes, if it's not OK to tell the physicist your table is flat, then your table is not flat (surely it's not both flat and not-flat).

Of course, the physicist with very exacting standards still does not have the most exacting standards (imagine his colleague who has an *electron* microscope). So even a table flat enough for him will not be flat enough for others (and so, the reasoning goes, not flat). Nothing, save something *absolutely* flat, will be safe from this sort of argument. So nothing is flat.

That's one way to think about the word "flat," but it's not the only way. What are our data? That "This table is flat" sounded plausible when you were looking for a place to set your coffee, but implausible when a physicist needed a spot to set his microscope. We might, then, propose the following:

- "X is flat" is true just in case X is flat enough for the speaker's purposes.

That makes "flat" context-sensitive. In a context where your interest is finding a place to set your coffee, "My table is flat" expresses a truth: the table is flat enough for your interests. But in a context where you are helping a physicist find a place to set his microscope, "My table is flat" expresses a falsehood: the table is not flat enough for this purpose.

It is important to understand that this view does *not* say that whether or not the table is flat depends upon the speaker's purposes. Nor does it say that a table that was once flat ceases to be flat when a physicist enters the room. The sentence "Five minutes ago the table was flat, but now that a physicist is here, it is not flat" does not express a truth in the context of helping a physicist find a spot for his microscope. What does express a truth in this context is: "Five minutes ago, the sentence 'the table is flat' expressed a truth, but now that sentence expresses a falsehood." This sentence expresses a truth not because anything about the table has changed, but because something about the meaning of the word "flat" has changed. The physical properties of tables don't change because of the interests of speakers, but the meanings of words do. Again, we are talking about the word "flat," and not about *flatness*.

Something like this is a very standard view about gradable adjectives, and it means that Unger's argument fails. Some philosophers have thought that we should think of "knows" as behaving similarly to any other gradable adjective (and that this will help us to understand the skeptical paradox). As we will see, there are ways in which "knows" differs from standard gradable adjectives. Still, there *are* striking similarities. It's easy to see why this might be relevant to the skeptical paradox. Perhaps in less exacting contexts "I know I have hands" is true, even though in more exacting contexts this same sentence is not true. Perhaps the meaning of "knows" varies from context to context.

3.5   "Knowledge" Contextualism

Let us turn to the view that "knows" is sensitive to context in much the same way that gradable adjectives are. Recall that gradable adjectives refer to properties that come in degrees. Does informational knowledge come in degrees?

Well, that depends upon which conception of knowledge we might be looking at; but we will find that, at least in the view we eventually articulate and defend in this book, knowledge actually does come in degrees. That may seem odd to some. Consider someone saying, "We both know that's a zebra, but I know that it's a zebra better than you do." But as we have seen, representations of information can come in degrees of accuracy or adequacy, and, even more importantly, as we will try to show, so does warrant. We think we will eventually provide an account of knowledge such that Wooj can be said to know where his litter box is. But so can the human beings who live with Wooj, and it seems highly likely that Wooj's human friends not only have different kinds of warrant for their knowledge; they also have more of it, since they can use cognitive capacities in generating their warrant that are much more sophisticated (and whose combinations are much more reliable) than those Wooj uses. We can ask an interesting question: how warranted do you have to be in order to know that you have hands?[1] The skeptic thinks you must be *very warranted* – warranted enough to rule out any possibility of error. The fallibilist thinks that you need not be that warranted – perhaps you need only be warranted enough to rule out normal possibilities of error (that your hands have been amputated, say). That is, the (traditional) fallibilist says that:

- "*S* knows that *p*" expresses a truth in context C only if *S* has strong, but not necessarily conclusive, warrant for *p*.

while the (traditional) skeptic says that:

- "*S* knows that *p*" expresses truth in context C only if *S* has conclusive warrant for *p*.

This is a serious disagreement, but notice that there is something that both agree to: whether a sentence of the form "*S* knows that *p*" (call these *knowledge ascriptions*) expresses a true proposition does not depend on the context of the assertion. The degree of warrant required for knowledge is *invariant* with respect to conversational context. We can, accordingly, call this *classical invariantism*. There are two varieties of classical invariantism: *fallibilist invariantism* and *skeptical invariantism*.

The *contextualist* thinks that invariantism is incorrect. She thinks that whether a knowledge ascription expresses a truth can vary from context to context, even when we hold fixed S's degree of warrant. An example from Cohen nicely illustrates the idea:

> Mary and John are at the L.A. airport contemplating taking a certain flight to New York. They want to know whether the flight has a layover in Chicago. They overhear someone ask a passenger Smith if he knows whether the flight stops in Chicago. Smith looks at the flight itinerary he got from the travel agent and responds, "Yes I know – it does stop in Chicago." It turns out that Mary and John have a very important business contact they have to make at the Chicago airport. Mary says, "How reliable is that itinerary? It could contain a misprint. They could have changed the schedule at the last minute." Mary and John agree that Smith doesn't really know that the plane will stop in Chicago. They decide to check with the airline agent. (1999: 58)

We are supposed to intuit that Smith speaks truly when he says "I know." We are also supposed to intuit that Mary speaks truly when she says "Smith doesn't know." How can this be? Smith believes, on the basis of his itinerary, that the flight stops in Chicago. His belief is, accordingly, pretty well warranted. He seems to think his belief is warranted enough to claim "I know it will stop in Chicago," while Mary seems to think it is not warranted enough to claim "Smith knows it will stop in Chicago." We might view this as a real disagreement: Smith and Mary agree that Smith's belief is warranted to degree X, but while Smith thinks this is sufficient for knowledge, Mary does not. We might then try to decide who is right, Smith or Mary.

The contextualist, however, wants us to approach the case differently. She wants us to notice that Smith and Mary are in two very different conversational contexts. Smith is answering someone with a very casual interest about the possibility of a stop in Chicago. Mary and John, however, have a very important business meeting in Chicago and need to know whether to take this flight. Perhaps "knows" is sensitive to such contextual factors. Perhaps given Smith's casual context, a comparatively low degree of warrant suffices to make "Smith knows that the flight stops in Chicago" true. For a more demanding context like Mary's, however, the same knowledge ascription might require a much higher degree of warrant. Perhaps, then, Smith and Mary *both* spoke truly – perhaps they are not contradicting each other after all. This motivates a general contextual thesis:

> **Contextualism.** "*S* knows that *p*" expresses a truth in context *C* only if *S* has strong enough evidence to meet the standards of *C*.

If this is right, then the traditional fallibilist and skeptic are both wrong: how warranted *S* needs to be to truly ascribe knowledge to *S* varies from context to context. However, they can both be right in the following sense: there may very well be "fallibilist" contexts in which strong but non-conclusive warrant is adequate. Likewise, there may be "skeptical" contexts in which nothing short of conclusive, or absolute, warrant will do.

At present, this is just a strategy for solving the skeptical paradox. A full contextualist solution requires some explanation of how our knowledge ascriptions are true in ordinary contexts and false in skeptical contexts. We will also need to hear something about how skeptical contexts arise in the first place. Contextualists have attempted detailed solutions in a variety of ways, but, for our purposes, it will be enough to take a closer look at just one such approach.

3.6 Cohen's Internalist Contextualism

Stewart Cohen (1988, 1999) argues that viewing "knows" as a context-sensitive predicate is the only satisfactory way to see ourselves out of the skeptical paradox. As we noted, knowledge requires warrant, and warrant comes in degrees. Cohen is an internalist – he thinks of warrant in terms of *rationality* or *justification*.[2] That is, someone is warranted in believing *p* just in case they are rational to believe *p*. But beliefs vary in degree of rationality. How rational must a belief be in order to count as knowledge? As a contextualist, Cohen holds that this varies from context to context. More precisely:

> **IC.** "*S* knows that *p*" expresses a true proposition in context *C* only if *S*'s belief is rational to the degree required by *C*.

How does **IC** get us out of the skeptical paradox? Recall that we seem to have tension between our ordinary knowledge ascriptions – "I know that I have hands" – and the skeptic's refusal to ascribe knowledge to anyone – "No one knows anything." Ordinarily, we think that our everyday knowledge ascriptions are accurate. But when we listen to the skeptic, we start to worry that she is correct. The solution, according to Cohen, is to recognize that everyday contexts require a relatively low degree of rationality. Even the skeptic will admit that our beliefs are rational *to some degree*. In ordinary contexts, that degree of rationality is sufficient for "*S* knows that *p*" to come out true. That this relatively low degree of rationality is all that ordinary contexts require is evidenced by our intuition that ordinary knowledge claims are true.

On the other hand, in a skeptical context, the standards of rationality are so high that they are unsatisifiable by fallible humans like us. Just how the skeptic gets us into such a context is controversial, but the idea is that he does so by making salient to us the possibility that we are radically deceived. At any rate, once the skeptic has got us into a skeptical context, none of our beliefs are rational enough for that context. And so the skeptic can truly assert "You don't know that you have hands" or "No one knows anything."

The skeptic's utterances here, though, don't *contradict* our knowledge ascriptions in ordinary contexts – both can be true because both say something different. Recall that the skeptical paradox involves the following three inconsistent but eminently plausible claims:

1. I know that I have two hands.
2. Since my knowing that I have two hands entails that I am not deceived about that (a brain in a vat or deceived

by Descartes' demon, etc.), and I also know *this* entailment, then if I know that I have two hands, then I also know I am not being deceived.

3. I don't know that I am not being deceived.

1 through 3 are mutually inconsistent but individually plausible. Cohen proposes getting us out of trouble by replacing each of these inconsistent theses with a contextualized counterpart. The contextualist counterparts are *not* inconsistent but explain why we found 1 through 3 plausible. Cohen proposes that we replace 3 with the following:

3*. In a skeptical context *SC*, "I don't know that I am not being deceived" expresses a truth (because my belief that I have hands is not as rational as *SC* requires).

3* explains the plausibility of 3. When we consider 3, we imagine it as uttered in a skeptical context (where a skeptic has gotten us worried about radical deception) and correctly intuit that it is true in such a context. Next, Cohen proposes that we replace 1 with

1*. In an ordinary context *OC*, "I know that I have two hands" expresses a truth (because my belief that I have two hands is as rational as *OC* requires).

1* explains the plausibility of 1. When we consider 1, we imagine an assertion of it in an ordinary context and correctly intuit that it is true in such a context. That leaves 2, the closure principle. Cohen argues, quite plausibly, for the following principle:

Contextualized Rationality: Our belief that we have hands is only as rational as our belief that we are not brains in vats.

This principle guarantees a contextualized version of the closure principle:

2*. If "I know that I have hands" expresses a truth in context *C*, then "I know that I am not a brain in a vat" expresses a truth in *C*.

For if "I know that I have hands" expresses a truth in context *C*, then my belief that I have hands is as rational as required by *C*. But then our principle guarantees that my belief that I am not a brain in a vat is also as rational as required by *C*. If, conversely, my belief that I am not being deceived is not as rational as required by *C*, then our principle guarantees that neither is my belief that I have hands. Thus closure is preserved and the plausibility of 2 is explained.

Cohen's solution to the skeptical paradox has fallen into place. We seemed to be confronted with three inconsistent theses 1 through 3. In fact, what is true are the following theses, which are perfectly consistent:

1*. In an ordinary context *OC*, "I know that I have two hands" expresses a truth (because my belief that I have two hands is as rational as *OC* requires).

2*. If "I know that I have hands" expresses a truth in context *C*, then "I know that I am not a brain in a vat" expresses a truth in *C*.

3*. In a skeptical context *SC*, "I don't know that I am not being deceived" expresses a truth (because my belief that I have hands is not as rational as *SC* requires).

But this all by itself does not constitute a solution to our paradox. Why, after all, are we genuinely worried about skepticism? When we're in the clutches of a skeptical argument, we're genuinely worried whether we know anything. We don't think, "Sure, right now I can't truly say that I know anything. But soon enough I'll return to an ordinary context where I can truly say I know many things."

The contextualist holds that our problem is a failure to recognize that (**A**) "knows" is a context-sensitive verb, and that (**B**) the skeptic covertly changes the context. The reason we ordinarily think we know we have hands is because we're ordinarily in contexts where "I know that I have hands" expresses a truth. The reason the skeptic makes us doubt that we know we have hands is because he lures us into a context where "I know that I have hands" expresses a falsehood. Since we don't notice that "knows" is context-sensitive or that the skeptic has changed relevant features of the context, we think that the skeptic has shown that "I know that I have hands" expresses a falsehood in any context – that is, we think that the skeptic has categorically shown that we don't know anything.

3.8 The Argument from Ordinary Language

Contextualism about knowledge ascriptions seems to offer a handy solution to the skeptical paradox. But is there independent reason to think that contextualism is true? According to contextualists, the best evidence for contextualism comes from ordinary language. Contextualism is a semantic thesis about the meaning of "knows." As such, the best evidence for the thesis will be evidence about the ordinary usage of "knows." The contextualist will present us with cases in which we imagine speakers making (or denying) knowledge ascriptions in various circumstances. Keith DeRose's famous pair of bank cases illustrate the strategy:

> **Bank Case A:** My wife and I are driving home on a Friday afternoon. We plan to stop at the bank on the way home to deposit our paychecks. But as we drive past the bank, we notice that the lines inside are very long, as they often are on Friday afternoons. Although we generally like to deposit our paychecks as soon as possible, it is not especially important in this case that they be deposited right away, so I suggest that we drive straight home and deposit our paychecks on Saturday morning. My wife says, "Maybe the bank won't be open tomorrow. Lots of banks are closed on Saturdays." I reply, "No, I know it'll be open. I was there just two weeks ago on Saturday. It's open until noon."
>
> **Bank Case B:** My wife and I drive past the bank on a Friday afternoon, as in Case A, and notice the long lines. I again suggest that we deposit our paychecks on Saturday morning, explaining that I was at the bank on Saturday morning only two weeks ago and discovered that it was open until noon. But in this case, we have just written a very large and very important check. If our paychecks are not deposited into our checking account before Monday morning, the important check we wrote will bounce, leaving

us in a very bad situation. And, of course, the bank is not open on Sunday. My wife reminds me of these facts. She then says, "Banks do change their hours. Do you know the bank will be open tomorrow?" Remaining as confident as I was before that the bank will be open then, still, I reply, "Well, no. I'd better go in and make sure." (DeRose 1992: 913)

DeRose judges (and hopes that we agree) that he speaks perfectly appropriately in **Bank Case A** when he says "I know it'll be open." He also judges that he speaks appropriately in **Bank Case B** when he says, in answer to the question "Do you know?," "Well, no." For a classical invariantist, this is puzzling. After all, DeRose's epistemic position in **Bank Case A** is identical to his epistemic position in **Bank Case B**. Fallibilist invariantists should hold that he knows in both cases, while skeptical invariantists should hold that he knows in neither case. Either way, the classical invariantist will have to explain why one of the assertions seems perfectly appropriate, even though it is false.

The contextualist, on the other hand, has an explanation ready to hand. She can say that both assertions seem appropriate *because both are true*. Though DeRose's epistemic position is the same in both cases, the conversational context is quite different. In **Bank Case A**, (i) nothing of great importance hangs on whether the bank will be open, and (ii) no one is concerned with the possibility that the bank has changed its hours (or that DeRose is misremembering or something). In **Bank Case B**, on the other hand, (i) it is of great importance that the bank be open, and (ii) DeRose's wife is explicitly concerned with the possibility that the bank has changed its hours. The contextualist will urge that the comparatively low standards in **A** are such that DeRose's belief is warranted enough for an utterance of "I know the bank will be open" to be true. In **B**, however, the standards are higher, so that DeRose's belief is not warranted enough for an utterance of "I know" to be true.

Contextualists seek to use these sorts of cases as the basis of an argument for contextualism. They rely on a sort of charity principle. The principle says that, all else being equal, the best explanation for why an utterance of a competent speaker seems appropriate is that the utterance is *true*. We might formulate the principle as follows:

> **Charity:** If a competent speaker S appropriately utters "p" in context C, and is not mistaken about any relevant matters of fact, then we should assume that S's utterance of "p" expresses a truth in C.

Why should we accept this principle? Well, when they are being honest, speakers use language to try to describe situations accurately. If someone inaccurately describes a situation, this can only be due to (i) linguistic incompetence (they misunderstand the use of word); (ii) a false belief about the situation; (iii) intentional dishonesty. Insofar as we are talking about honest speakers with no false beliefs about the situation, (ii) and (iii) will not be live explanatory options. Although competent speakers make mistakes, they do so infrequently and when they do so, their utterances generally do not seem appropriate. These remarks are no doubt sketchy, but they are plausible and it is this sort of thinking that undergirds **Charity**.

With **Charity** in hand, the general contextualist argument falls into place. First, the contextualist presents us with two cases: in one, **LOW**, a speaker utters "S knows that p," and in the other, **HIGH**, a speaker utters "S does not know that p." In both cases, the speaker is speaking of the same agent, S, and S's epistemic position is held fixed with respect to p. If the cases **LOW** and **HIGH** are selected well, then we will have the intuition that the knowledge ascription in **LOW** is appropriate and that the knowledge denial in **HIGH** is also appropriate. The contextualist presents us with the following argument:

1. The utterance of "S knows that p" in **LOW** is appropriate.
2. The utterance of "S does not know that p" in **HIGH** is appropriate.
3. The speakers in **LOW** and **HIGH** are competent and are not misinformed about any underlying matters of fact.
4. So, by **Charity**, "S knows that p" expresses a truth in **LOW** and "S does not know that p" expresses a truth in **HIGH**.
5. Hence, knowledge contextualism is true.

There are several ways for classical invariantists to respond. First, they might argue that ordinary speakers are not (entirely) competent in their use of the word "knows." The idea would be that it takes special training in epistemology to get really good at applying "knows." This strikes us as rather implausible: perhaps ordinary speakers aren't competent, but surely epistemologists aren't much better. After all, most results in epistemology hang on our pre-theoretical intuitions about appropriate and inappropriate uses of "knows." Another strategy would be to deny that the utterance in **HIGH** (or **LOW**) really does seem appropriate. But, if the contextualist selects her cases well, this is difficult to argue with a straight face. Finally, the invariantist might offer a charitable explanation of *why* speakers systematically make mistakes when confronted with cases like **LOW** and **HIGH**. This strategy seems to be the best option for invariantists. As we shall see, Williamson employs this strategy to great effect.[3]

3.9   Williamson's Objection to Contextualism

Timothy Williamson (2005) contends that the data don't favor contextualism over classical invariantism. The contextualist seeks to avoid attributing error to competent speakers who are not confused about any underlying matters of fact (and don't seem to be speaking loosely or metaphorically). We have seen evidence that competent speakers might attribute knowledge to a subject in one context while denying knowledge to the very same subject in a different context. The contextualist can explain how both speakers speak truly, while the classical invariantist must think that at least one of them is mistaken. This the contextualist regards as a reason to prefer contextualism over classical invariantism.

The trouble with this strategy, according to Williamson, is that there are cases in which the contextualist will have to attribute error but the classical invariantist will not. This is a result of the semantic blindness that contextualists postulate to explain the allure of skepticism. Ordinary speakers don't recognize that skeptical considerations change the context – instead they tend to take the considerations as showing that they were wrong in their original knowledge ascriptions. Consider the following example, a modified version of one of Williamson's:

A student is engaged in a rigorous conversation with an epistemology professor – standards are very high:

Professor: Do you know where your car is?
Student: Sure I know where my car is; it's in the parking garage.
Professor: But how do you know it hasn't been stolen since you left it there? Cars do get stolen from the garage now and then.
Student: True . . . I guess I was wrong – I don't really know where my car is. (Williamson 2005: 220)

Here we have three interesting ascriptions:

i. The student's initial utterance of "I know where my car is" in an ordinary context.
ii. The student's later utterance of "I don't know where my car is" in a skeptical context.
iii. The student's later utterance of "I was wrong" in a skeptical context.

The contextualist can allow that i and ii are both true. Initially, ordinary standards were in place and the student spoke truly when she said "I know where my car is." The professor then managed to raise the standards and so the student spoke truly again when she said "I don't know where my car is." However, according to contextualism, even in the skeptical context, it remains true that what the student said originally (in the ordinary context) was true. According to contextualism, then, iii is false. And though iii seemed like a perfectly ordinary thing for the student to say in light of the professor's probing, the contextualist must regard it as an error.

So all views are forced to attribute some error to ordinary speakers – we should expect nothing less from a real paradox. Still, the contextualist might claim some advantage over fallibilist invariantism here. The fallibilist invariantist must regard i as true, but ii and iii as errors. The contextualist is forced to attribute *less* error than the fallibilist invariantist in this dialogue. Of course, she can't claim this advantage over the *skeptical* invariantist, for the skeptical invariantist will regard ii and iii as false but i as true. And, of course, we can imagine a low standards analog of our original case. After meeting with his professor, our student drives to a bar (with "notoriously low standards") to meet a friend:

> *Student*: Then I realized that I didn't really know where my car was – it had been stolen for all I knew.
> *Friend*: What? Of course it hadn't been stolen . . . That practically never happens and you've got an alarm. Anyway, if you didn't know where your car was, how did you manage to drive here after class?
> *Student*: I didn't even think of that. Of course I knew where my car was. That philosophy professor always tricks me into saying things that aren't true! (Hawthorne 2004: 221)

Here the contextualist and the fallibilist invariantist will each be able to view two out of the three utterances as true, while the skeptical invariantist will only be able to recognize one of them as true.

How should we adjudicate this dispute? We could try to compile an exhaustive list of all the relevant data, tally the errors that each view must attribute, and then declare as winner the view that attributes the least amount of error (and hope that there isn't a tie). But attributing error to competent speakers isn't so bad if we have available a good explanation of why they might make such errors. This suggests a better way to resolve the dispute. All views will be forced to attribute error to competent speakers. Accordingly, they must offer an explanation of how competent speakers make such errors. The view with best explanation wins.

Williamson, a fallibilist invariantist, offers just such an explanation. His explanation invokes the *salience bias* (2005: 225–6). The salience bias is a well-known psychological effect. In forming judgments, we tend to give more weight to considerations that are psychologically salient at the time of judgment. For example, your overall evidence may be that a friend of yours is very trustworthy. However, if you are currently thinking about a lie she has just told you, you will tend to give this significantly more weight in thinking about how trustworthy she is – indeed, you may (unjustifiedly) judge that she is not very trustworthy.[4]

In judging whether someone knows that p, we take into account various ways that that person may have made a mistake about whether p. The salience bias predicts that if an error possibility is psychologically salient, we will give that possibility a lot of weight in judging whether the person knows – even if the error possibility in question is not really relevant. This, Williamson argues, is precisely what happens in DeRoses's **Bank Case B** (and other "high standards" cases). And, in Cohen's example of LA Airport, because Mary and John are considering the possibility that Smith's itinerary is a misprint (an error possibility for Smith's belief that the plane stops in Chicago), they decide that Smith's inability to rule out this possibility precludes his knowing. We judge that Mary and John are right because, in thinking about the case, we too are subject to the salience bias. But, as a fallibilist, Williamson insists that, *as a matter of fact*, Smith does know that the plane will land in Chicago – the unlikely possibility that his itinerary is a misprint does not really prevent him from knowing. Still, given the salience bias, it is easy to see why competent speakers might mistakenly conclude that Smith does not know – and why we mistakenly judge that they speak appropriately.

One might think this is question-begging – doesn't Williamson just assume that fallibilist invariantism is correct in offering this explanation of the cases? But that's not the right way to think about the situation. The burden of proof is on the contextualist: she must establish that "knows" is context-sensitive. She attempts to do so by presenting cases and arguing that contextualism best explains our intuitions about the cases. What Williamson offers here is a (compelling) fallibilist invariantist explanation of our intuitions. If his explanation is as good as, or better than, the contextualists', then we have been given no compelling reason to accept contextualism.

The contextualist charges the classical invariantist with violating **Charity**. As we have seen, both invariantists and contextualists must violate **Charity**. Williamson offers a plausible account of why competent speakers mistakenly deny knowledge in "high standards" cases. To respond, the contextualist must offer an explanation of why competent speakers fail to notice that "knows" is context-sensitive. This, it seems to us, is where the future of the debate between contextualism and invariantism lies. We don't hope to resolve that debate here, but we do think Williamson has given the invariantist an edge, at least for the moment.

Let us conclude this chapter with a final challenge for invariantism and then some remarks about how contextualism relates to the analysis of knowledge offered in the rest of this book.

3.10   A Final Challenge for Fallibilist Invariantism

We have seen some reason to think that fallibilist invariantists can explain away the intuitions that are supposed to support contextualism. But they face a further difficulty. Let us return to DeRose's **Bank Case B**. The fallibilist invariantist must say that DeRose is wrong – he does know that the bank will be open on Saturday. Of course, given how important it is that his wife's check get deposited, we think DeRose would be irrational not to double check. This suggests that what DeRose should have said was, "Yes, I know that the bank will be open tomorrow – but I had better make sure it is." To many ears (present authors included), this sounds bad. If you know the bank will be open, then surely you don't need to check. Many find the following principle very attractive:

> (**KPR**) If S knows that p, then S may take p as a premise in practical reasoning.

If **KPR** is right, however, DeRose would be perfectly rational not to double check. For, given that he knows the bank will be open, he can reason as follows: "My wife needs to get her check deposited before Monday; the bank will be open on Saturday; so there is no need to go to the bank right now." Assuming **KPR**, and fallibilist invariantism, we have to regard this reasoning as appropriate. This seems a difficult pill to swallow.

This phenomenon is fully general. All we have to do is imagine cases where S believes p on grounds that are less than fully conclusive (i.e., S could be, but isn't, wrong about p; fallibilists have to allow that there are such cases). Now stipulate that the question whether p is of very great practical importance to S (make S's life, loved ones, or financial stability hang on whether p). It will then seem irrational for S to assume p without further investigation. We will then have a violation of **KPR**. The fallibilist invariantist's options, then, are either to deny **KPR** or to deny that S would be irrational to assume p in such cases. These are unattractive options.

3.11 Subject-Sensitive Invariantism

This problem has led many theorists to a new view called *subject-sensitive invariantism.* According to subject-sensitive invariantists, whether one is warranted enough to know that p depends, in part, on how practically important p is for S. More precisely, subject-sensitive invariantists hold:

> (SSI) S knows that p (at t) only if S's degree of warrant is high enough for S to be rational in taking p as a premise in practical reasoning at t (and how much warrant is required to rationally take p as a premise depends on how important, practically speaking, p is for S at t).[6]

SSI tells us that DeRose does not know that the bank will be open on Saturday, for his degree of warrant is not high enough to rationalize assuming that the bank will be open in his reasoning (getting his wife's check deposited is just too important). Still, the spirit of fallibilism is preserved: when the practical stakes are lower, as in **Bank Case A**, DeRose can reasonably assume that the bank will be open, and so does know. In general, **SSI** allows that we can know on less than conclusive grounds so long as the stakes aren't too high.

It's important to see how **SSI** differs from contextualism. According to the contextualist, the meaning of "S knows that *p*" depends on features of the *speakers'* conversational context – the degree of warrant required to make a knowledge ascription true depends on the interests of the ascribers. The claim is that what a sentence of the form "*S* knows that *p*" says depends on who says it. SSI, on the other hand, is a version of invariantism: "*S* knows that *p*" always means the same thing, whoever says it and in whatever context. Subject-sensitive invariantists hold that what "*S* knows that *p*" says (in anyone's mouth) is that *S* has enough warrant to rationally assume *p* in practical reasoning.

What is interesting about the view (and what makes it seem similar to contextualism), is that a subject may know that *p* at one time and fail to know that *p* at a later time, *even though her warrant for p remains unchanged*: the question whether *p* may acquire greater practical importance for her. In **Bank Case B**, DeRose did know that the bank is open on Saturdays – until he picked up his wife and she told him that her check absolutely had to be deposited by Monday; then he no longer knew, since he was no longer rational to assume the bank would be open Saturday.

SSI, then, allows us to preserve the spirit of fallibilism, while hanging on to the link between knowledge and practical reasoning. These are benefits. The cost is that we need to accept that *S* can go from knowledge to ignorance with no change in epistemic position. This seems manifestly absurd. Consider the following case:

> **Remote control:** Suppose you believe, with a high degree of warrant, that the remote is on the coffee table. You're alone at home, you have no pets, you were just in the living room 15 minutes ago, and you clearly remember leaving the remote on the coffee table. You have a good track record with this sort of memory belief. Any fallibilist should say that you know that the remote is on the coffee table. Certainly, you could appropriately take that as a premise in your present reasoning. But then suppose an evil super-villain shows up and offers you a bet: if the remote is on the coffee table, you get a Twix bar, if it is not he will kill 1,000,000,000 innocent people. Surely you should not accept this bet! But that means that this reason-

ing is not appropriate: "The remote is on the coffee table, so if I accept the bet I'll get a Twix bar and no one will die." But then, by **SSI**, you no longer know that the remote is on the coffee table.

It seems ridiculous that an evil super-villain could render you ignorant just by offering you a high-stakes bet. But this is just what **SSI** commits us to. To avoid this result, but hang on to our fallibilist invariantism, we will have to either deny **KPR** or allow that seemingly inappropriate reasoning is, after all, appropriate. And we will have to do so in a way that explains our strong intuitions to the contrary. This is the challenge that fallibilist invariantists face. Many potential solutions exist in the literature, but we leave it to the interested reader to investigate further.

3.12 Conclusion

In this chapter, we have discussed an interesting semantic view called contextualism. We have seen how contextualists attempt to solve the skeptical paradox. We have considered the evidence that contextualists use to defend their views and one plausible invariantist explanation of the evidence. We then considered the major challenge for fallibilist invariantism that has led some to a view called subject-sensitive invariantism.

As we said at the outset, however, most of the issues we have covered in this chapter are orthogonal to the main concern of this book: the correct analysis of knowledge. The analysis of knowledge that we will eventually offer in the next chapters could be treated as a version of fallibilist invariantism, subject-sensitive invariantism, or even contextualism (perhaps with some minor modifications). Our own analysis of the concept of knowledge is, then, officially neutral on this topic. As we said in our first chapter, however, work continues to be done in this and all of the other areas we have covered in this book, and we may reasonably expect new arguments on most of our topics to be offered in the coming years.

Current Trends

In a way, a current trends section for this chapter is otiose: we have done our best here to introduce readers to the cutting edge of the debate about epistemic contextualism and related theses, though anyone wishing to be completely up-to-date should also have a close look at DeRose's externalist form of contextualism (in De Rose 1992, 1995, and 2005). It seems to us that the biggest challenge facing the contextualist is summed up well by Jason Stanley (2005: 47): "The alleged context-sensitivity of knowledge ascriptions has no other parallel among the class of uncontroversial context-sensitive expressions." Contextualists have tried to explain their thesis by reference to other context-sensitive linguistic categories, such as gradable adjectives and indexicals. But, as Stanley and others have argued, "knows" really doesn't behave much like a gradable adjective or indexical. To solve this problem, contextualists will need to get much more sophisticated in their appeal to linguistics and find a class of context-sensitive words that a semantics for "knows" can be accurately modeled on. For a glimpse into the future of this topic, see Schaffer and Szabo (forthcoming).

One topic that we left out of this chapter, but that deserves mention, is John MacFarlane's relativist semantics for "knows" and other epistemic modals. See, for example, his 2005 and forthcoming. Once again, we stress that this work is primarily in the philosophy of language and not epistemology proper, but MacFarlane hopes that interesting epistemological consequences can be drawn from his views.

4
Warrant as Justification

> Thus foundationism has become a philosophical hydra, difficult to come to grips with and seemingly impossible to kill.
> BonJour 1978: 1

4.1 Justification and Evidence

As we said in chapter 1, many epistemologists have understood warrant to consist in justification, and, in this chapter, we will explore what the options are for this sort of approach, and also say a few things about some of the challenges such an approach faces. We also said in chapter 1 that those who regard warrant as consisting in justification are often called "internalists," because justification is typically understood as a relation between states *internal to* the mind of the one justified. Again, speaking very broadly, justification is typically understood as a relation that obtains between the state that is justified and the states that do the justifying – for example, between a belief that is justified, and the believer's other beliefs that justify the target belief.

A rough-and-ready way to begin to understand how justification works is to think of justification as whatever one can offer as an answer to the challenge, "Why do you believe that?," or, if one is claiming actually to know something, then to the question "How do you know that?" When one answers these sorts of questions, one is typically supposed to provide *evidence* or *reasons* for the belief in question. So suppose Frank claims to have $500 in his checking account, and someone else asks him why he believes that. Frank answers, "Well, all I can say is that I *hope* I have that much money in my account!" In this case, it seems as if Frank has no evidence for thinking he has $500 in his account. Since Frank has no evidence to produce, we regard him as *unjustified* in his belief. Of course, even if his belief is unjustified, it might still be true. What's at issue is whether Frank has any *reasons* or *evidence* or *justification* for thinking that it is true.

Even if Frank *does* have adequate evidence, his belief *still* might not be justified. For Frank might not have noticed his evidence. We can imagine, for example, that in the case above Frank (a) remembers depositing $200 in his bank account yesterday, (b) saw that before he made his deposit his balance yesterday was $300, and (c) hasn't spent any money in the meantime. But, for whatever reason, Frank might not have put (a), (b), and (c) together and he might only believe that he has $500 because of wishful thinking. So even if Frank has adequate evidence, it seems that if his belief is not *based on* that evidence, he won't be justified. We'll say more about what it is for a belief to be based on some evidence in the next chapter; for now, the basic idea is clear enough. When you have evidence for a belief, but your belief is not based on the evidence, we can say that your belief is *justifiable* but not *justified*.[1]

Further, justified belief comes in two varieties. To illustrate, suppose now that Frank does not have adequate evidence, but thinks he does. Suppose, for example, that Frank was taught to trust the tarot cards.[2] If the cards tell Frank that he has $500, he will (understandably) believe that he has $500 and also think that his belief is very well-supported. But, of course – and hopefully this won't come as a shock, dear readers – that the tarot cards were thus-and-so is *no evidence at all* that Frank has $500 in his bank account. So when we talk about justification, we can mean two things: we can mean either what seems to the epistemic agent herself to be evidence for her belief, or we can mean *what really is* evidence for the agent's belief. Let's call the first one *subjective* justification and the second one *objective* justification. In this example, Frank's belief is subjectively justified but not objectively justified.

So far, we have distinguished between *justifiable* and *justified* belief. We have noted further that there are two types of justified belief: *subjectively* justified belief and *objectively* justified belief. Later in this chapter, we will have more to say about how these need to be related. It should already be obvious, though, that if justified belief is required for knowledge, it is objectively justified belief that is required. Merely justifiable belief, or even subjectively justified belief, are not good enough. The reason is simple: if a merely justifiable belief (or a subjectively justified belief) turns out to be true, this will be a matter of *luck. Luck isn't good enough for knowledge.* So, if the internalist thinks justification is a necessary component of warrant, she needs to be talking about objectively justified belief.

We must notice one further feature of justification: it comes in degrees. You can be more or less justified – have more or less evidence – for a belief. How much is required for warrant? There may not be a general answer, but it is clear that *some* evidence is not always *enough* evidence. For example, if all you know about hamburgers is what you tasted at the burger place round the corner on one occasion, you have some evidence for thinking that all hamburgers are greasy and disgusting. But do you have enough to be *warranted* in believing that all hamburgers are greasy and disgusting? Surely not – your sample of one greasy and disgusting hamburger from one restaurant is just not enough evidence.

So when we consider different accounts of justification as warrant, we will have to bear these distinctions in mind: (*i*) is the justification a matter of justifiable or justified belief, (*ii*) is the justification subjective or objective, and (*iii*) is the justification really adequate for warrant?

4.2 The Regress of Justification

It is very traditional to differentiate theories of justification by how they respond to a skeptical argument called *the regress of justification.* Think about what it means to justify some claim of knowledge. Someone challenges the claimant: "How do you know that *p*?" The claimant then makes some response, in which the claimant provides *evidence* for thinking that *p* is true. Call this evidence *q*. But now the challenger can challenge again: "How do you know that *q*?" To this challenge, the claimant must now provide *other* evidence. Call this evidence *r*. But now the challenger can challenge again . . . and so on. It looks like we have created a regress. We either have to go on forever, go in a circle, or stop with a belief that doesn't require another belief as evidence. And now perhaps the skeptic can use this regress to argue that no belief can be justified. The argument might go something like this:

1. A belief can be justified only if it is justifiedly inferred from another belief. (That is, nothing can be justified all by itself, or justified by something else that is not a belief).
2. A belief can be justifiedly inferred from another belief only if that other belief is itself justified.
3. Therefore, either a belief can be justified by circular reasoning or it can be justified via an infinite chain of reasoning, or no belief can be justified.
4. No belief can be justified by circular reasoning.
5. No belief can be justified by an infinite chain of reasoning.
6. Hence, no belief can be justified.

If we are to avoid skepticism, we must reject one of the premises of this argument. Which premise one rejects determines which theory of justification one accepts (or so the tradition goes).

Premise 1 calls for justificatory inferences to be made entirely and only from beliefs to other beliefs. So let us call the acceptance of this premise a commitment to *doxastic inferentialism*. We can then characterize as *non-inferentialism* the theory of justification that rejects premise 1. Non-inferentialists think that (at least some) beliefs can be justified by something other than inference from other beliefs. Some have held that some beliefs can be self-justifying; others have held that perceptual experience or rational intuition can justify belief; and still others have held that it is the coherence in one's system of beliefs that justifies each belief in that system.

The theory of justification that rejects premise 2 (and accepts premises 1, 3, 4, and 5) is *unjustified foundationalism*. Unjustified foundationalists think that even if your belief that q is unjustified, if q is a good reason for p, you can infer p from q and end up with a justified belief that p. This is a form of what is called "foundationalism," because it stops the regress of justification by finding some (foundational) beliefs that confer justification on other beliefs, which do not themselves need to be justified by other beliefs within the justification system. It is called "unjustified foundationalism" because, unlike other forms of foundationalism, in this version the foundational beliefs confer justification on other beliefs, but are not justified themselves.

Linear Coherentism is the theory of justification that rejects 4 (and accepts 1, 2, 3, and 5). Linear coherentists think that your belief that p can justify your belief that q, and your belief that q can justify your belief that p. In other words, justification can go in circles.

Infinitism is the theory of justification that rejects 5 (and accepts 1, 2, 3, and 4). Infinitists think that you can justify your belief that p through an infinite chain of inferences.

We will find that, contrary to tradition, no epistemologist has endorsed infinitism or linear coherentism. A few have endorsed unjustified foundationalism, but the problems with that view seem to us (and many others) to make it quite implausible. Nearly all contemporary theories of justification are versions of non-inferentialism, if we divide theories up in this way. Later in this chapter, however, we will argue that there is a better way of dividing up theories. But, first, let us see why infinitism, linear coherentism, and unjustified foundationalism have proven so unpopular.

4.3   Unjustified Foundationalism

Various versions of unjustified foundationalism have been offered in the literature,[3] but the view has not gained much popularity. To see why, consider Green who arbitrarily believes that *q*: there are 300,879,982 grains of sand on Myrtle Beach. Suppose Green then infers that *p*: there is an even number of grains of sand on Myrtle Beach. The question is whether Green's belief that *p* is justified. Plainly, *q* is a reason for *p*. It seems pretty clear, though, that even if it is true that there are an even number of grains of sand on Myrtle Beach, Green surely does not *know* that there are, since his only justification for that belief is itself wholly unjustified. We can grant that, *from Green's (subjective) perspective*, there is nothing wrong with his belief that *p*. He has a reason, *q*, for his belief that *p* and he is not aware of any reason for doubting *q*. But this just shows that Green's belief is only *subjectively* justified. From an objective perspective, Green's reason for believing *p* is arbitrary, and arbitrary reasons are not good enough for objective justification.

Now, it might seem that identifying some apparently basic beliefs as "innocent until proven guilty" would be a more promising way to go than having the source of justification being simply arbitrary, as in our example with Green. More would need to be said, of course – we might have to characterize what sorts of other features such beliefs would need to have in order to merit counting them as "innocent until proven guilty." But notice that once we have supplied such grounds, the very property of being "innocent until proven guilty" would supply a ground of justification for such beliefs. Hence, such beliefs would now qualify as *justified* beliefs and so the theory would now not actually be a form of *unjustified* foundationalism; it would now appear to be a form of *justified* (or what we will call "traditional") foundationalism.

So this reveals why so few epistemologists are inclined to pursue unjustified foundationalism as a theoretical option. In brief, what is unappealing about such an approach is the simple fact that it allows beliefs that are not themselves justified to justify other beliefs. Moreover, such a theory cannot go on to give any good reason for thinking that the unjustified beliefs should be regarded as conveying justification to other beliefs, because whatever such reasons might be given would have the consequence of overthrowing the original claim that such beliefs really were unjustified themselves.

4.4 Linear Coherentism

Linear coherentism holds that all chains of justification must eventually form a circle – and that such circular reasoning yields justified beliefs. No epistemologist we know of has endorsed this view. It is easy enough to see why. Let us consider a very simple example, and let "*p*" stand for "The moon is made of Schabziger cheese." Let "*q*" stand for "The moon is made of a dairy by-product and blue fenugreek." Finally, let "*r*" stand for "The moon is made of a dairy by-product and *Trigonella Caerullea*." In fact, *q* is a reason for *p*, *r* is a reason for *q*, and *p* is a reason for *r*, since Schabziger cheese actually is made of skimmed cow's milk and blue fenugreek, which is none other than the herb, blue melilot, whose scientific name is *Trigonella Caerullea*. But it's ridiculous to think that you could justify your belief that the moon is made of Schabziger cheese by your belief that *q* if the only reason you had for believing *q* is your belief that the moon is made of Schabziger cheese! Circular reasoning, even if the inferences made within such reasoning work in the way the linear coherence theory requires, does not really confer justification, because each new inference can end up conferring only another step in a circle of absurdity.

4.5 Infinitism

Infinitism is the view that we can achieve justified beliefs by carrying out infinite chains of reasoning. Like linear coherentism, this is a view that has not seen any defenders, as far as we know. However, at least one epistemologist, Peter Klein, has claimed to endorse this view.[4] As a matter of fact, for reasons we will explain, we really think his view commits him to a form of unjustified foundationalism, rather than infinitism, but to see this, it will be worth attending to some of the details of his actual view.

Klein thinks that the regress argument teaches us that justifiability is about being in a position to respond to a challenge – a challenge of the form "How do you know that *p*?"

So Klein concludes that for a belief that p to be justifiable, it must be the case that S *could* produce a reason for p were she challenged. And, of course, she must be able to produce a reason for her reason, and so on. Hence, Klein adopts the following principle:

> **PJ.** S's belief that p is justifiable iff there is an infinite series of non-repeating propositions available to S such that, beginning with p, each succeeding member is a reason for the immediately preceeding one. (2007a: 11)

Klein of course recognizes that we are finite beings. It would be a bad idea for a finite being to try to carry out an infinite defense of her belief that p – she could never complete the task. But, of course, it is *irresponsible* to hold a belief without providing *any* defense for it. So how far down the chain of available reasons must a responsible agent go? Klein says that depends on the context the agent is in: how important is it that she's right about p (do lives hang in the balance)? How important is it that she's right to the people who are asking her whether p? And so on. This leads Klein to endorse the following theory of justified belief:

> **DJ.** S's belief that p is justified iff p is justified for S, S's has cited, as a reason for p, the first member of the series of propositions justifying p, and for each proposition in the series, S has cited, as a reason for it, its successor if the epistemic context requires it. (2007a: 11)

Klein claims to be an infinitist, not an unjustified foundationalist. He certainly is an infinitist about *justifiable* belief, as his principle **PJ** demonstrates. But the regress argument concerns *justified* belief. And it is clear that Klein's account of justified belief, as represented by **DJ**, is a version of unjustified foundationalism. According to **DJ**, every justified belief will have been actually supported by a finite chain of reasons and the last member of that chain will not have been supported. Hence, the last member in any chain of reasons that S has used to support a belief will itself be an *unjustified* belief. This means that a belief can be justifiedly inferred from an unjustified belief, which is just to deny premise **2** of the regress argument.

We mentioned above that Klein calls himself an "infinitist," but the infinitist part of his view is about *justifiable* belief, not *justified* belief. The regress argument concerns *justified* belief. But no one has held the infinitist view of *justified* belief because to suppose that we can carry out infinite chains of reasoning is absurd: at some point, we all die and when we die, even if we have gone through millions of steps in a chain of reasoning, there will still be infinitely more steps to go. And we have already seen why unjustified foundationalism has not seemed to many epistemologists to be a plausible account of warrant.[5]

4.6 Non-Inferentialism

Non-inferentialism, recall, is the theory that (at least some) beliefs can be non-inferentially justified. This stops the regress of justification because in asking what justifies these beliefs, we need not refer to other beliefs about whose justification the same question would arise. But non-inferentialism is a broad church; among its congregation we find:

- *Traditional foundationalists*, who think that some beliefs (for example, beliefs about our own present experiences) are immediately justified (because they are immune to Cartesian doubt), but that all other justified beliefs must be inferred from these.
- *Modest foundationalists*, who do not require that immediately justified beliefs be immune to Cartesian doubt. They will typically extend the class of immediately justified beliefs to include beliefs about our immediate physical environment.
- *Holistic coherentists*, who reject the idea that justification is a property that some beliefs get immediately and then transfer to other beliefs via inference. They think, on the contrary, that justification is something conferred on a belief to the degree that it coheres with the rest of one's beliefs

We will discuss modest foundationalism and holistic coherentism in detail in the following sections, but first we

should make some remarks about traditional foundationalism.[6] As we have noted, foundationalists hold that there are
non-inferentially justified beliefs (also called *basic beliefs*).
The thought behind traditional foundationalism is that if
there are such beliefs, they must be *self-justified*. Furthermore, traditional foundationalists assume, plausibly enough,
that the only way a belief could be self-justified is if merely
holding the belief guarantees that it is justified – if the belief
is indefeasible. We will say that a belief that *p* is *indefeasible*
for *S* if and only if *S*'s believing *p* entails that *S* is justified
in believing *p*.[7] Traditional foundationalists try to identify
some feature of foundational beliefs that guarantees their
indefeasibility. They might, for example, hold that such
beliefs are *incorrigible* (impossible to be mistaken) or that
we have some sort of *direct access to* or *awareness of* the
very thing that makes the belief true. For example, Descartes' "I think therefore I am" might be an example of an
incorrigible belief; or it might seem that we have direct
awareness of the conscious experiences that make beliefs like
"I *feel* cold" or "That *looks* red" true. Beliefs about the
external world, on the other hand, are not incorrigible and
we do not seem to be directly aware of their truth-makers.
So traditional foundationalists have thought that the foundations of knowledge are beliefs about our own present conscious experiences and perhaps about simple *a priori* truths.
From these self-justified foundational beliefs, we can infer
other beliefs that will inherit justification from the foundational beliefs.[8]

We discuss two influential objections to traditional foundationalism. The first objection is due to BonJour (1978).
BonJour argues that there can be no self-justifying (or indefeasible belief). What is it about beliefs concerning our conscious experiences that make them self-justified? We looked
at two possible answers, and no doubt there are other possibilities that a foundationalist might appeal to. The general
point, however, is that the foundationalist must identify some
feature φ that all basic beliefs have, such that having φ makes
those beliefs highly probable. After all, epistemic justification
is about truth (or accuracy), so if foundational beliefs are
self-justified, they must have some feature that makes them
likely to be true. But then, surely, we are not justified in our

foundational beliefs unless we are justified in believing that they have feature φ and that beliefs with feature φ are likely to be true.[9] That is to say, that they are not foundational after all, for their justification depends on the justification of other beliefs.

The second problem with traditional foundationalism is that, even if beliefs about our current mental states are incorrigible and foundational, this would seem to be too austere of a foundation to support knowledge of the external world. To move from beliefs about our own experiences to non-foundational beliefs about the external world, we must use rules of inference. Traditional foundationalists have also typically required that we be justified in accepting the rules of inference that we use. Now there are two types of rules of inference: *deductive* and *non-deductive* (or *ampliative*).[10] Clearly, deductive inference rules will not take us from "this cup looks red" to "this cup is red" – Descartes' evil demon thought-experiment shows that our experiences don't logically entail anything about the external world.

So, if the traditional foundationalist is to secure us justified external world beliefs, she will have to allow us to use non-deductive inference rules. She will also have to allow that we are justified in believing such rules. But then our knowledge of non-deductive inference rules must itself be either inferentially or non-inferentially justified. It looks like they cannot be inferentially justified, for that would require deriving them from our basic beliefs and the rules of deductive inference (as the deductive inference rules are the only alternative to the non-deductive rules). But deductive rules will never entail the truth of, for example, inductive generalizations. On the other hand, it seems implausible that our belief in non-deductive inference rules could be non-inferentially justified in the traditional sense: they certainly seem far from incorrigible or "demon-proof."

These objections may not be insurmountable, but they have been very influential. And whether or not they are surmountable by the traditional foundationalist, they are not problems faced by modest foundationalism. Rather than pursue the matter further, we will turn to a different skeptical argument that, we think, does a better job of dividing up theories of justification. We will then be in a position to see a more fundamental problem with both traditional and modest foundationalism.

4.7 The Problem of the Criterion

It seems to us that the best of way drawing distinctions among different types of theories is by asking how they respond to a version of the skeptical argument known as *the problem of the criterion*. The argument makes use of the following premise:

> **KR.** A belief source K can produce justified beliefs for S only if S is justified in believing that K is reliable.

We obviously believe that some belief sources are reliable and others are unreliable. Given this fact of epistemic life, it would seem like a bad policy to trust a belief source blindly before we know whether it is reliable. Now to make the problem of the criterion concrete, consider a particular belief source: sense perception. Most of our knowledge about the world comes from sense perception. If knowledge requires justification, and **KR** is true, then we had better be justified in believing that sense perception is reliable. Of course, intuitively, we *are* justified in thinking sense perception is reliable. A problem arises, however, when we reflect on *how* we might get such justification. It seems that the only way we can learn about the reliability of sense perception is by our experience using such faculties. You might, for example, discover that your ability to recognize faces at 500 yards or more is very unreliable by seeing faces from that distance and then getting closer to confirm or disconfirm who you thought you saw. And, of course, psychologists who study our perceptual faculties run all sorts of interesting experiments that teach us about where and when our faculties are reliable and unreliable. But now there seems to be a real problem:

1. Sense perception can produce justified beliefs for us only if we are justified in believing that sense perception is reliable.

2. We can be justified in thinking that sense perception is reliable only if we have justified perceptual beliefs that provide support for this conclusion.
3. Either *(i)* we must have justification for thinking that sense perception is reliable prior to gaining justification for our sensory beliefs, or *(ii)* we must have justification for our sensory beliefs prior to gaining justification for thinking that sense perception is reliable.
4. By 2, *(i)* cannot be the case.
5. By 1, *(ii)* cannot be the case.
6. Hence, sense perception cannot produce justified beliefs.

The argument, in a nutshell, says that since we need to be justified in thinking that sense perception is reliable before it can produce justified beliefs, and that the only way to find out whether sense perception is reliable is to use justified beliefs generated by sense perception, there is no way for sense perception to generate justified beliefs. That's a very skeptical conclusion, and it generalizes to other belief-sources like memory, deduction, and induction. We leave it to our readers, however, to spell out the versions of the argument that concern these other belief-sources.

Once again, if we want to avoid skepticism, we will have to reject one of the first three premises of this argument. Which premise we reject will determine which sort of theory of justification we endorse.

Dogmatism is the view that rejects premise 1 (and accepts 2). Dogmatists think that we can get justified beliefs from, for example, perception even if we aren't justified in believing that perception is reliable. We should note that modest versions of foundationalism count as dogmatist theories in our sense. It is somewhat unclear (and it depends on the particulars of the theory) whether traditional foundationalism will count as versions of dogmatism or apriorism.

Apriorism is the view that rejects premise 2 (and accepts 1 and 3). Apriorists think that we have *a priori* justification for thinking that sense perception is reliable and that this is what enables sense perception to produce justified beliefs for us.

Holistic coherentism is the view that rejects premise 3 (and accepts 1 and 2). Holistic coherentists do not think that the justification for either belief is prior to the other – it is only when we have enough together in a coherent way that *any* of them become justified; and then they become justified all at once.

It's worth remarking that many important theories of justification are versions of dogmatism and many other important theories of justification are versions of holistic coherentism, though dogmatism seems to be the more common view. Some noteworthy versions of dogmatism are:

- *Evidentialism*, as advanced in Earl Conee and Richard Feldman (2004).
- *Traditional foundationalism*, as advanced in Laurence BonJour (2001).
- *Traditional foundationalism*, as advanced in Richard Fumerton (1995).
- *Unjustified foundationalism*, as advanced in Peter Klein (1999, 2000, 2005a, 2005b, 2007a, 2007b, and 2011).
- *The Defeasible Reasons Theory*, as advanced in John Pollock (1974) and also Pollock and Cruz (1999).
- *Dogmatism*, as advanced in James Pryor (2000).

(Most forms of externalism also qualify as dogmatist theories, in the sense that they treat our cognitive processes as conferring warrant on their products, but do not require warrant from some other source themselves. We discuss externalism in chapter 6.)

Some noteworthy versions of holistic coherentism are:

- *Negative coherentism*, as advanced in Gilbert Harman (1973).
- *Positive coherentism*, as advanced in Keith Lehrer (2000a).
- *Positive coherentism*, as (formerly) advanced in Laurence BonJour (1985).
- *Positive coherentism*, as (formerly and tentatively) advanced in Stewart Cohen (2002).

Apriorism is the view most associate with Descartes, who sought an *a priori* proof that a non-deceiving God exists and endowed us with reliable sensory faculties. The perceived failure of Descartes' project provided much of the impetus for the rise of contemporary dogmatism. But apriorism has not received much attention from contemporary epistemologists. Accordingly, we won't discuss apriorism any further in this chapter.

Our aim here is not to survey all these views – excellent critical surveys already exist.[11] Instead, we will examine a recent (and influential) dogmatist theory and notice a serious problem – a problem that is shared by all versions of dogmatism. We will then examine a version of holistic coherentism. This view, we contend, avoids the problem that beleaguers dogmatism.

4.8   Dogmatism and the Problem of Easy Knowledge

Distinctive of dogmatism is the claim that some belief sources can produce justified beliefs for *S* even if *S* does not know that such sources are reliable. A recent influential version of dogmatism is in Pryor (2000).[12] One of the main theses of Pryor's view is the following principle:

> **PFJ.** If (i) *S* has an experience as of *p*'s being the case, (ii) *S* has no reason to think that her experience is misleading, and (iii) *S* believes *p* on the basis of this experience, then *S* is justified in believing that *p*.

The idea is that, absent a special reason for doubt, you are justified in taking your experiences at face value. If you have an experience as of there being a large red cylinder in front of you, and you believe, on this basis, that there *is* a large red cylinder in front of you, you will have formed a justified belief (provided that you have no reason for thinking that your experience is misleading in this case).

Now there are some questions that we might ask Pryor. Let us imagine you see a bright red apple on the table. Your visual experience in this case will consist of a particular two-dimensional array of variously colored light. What are you having an experience "as of"? Is it an experience as of a two-dimensional color array? Is it an experience as of a red three-dimensional object? Is it an experience as of a bright red apple? Or perhaps it is an experience as of a Washington-grown, pesticide-free, Red Delicious apple? Though I may be seeing a Washington-grown, pesticide-free, Red Delicious apple, surely my visual experience alone is not sufficient justification for *believing* that I am seeing a Washington-grown, pesticide-free, Red Delicious apple. My justification for that belief would need to include knowledge about where apples are grown, where this particular apple came from, what farms don't use pesticides, and so on.

So, for Pryor's view to be plausible, he'll need an account of what a particular experience is "as of" that doesn't allow the absurd result that you could have non-inferential perceptual justification for believing that you are looking at a Washington-grown, pesticide-free, Red Delicious apple. Of course, Pryor offers such an account and we need not pause here to evaluate it. We note the issue simply to help the reader understand the nature of the view.

PFJ explains how we acquire basic, non-inferentially justified beliefs. These basic beliefs will, further, count as evidence for other propositions. If, for example, you open the cabinet and see a nearly empty bottle of whisky, you perhaps acquire a non-inferentially justified belief that the whisky bottle is nearly empty. This may count as strong evidence that your roommate pilfered most of your whisky. So, on the basis of your justified belief that the whisky bottle is nearly empty, you could justifiedly infer that your roommate pilfered most of your whisky. This belief could in turn serve as the evidential basis for still further beliefs (e.g., that your roommate is a cheapskate, that his borderline alcoholic girlfriend must have been over last night, and so on).

This version of dogmatism has many points in its favor. For one, it avoids the skeptical conclusion of the problem of the criterion. Further, it explains how we can begin to acquire justified beliefs about the world around us even before we know much about our belief-forming processes or their varying degrees of reliability. Finally, it is rather plausible that, if you have an experience as of *p*, then you are justified in taking that experience at face value (absent special reasons for doubt) – at least, it seems as though we ordinarily conduct our epistemic business in this way.

There is, however, a rather serious problem with dogmatism, and it is one that epistemologists have begun to appreciate only recently. Stewart Cohen has called it "*the problem of easy knowledge*" (2002). Let's suppose we are considering a version of dogmatism that entails the following:

> E. If (i) S has an experience as of O being the color X, (ii) S has no reason to think that her experience is misleading, and (iii) S believes O is the color X on the basis of this experience, then S is justified in believing that O is the color X.

It's an intuitive enough principle. If something looks red to you, that's all the reason you need for thinking that it is red. One way of encountering the problem of easy knowledge, however, is via what is known as the closure principle:

> JClosure. If S justifiedly believes that p, and S competently deduces q from p, then S justifiedly believes that q.

This principle is also quite intuitive. If you grant that someone is justified in believing that p, and you agree with them that p entails q, how on earth could you fault them for thereby believing q, once they have made the deduction? Consider now the version of the closure principle for knowledge:

> KClosure. If S knows that p, p entails q, and S competently deduces q from p, then S knows that q.

If justification is required for knowledge, it is hard to see how **KClosure** could be true but **JClosure** false. Perhaps unsurprisingly, some epistemologists have denied one or another version of closure. Nevertheless, as we shall see in chapter 6, the theoretical costs of denying closure are quite high.

Back to the problem of easy knowledge. Suppose Plum has an experience as of O being red and has no reason for thinking this experience is misleading. He forms the belief that O is red on the basis of experience. According to E, Plum is justified in believing that O is red. But if O is red, this entails that O is not white with red lights shining on it, and Plum knows this. So suppose Plum competently deduces that O is not white with red lights shining on it. Is he thereby *justified* in believing that O is not white with red lights shining on it? It is not so clear that he is. Imagine the following conversation at a furniture store (Cohen 2002: 315):

> *Dad*: Here you go son, this is a fine red table for your room.
> *Son*: But, Dad, how do you know it's not a white table with red lights shining on it?
> *Dad*: Well, Son, it *looks* red, so it *is* red. And if it is red, then it is not white with red lights shining on it.
> *Son*: ?!

The "reason" Dad gives Son for thinking that the table is not white under red lighting is patently absurd. Ordinarily, of course, Dad *would* be justified in believing that the table is not white with red lights shining on it – only the skeptic denies that – but surely Dad cannot know this simply by carrying out the absurd reasoning above. Justification that the table is not white with red lights shining on it is simply not that easy to come by – it depends on all sorts of other knowledge (such as how often furniture stores have red lights, how a white table under red lights usually differs in appearance from a red table under white lights, and so on).

But even without closure, we encounter the problem of easy knowledge. It is often seen as a virtue of dogmatism that it can explain how we *do* eventually come to know that perception is reliable. Once we have a complete enough picture of the world around us and our perceptual faculties (which **PFJ** explains how we can acquire), we can then infer various things about the reliability of our faculties. Dogmatism seems to be in a good position to explain how, for example, modern vision science is possible.

But if dogmatism is right, there is a much easier way of determining whether our color vision is reliable – a way that is much *too* easy. Suppose Son asks Dad whether color vision is reliable. Dad picks up a stack of colored construction paper and tells Son that they can investigate the matter together.

(Dad picks up a red piece of paper.)
Dad: Well, this one is red. And it *looks* red. So color vision
worked that time.
(Dad picks up a blue piece of paper.)
Dad: Let's see . . . this one is blue. And, why, what do you
know – it *looks* blue. Color vision worked again!
(Hundreds of sheets later.)
Dad: Well, Son, our color vision got it right 345 times out of
345. That seems pretty darn reliable to me!

Once again, this procedure is patently absurd. Surely this
is no way of coming to justifiedly believe that color vision is
reliable! The trouble is, according to principle E, there is
nothing wrong the procedure. For each time Dad flips over
a piece of paper and sees that the paper is color *X*, E says
that Dad justifiedly believes that the paper is color *X*. Furthermore, if something looks color *X* to us, dogmatists will
presumably allow that we can justifiedly *believe* that something looks color *X* to us. But if we assume that enumerative
induction is a way of gaining knowledge of reliability – and
how else could we learn about reliability? – then the dogmatist will have to allow that Dad's procedure is a good one.
   That is an unacceptable result. For all its intuitive appeal,
dogmatism makes knowledge about our reliability *much too
easy*. Perhaps, then, holistic coherentism is a better response
to the problem of the criterion.

4.9   Our Epistemic Mission as a Part of Our Life Missions

If dogmatism is false, then it must be that we can have justified perceptual beliefs only if we have a justified belief that
perception is reliable. How do we acquire justification for
thinking that perception is reliable? Let us approach this
question by wondering first why we believe that perception
is reliable.
   The dogmatist, no doubt, is motivated in part by the old
saying, "seeing is believing." The fact is that we have certain
cognitive equipment, such as perceptual capacities (sight,

hearing, taste, touch, smell, and kinesthetics), and the way these work is to generate new beliefs in us. If you now ask, "But what justifies these beliefs?" we might be inclined simply to answer that they don't require inferential justification (given the automatic nature in which they arise in us, it is not as if we infer them from anything else). Their justification is immediate and derives from the nature of our perceptual faculties.

But this is moving a bit too fast. It is one thing to talk about how perceptual beliefs and other cognitive states come into being, and another to ask in virtue of what (if anything) they qualify *as justified*. We should grant the dogmatist that simple perceptual beliefs are not usually formed by inference from other beliefs. But we have seen that we must disagree with the dogmatist that their justification does not depend on other beliefs. In particular, it seems that the justification for our perceptual beliefs must depend, in part, on our justification for thinking that perception is reliable. This now leads to what may at first seem to be a rather puzzling question: granting that we have processes that automatically produce beliefs in us, do we also have some *reason* or *evidence* for thinking that these processes are reliable?

One way to approach this question might be to ask what it would be like to reject perception as unreliable. This would be like the case of someone whose response to Descartes' evil demon scenario was a little overboard: rather than feeling a certain nagging doubt, imagine someone becoming convinced that the scenario was true, and therefore also convinced that everything she experienced via the senses and other automatic cognitive processes was actually *false*. Think about what would happen to such a person. She wakes up in the morning, but is convinced that what looks like solid floor beneath her is actually not solid or a floor at all. What looks like food is actually not at all nourishing. She can't really stop breathing, although she is convinced that aspirating the air will not help her to survive. But it doesn't matter what she does or doesn't do, because whatever things appear to be, they're actually completely different. Having no basis on which to make any judgment of any kind about her environment, she finds she has no reason one way or another to do anything at all: no reason to eat or drink, no reason to dodge what looks like traffic, no reason not to jump from cliffs or play with fire. If one really rejects all of the beliefs one's cognitive capacities automatically cause, one would obviously not survive for long.

But notice that the case is actually trickier than this quick sketch, because the way in which our cognitive capacities seem to work is to induce belief, but then the over-riding beliefs of our bizarre case would either need to have the capacity actually to block or negate the automatic processes, or else what would really be occurring is that the processes would continue as normal, causing our heroine to believe just like everyone else, but she would also be generating negating *meta-beliefs* of such a sort as to suffer from the most massive case of cognitive conflict. At the base level, her capacities would continue to make her believe things about her world, but then she would also generate the meta-belief that all of these other beliefs were false. In either case, the outcome would be disabling – either she would find a way to block her ordinary processes from forming beliefs as usual, or else she would be busily meta-cognitively rejecting every belief she could consider, even as she could not control such beliefs arising in her.

Of course, if someone really was in a world controlled by a Cartesian demon, one would be better off, as far as trying to believe only what is true and not to believe what is false, attempting our heroine's bizarre strategy – for this strategy would actually be the most effective one in a demon-world. But if we situate our epistemic mission within our broader life-missions (such as survival, social acceptance, and the many other things we pursue as crucial to our well-being), then plainly our heroine's bizarre epistemic strategy would be an extremely poor fit. From this, we can conclude that our life-missions have consequences upon how we are to practice our epistemic mission, such that *it is simply not a real option for us **not** to rely on our ordinary automatic cognitive processes.*

That does not prove at all that we cannot ever be given reasons for doubting any of the effects of our ordinary automatic cognitive processes, even to the point of mistrust. Consider all of the famous optical illusions – the apparently bent stick in water that we know is straight, or the mirage of water in the road we know is completely dry. We can and do mistrust and reject the appearances of perceptions when we have sufficient evidence for regarding them as unreliable. As we look at the stick in the water, we actually *do not* believe that it is bent, so, in this case, seeing is not believing. Instead, our meta-cognitive self-assessment works in such a way as to block the customary link between perception and belief. What we can't do is to achieve that same effect globally – rejecting all of our spontaneously generated beliefs – without completely abandoning or confounding too many of our other life-missions. So, we are selective in this process, and treat the automatic cognitive processes with the respect that they deserve, as measured by their roles in our other life-missions. In other words, it is a kind of default, within the way that we cognitively process, that we regard the effects of our automatic cognitive processes as being reliable indicators of truth.[13]

> **DR.** To fulfill our overall life-mission, we must treat our automatic cognitive processes – in particular, perception – as generally reliable (while recognizing that we can come to discover localized domains of unreliability).

Unfortunately, **DR** does not provide us with *evidence* for the reliability of perception. We must distinguish here between *practical* and *epistemic* reasons for belief. A practical reason for believing that *p* says that it is in your best practical interest to believe *p*, regardless whether *p* is true or you have any evidence. Consider an example: if someone offers you $1,000,000 to believe that the moon is made of green cheese, it may very well be in your interest to believe that the moon is made of green cheese. The fact that there's $1,000,000 in it for you is a practical reason for you to believe that the moon is made of green cheese. An epistemic reason for believing *p*, on the other hand, is something that counts as evidence for *p*, or that makes *p* likely to be true. The fact that someone has offered you $1,000,000 is not *evidence* that the moon is made of green cheese; nor does it make any likelier that the moon is made of green cheese.

Having distinguished between practical and epistemic reasons, it is pretty clear that epistemic justification – of the sort required for knowledge – concerns epistemic reasons. You can't know that the moon is made of green cheese on the basis of the fact that someone offered you $1,000,000 to believe so. To know that the moon is made of green cheese requires evidence – satellite images perhaps, the testimony of knowledgeable scientists, or perhaps a visit to the moon.

As **DR** suggests, it may be in our best overall interest to believe that perception is reliable, but this is a practical rather than epistemic reason. **DR** explains why we originally trust our perception as reliable, but it cannot be the explanation of how that trust gets *justified*. The only way we can see of explaining that justification is holistic coherentism, to which we now turn.

4.10   Holistic Coherentism and Justification

Let us reconsider the picture the dogmatist gave us of justification. Her view is that justification for individual beliefs is *generated* (*ex nihilo*, as it were) from perception: the experience as of a red apple creates justification for believing that there is a red apple. This justification can then be *transferred* to other beliefs by means of inference (if there's a red apple, then Suzie forgot to eat her snack). The problem with this picture is that it creates the problem of easy knowledge.

But consider a different picture of justification. The holistic coherentist suggests that justification for a belief is generated by the *overall coherence* of the system of beliefs within which it is situated and the degree to which the belief fits into (or coheres with) that system. After enough time in the world, we will form an overall picture of ourselves and our environment (a system of beliefs). If this system has a high degree of coherence, then particular beliefs within the system earn their justification by adding to the overall coherence of the system.

Perhaps an analogy will help. A large ship at sea keeps the crew out of the water, not in virtue of any particular plank of wood, but because there are numerous planks of wood fitting together in the right way. Any particular plank of wood contributes to the ship's seaworthiness by fitting in its spot and plugging a potential leak. This might be contrasted with a building: what supports a man on the fifth floor is, ultimately, the foundational pillars on the ground – those provide support independently of the rest of the structure, which merely adds height. In the ship, however, each plank is of roughly equal importance and, without enough planks, the ship can't float in the first place.

The holistic coherentist views justification as analogous to a ship at sea. None of our beliefs can be justified until we have enough of them fitting together to have a coherent picture of the world. At that point, a bit of magic happens and they all acquire justification "at once" (all those that cohere well, that is). The key thesis for the holistic coherentist is the following:

> **HC.** S's belief that p is justified just in case p coheres well with S's belief system, which itself has a high degree of coherence.

Notice how different holistic coherentism is from linear coherentism: for the holistic coherentist, no circular inferences take place. If asked what ultimately justifies a belief, the holistic coherentist does not point to another belief, and then another and another until she winds up in a circle. Instead, she points to the *fact* that the belief fits into a coherent system.

Principle **HC** explains why perceptual beliefs can be justified only if we also have justified beliefs about the reliability of perception. Imagine someone with a very simple belief system which contained no beliefs about the reliability of his faculties. His belief system is lacking in coherence: he finds himself with perceptual beliefs which he has no reason to trust, yet he trusts them anyway. This creates incoherence between his first-order perceptual beliefs and meta-cognitive beliefs about perception. His first-order beliefs presuppose that his perceptual faculties are reliable, but his meta-cognitive judgment must be that he has no idea whether they are reliable. As far as **DR** goes, it may be perfectly reasonable for this person to run his epistemic life as he does; nevertheless, it's clear that he lacks justification for his beliefs.

And now we're in a position to see how we can, in fact, learn that our perception is reliable. As we begin our epistemic lives, we have implicit trust in our perceptual faculties, in accordance with **DR**. This allows us to acquire a large stock of perceptual beliefs – to exercise our innate cognitive equipment. As time goes on, some of the perceptual beliefs we acquire are about circumstances in which perception seems to work quite well and circumstances in which it doesn't. By this point, we have achieved a fairly sophisticated understanding of our own environment and our perceptual faculties. Our belief system is coherent, and our beliefs about perception cohere well with the system. By principle **HC**, then, they (along with the rest of our beliefs) acquire *justification*.

Holistic coherentism, then, provides a solution to the problem of the criterion *without encountering the problem of easy knowledge*. Holistic coherentists embrace the idea that we must be justified in thinking that perception is reliable if we are to be justified in our perceptual beliefs. They also endorse the claim that knowledge about the reliability of perception is itself perceptual. What they reject, however, is the idea that there are priority relations between justified beliefs. It's not as though you need to be justified in believing that perception is reliable *before* you can be justified in using perception (or vice versa). Rather, justification arises once you have both ordinary perceptual beliefs and beliefs about the reliability of perception – the coherence of such a system creates justification all at once. What is more, this solution avoids the problem of easy knowledge, because knowledge can only be the result of a system that has been built up over time and as a result of both experience and reflection on that experience. We can tentatively conclude, then, that some version of holistic coherentism is the best account of epistemic justification.

4.11 Coherentism, Dogmatism, and Doxastic Inferentialism

It's now time to fill a promissory note. We said in section 4.2 that our own view rejected the first premise of the regress of justification argument – the premise that asserts the principle we called "doxastic inferentialism." The way in which theories that reject doxastic inferentialism are able to avoid regress skepticism is by contending that there are some non-inferentially justified beliefs. As we have seen, not all theories that accept non-inferentially justified beliefs imagine that the structure of justification depends upon self-justified beliefs as foundations. So, in our discussion of the problem of the criterion, we have seen that there are more sophisticated ways of thinking about non-inferential justification.

According to the dogmatist, perceptual beliefs are non-inferentially justified. If you have an experience as of a red apple and form a belief that there is a red apple on that basis, then you are justified – you don't have to infer that belief from other beliefs. According to the holistic coherentist, in a way, it turns out that *all* beliefs are non-inferentially justified. Beliefs are justified in virtue of adding to the coherence of an adequately coherent system of beliefs. Inference, according to the coherentist, neither creates nor transfers justification, strictly speaking.

We think the divide between dogmatists and holistic coherentists is one of the central divides in epistemology, with well-developed theories on both sides. This is a divide that cannot be captured, however, via the regress argument. As far as that argument goes, nearly all epistemologists are in agreement. This suggests that differing solutions to the problem of the criterion offer a much better way to understand the landscape of contemporary epistemology. As we shall see in the next section, moreover, the approach we have endorsed here also provides an important and novel advantage in an area of epistemology that has received a great deal of attention recently.

4.12   Testimony

We have argued that justification requires a broad and coherent body of beliefs. Most adult humans have such a body of beliefs. But how do we acquire this vast store of beliefs about the world? The discussion in the previous chapter made it sound as though most such beliefs are derived from perceptual experience. In a way, of course, this is correct: virtually everything we know about the external world must come to us through the medium of our senses. But putting things in this way is misleading in an important respect. Consider the following things you probably believe:

- That Christopher Columbus sailed the ocean blue in 1492.
- That the world existed before you were born (!).
- That the Moon orbits the Earth.
- That coffee contains caffeine.

Each of these beliefs of yours is based on the *testimony of others*. The first two beliefs in the list we might call *historical* beliefs; they are beliefs about events before you were born. Clearly, any justification you have for historical beliefs must rely heavily on the testimony of others (whether that be from historical documents, textbooks, or conversation with a friend). The second two beliefs in the list we can call *scientific beliefs*; they are beliefs about scientific matters. A great many – probably *most* – scientific beliefs concern subject matters in which you are no expert. In such cases, you rely almost entirely on the expertise of scientists.[14]

Historical and scientific beliefs are but two categories of belief that depend heavily or entirely on testimony. And there are many others. To name but one example: you've likely never been to China, but believe quite a few things about it. Where could these beliefs have come from if not testimony?[15]

So a moment's reflection reveals that our body of beliefs depends heavily – perhaps ineliminably – on the testimony of others. This raises an immediate worry. Is the testimony of others really very reliable? At first glance, it doesn't seem like it. People lie. People say things about which they have no knowledge. News reporters are often lazy in checking their facts. And politicians are notorious for misleading their constituents. Testimony, it would seem, is a rather fragile basis for our beliefs.

But perhaps testimony is reliable; perhaps lies, deception, and laziness are the exceptions that prove the rule. Still, if we're to base our beliefs on testimony, don't we need to *know* that testimony is reliable? And wouldn't we have to gain such knowledge without relying on testimony? But without recourse to things we learned from others, would we really have enough resources to justify our trust in testimony? The fact that many of our beliefs are based on testimony, then, generates another version of the problem of the criterion. This problem has exercised many philosophers in recent years, and two views have arisen:[16]

Reductionism. Our justification for testimonial beliefs comes from perceptual evidence that testimony is reliable (which evidence does not itself depend on testimony).[17]

Anti-reductionism. Our justification for testimonial beliefs is basic – if someone tells you that *p*, then that gives you justification for believing that *p*, unless you have some special reason to doubt *p* or the trustworthiness of the testifier.[18]

The idea behind reductionism is simple enough. When you receive a bit of testimony, you are often in a position to check it yourself. For example, if a weather forecaster predicts rain in the afternoon then you can simply watch for rain in the afternoon to find out if the forecaster was right. If you do this often enough, you can get a feel for how reliable the forecaster is. If you discover that the forecaster is sufficiently reliable, then in the future you justifiedly believe his predictions. The key point to notice is that your justification wouldn't rely on any sort of ineliminable trust in testimony. Through ordinary perceptual experience you've learned that this forecaster usually gets it right: you have personally verified his reliability.

The reductionist claims that reliance on non-testimonial evidence is the only way testimony can give us justified beliefs. If you believe *p* on the basis of testimony, then you had better have reason – derived from personal experience – for thinking that the person who told you that *p* is reliable (in the present circumstances, anyway). Now reductionists don't want to be skeptics. And they recognize that the vast majority of our beliefs are based on testimony. So consider the horde of testifiers on whom you've relied in the past – reporters, authors, scientists, governmental agencies, doctors, strangers, mechanics, advertisers, family, preachers, talk-show hosts, Wikipedia, Dictionary.com, and so on. The reductionist is committed to claiming that you have done enough personal verification to believe reasonably that most of these testifiers are reliable.

But this is unrealistic. As a child, you implicitly trusted your parents. No doubt, you were eventually able to verify much of what they told you. But your parents tell you so much about the world that the small percentage you are able to check is hardly adequate to establish their general reliability. Nevertheless, you mostly believed what they told you. And a lot of what they told you was about who else you should believe – your teachers, some books but not others, some TV shows but not others, etc. In effect, you come to have beliefs about who is reliable and who isn't from your parents (and other close childhood influences). No doubt, the very people your parents told you to trust may have led you ultimately to doubt other people you were told to trust. If you were brought up trusting intellectual books, you may eventually have read and trusted some books that led you to doubt (say) your high-school history teacher. Eventually, you end up with a pretty sophisticated system of beliefs about who to trust and who not to trust and you can probably offer some pretty good reasons for those beliefs. But this all seems to rest on an early and unverified trust in beliefs supplied by your parents. If all you had recourse to were beliefs based on personal experience, it is doubtful that you would be able to establish the statistical reliability of very many of the testifiers on whom you've relied.

Reductionism, then, would seem to lead to deep skepticism about most of our beliefs. That is a serious problem with reductionism. Anti-reductionism avoids this problem. Anti-reductionists claim that testimony is a unique source of justification: the fact that someone told you that *p* is, all by itself, a reason to believe *p*. Anti-reductionism, however, has its own problems. To our minds, the most serious is that, like the dogmatism discussed in the previous chapter, anti-reductionism allows for "easy knowledge." If anti-reductionism were right, it would be too easy to find out that a testifier was reliable: you could simply believe everything she says, infer that everything she has ever told you is true,[19] and so conclude that she is very reliable. That, however, would be a very unreasonable way to proceed!

We think neither reductionism nor anti-reductionism is promising. But they are not the only options: a holistic coherentist account of justification offers a very different epistemology of testimony. Recall that our version of coherentism embraces the following principle:

> **KR.** A belief source K can produce justified beliefs for S only if S is justified in believing that K is reliable.

Restricting the principle to testimony, we get:

> **TR.** Testimony can produce justified beliefs for S only if S is justified in believing that testimony is reliable.

The reductionist also embraces **TR**. But the anti-reductionist will be quick to point out that this leads to skepticism: without relying on testimonial beliefs, we will not be able to establish the reliability of testimony. But if we recall what we said earlier about the problem of the criterion applied to perception, we can now see that both parties are endorsing the following false dilemma, as applied to testimony:

> Either (*i*) we must have justification for thinking that testimony is reliable prior to gaining justification for our testimonial beliefs, or (*ii*) testimony can produce justified beliefs for S even if S has no justification for thinking that testimony is reliable.

There is, as we have seen, a third option: according to the holistic coherentist account, neither our justification for our testimonial beliefs nor our justification for thinking that testimony is reliable needs to be *prior* to the other. According to the holistic coherentism that we have advocated, beliefs are justified only insofar as they cohere well with a broad system of beliefs that is itself coherent. A sufficiently coherent system of beliefs will include beliefs about the reliability of belief sources (testimony, perception, reason). But these reliability beliefs are themselves justified by their coherence with the rest of the system, not by some antecedent source of justification.

As children, we implicitly trust the testimony of a great many unverified sources. This is a crucial step in acquiring the beliefs that we do. But it is only once we have developed a broad and sophisticated body of beliefs (one which includes beliefs about when and what sort of testimony to trust) that we begin to have *justified* beliefs. And these beliefs are justified "all at once" – beliefs *about* testimony and beliefs *based on* testimony becoming justified by fitting together into a broad and coherent system of beliefs. We conclude that holistic coherentism offers the best available account of testimonial justification.

4.13 Holistic Coherentism and the Possibility of Animal Knowledge

We conclude this chapter with a dilemma. It is tempting to think that knowledge requires justification. In this chapter, we have examined the notion of epistemic justification and concluded that holistic coherentism is the best account of justification. However, it seems likely that animals and small children do not have the sorts of systematic, coherent belief systems required of epistemic justification. We seem to be faced with a choice: we can either (i) say that knowledge requires justification and that animals and small children do not know things, or (ii) say that knowledge does not require justification and accept that easy knowledge is, contrary to intuitions, possible. This is, to say the least, an awkward choice. In chapter 8, however, we will see that there is a way to avoid this dilemma.

Current Trends

We discussed some of the standard objections to traditional foundationalism. Although we do not accept this view ourselves, any claims that traditional foundationalism is dead would be an exaggeration, since there has recently been a notable resurgence of interest in the view. Fumerton (1995) and BonJour (2001) are but two examples of epistemologists defending sophisticated versions of traditional foundationalism. For an excellent collection of essays on the topic, see DePaul (2001).

The problem of easy knowledge has been a significant topic of discussion since the publication of Cohen's 2002. Additional entries in the literature are Van Cleve (2003), Bergmann (2004), Markie (2005), Cohen (2005), Black (2008), Kornblith (2009), and Cohen (2010). Interestingly, Cohen's most recent work on the topic has advocated a kind of apriorism. The most startling feature of this view is that it grants us *a priori* knowledge of contingent truths.

As we indicated in our section on the subject, the epistemology of testimony has been a focus of significant recent debate. As we indicated there, the debates in the literature have tended to support either the reductionist position (Adler 1994; Fricker 1994; and Lyons 1997) or the anti-reductionist position (Coady 1992; Burge 1997; Foley 1994; and Audi 2002). Our own holistic coherentist defense of testimonial justification is, as far as we know, novel, and presented here for the first time.

Unfortunately, holistic coherentism has not received much support or attention in recent years (with the notable exceptions of Lehrer (2000a) and Cohen (2002) – whose endorsement is only tentative in any case). But we hope that our arguments in this chapter provide some reason for enterprising young epistemologists to take up the torch!

5

Justification, Defeaters, and Basing

According to the inherited lore of the epistemological tribe, the [justified true belief] account enjoyed the status of epistemological orthodoxy until 1963, when it was shattered by Edmund Gettier with his three-page paper "Is Justified True Belief Knowledge?" . . . Of course there is an interesting historical irony here: it isn't easy to find many really explicit statements of a JTB analysis of knowledge prior to Gettier. It is almost as if a distinguished critic created a tradition in the very act of destroying it.

Plantinga 1993a: 6–7

5.1 Defeated Justification

One of the problems for justification as an account of warrant is that one's justification can be *defeated*. The way in which this happens is for something to go wrong in one's evidence, where what has gone wrong is not one's *fault* – where any normal person would accept one's evidence as justification, and yet the evidence itself is flawed. The famous origin of this problem is found in a very important paper by Edmund Gettier (1963). Gettier actually gives a couple of cases, so let us begin with these. What follows is our own paraphrase of Gettier's examples.

Smith and Jones are roommates and are both candidates for a job. Smith happens to notice that Jones has 10 coins on top of Jones's dresser, which Jones then sweeps into his hand and then pocket, as he leaves for his job interview. Smith also sweeps his own coins into his hand and pocket, but fails to notice how many coins were included. When Smith is called into his own interview, the interviewer informs him that the job will go to Jones, instead. Although he is sorry to receive this news, Smith is still good at making inferences, and infers that the one who will get the job has 10 coins in his pocket. Smith believes this. But now, the interviewer informs the company president of her decision, and is overruled by the company president, who prefers Smith for the job. So, in fact, the offer will actually go to Smith, who will gladly accept. And it turns out that the number of coins Smith happened to put into his pocket that morning was the same as for Jones: Smith has 10 coins in his pocket. Hence, Smith's belief that the one who will get the job has 10 coins in his pocket is true, and given Smith's evidence, Smith is also justified in this belief. But Smith surely does not know that the one who will get the job has 10 coins in his pocket because, as it turns out, all of Smith's evidence for this belief is completely irrelevant, as all of that evidence has to do with someone *other* than the one who actually gets the job.

In the second example, suppose that Smith has good reason to believe that Jones owns a Ford – he always sees Jones driving a Ford and has often driven with Jones in that Ford. Now suppose that Smith has another friend, Brown, but Smith has no idea where Brown is right now. Knowing that one may validly infer any disjunction from something that is true (that is, if p is true, one may always infer that either p or q is true, for any value of q, since the truth value of the disjunction will be true if either or both of the disjuncts are true), Smith creates the following disjunction in his mind:

r. Either Jones owns a Ford or Brown is in Barcelona.

Well, it turns out that Jones never did own a Ford – he has always preferred to use a rental car. But, as it turns out, Brown really is in Barcelona. Smith believes that *r*, and is justified in his belief. Moreover, *r* is true, but all of Smith's evidence for believing *r* has to do with Jones, and all of his evidence is misleading. Smith actually has no evidence concerning Brown, and yet it is because of Brown and Brown's current whereabouts that Smith's belief is true. So, as with the other case, it appears that Smith's justified true belief cannot count as knowledge, because all of Smith's evidence for his belief is irrelevant. In both cases, it seems to be *just luck* that the beliefs happen to be true.

5.2 Defeating Defeaters

Many similar examples can be (and have been) proposed with the same basic problem. Each of these examples is a case in which epistemologists would say the justification is *defeated*, because some *other* evidence "out there" shows that what the epistemic agent counts as justifying his belief is actually false. So, what we need, in order to surmount the Gettier problem, is some stipulation to the effect that the justification is not defeated. Now, one way to try to achieve this result is to add, as an addition to our justification condition, that there is no *other* information "out there" that would defeat the justification.[1] But this gives rise to new problems, including misleading defeaters and false (or defeated) defeaters.

A misleading defeater is one that could lead someone to think his justification was defeated, even when it is not actually defeated. To see how this might work, consider the following case, modified from one given by Lehrer and Paxson:[2] I see someone walk into a library and then take a book from the shelf and stick it under his jacket and then leave the library. I recognize the man as Tom Grabit, whom I have known for a few years now and see and talk with often, and whom I have come to recognize (for good reason until now) as an honest and law-abiding man. But suppose further that unbeknownst to me, Tom has an identical twin brother, John, a kleptomaniac with a long arrest and conviction record for stealing books from libraries. Were this fact to come to my knowledge, I might no longer feel any confidence in my justification for thinking that Tom stole the book. But if we now add that (also unbeknownst to me) Tom's brother was nowhere near the library on the day of the theft, we will see that this "defeater" is a *misleading defeater*, because it actually was Tom who stole the book, and my justification for thinking that it was Tom is unaffected by this additional (and true) information.

A false defeater will be one that might also be taken as defeating one's justification, but the defeater itself is false. A case of this sort would be where I see Tom Grabit steal the book and believe this, but unbeknownst to me Tom's mother has claimed that Tom was not anywhere near the library that day, but instead, Tom's evil twin brother was there and stole the book. However, also unbeknownst to me, Tom's mother is a pathological liar, and Tom has no evil twin. Just confronted with Tom's mother's testimony, I might regard my justification as defeated. But the defeater (the mother's testimony) is false – that is, there is still other information out there that defeats this defeater (i.e., that the mother is lying about the brother).

So, while we can see why we require that the justification not be defeated, we must also have some way of making sure that we don't count justification as defeated, if the only defeaters out there are themselves either misleading or false. Let us call any consideration that would lead us to regard a certain defeater as either misleading or false a "defeater-defeater," because any consideration that would allow us to dismiss a defeater would defeat that defeater *as* a defeater. So, we might now say that our justification will be undefeated, just in case all defeaters to that justification are themselves defeated.

Now, one might think that it would be enough simply to insist that one's justification does not depend on anything that is actually *false*. This provision would actually handle all of the problem cases we have imagined so far, but cases can be imagined in which this condition remained true, but we would still conclude that the justification was defeated. Consider another twist on the Grabit case:[3] I see Tom Grabit steal the book, but unbeknownst to me Tom has an identical twin brother, John, a kleptomaniac with a long arrest and conviction record for stealing books from libraries. Moreover (also unbeknownst to me), reliable eyewitnesses place John in the library at the exact time I claim to have witnessed the crime. In this case, it seems that I cannot know that Tom stole the book (even though, in this case, he really did), because something I do not know reveals my justification as inadequate. My justification does not depend on anything that is false;

however, given all of the relevant information, it is shown to be inadequate.

It might yet be objected that this is actually not a case in which my justification does not depend on anything that is false, because the way in which I treat my evidence shows that I regard it as *adequate*, when, in fact, it is *not adequate*. But this additional commitment on my part reveals the falsehood that defeats my justification: in addition to the evidence that I have, I have made a meta-cognitive assessment of my evidence, and that assessment is false, and my justification requires that my assessment be true and not false.[4]

Whether or not these considerations are sufficient to provide an adequate account of what it means for justification to be undefeated continues to be a matter of debate – one that we do not claim to end here. But at least the strategies we have reviewed show in general terms why epistemologists are convinced that, if and insofar as justification is a requirement of knowledge, it must be *undefeated* justification that satisfies such a requirement. As we will see, these same strategies will come in handy again when we consider forms of warrant other than justification, for which the familiar Gettier problems also arise.

5.3 The Basing Relation

We have been discussing some of the specific problems that arise when we think of warrant in terms of justification. Yet another such problem concerns what is called the "basing relation," which we mentioned in section 4.1. There we distinguished between a belief that is justifiable and one that is justified. The difference, we said, is that a justified belief must be *based on* the evidence that makes it justifiable. We can call the relation between a belief and its basis "the basing relation." If we think of warrant in terms of justification, it must be justified belief, rather than merely justifiable belief, that we're after. Accordingly, an account of warrant will involve an account of the basing relation.

What sorts of things can we base our beliefs on? What sort of relation is the basing relation? In answer to the first question, we note that our beliefs can be based on all sorts of things: on other beliefs, on experiences, memories, and even emotions. Perhaps some of our beliefs are baseless. In answer to the second question, epistemologists have offered several accounts of the basing relation. We are convinced that none of them are adequate, and will propose a new account here.

5.4 Causal Theories of Basing

Very many epistemologists have supposed that the basing relation is a *causal relation*: the bases of a belief are the causes of that belief. This is why so many epistemologists have maintained that justified beliefs must be properly caused. A typical causal theory of the basing relation looks something like this:

> **CTB.** *b* is a basis of *S*'s belief that *p* iff *b* caused *S* to believe that *p*.

There are three problems with this sort of theory. The first is called *the problem of deviant causal chains*.[5] Suppose Rex is sitting in a coffee shop when he notices the lovely Susan enter. Startled, Rex spills his hot cup of coffee on his leg and feels searing pain. Pretty clearly, Rex's belief that he is in pain is not based on his belief that Susan has just entered the coffee shop. But this is just what the causal theory would seem to imply. After all, his belief about Susan caused his belief about pain. This has turned out to be an incredibly difficult problem for causal theorists to solve.

The second problem for causal theories – and it is one that has not been widely appreciated – involves the possibility of two beliefs being based on each other. As I work on a crossword, my belief that one-across is "aero" might be (partly) based on my belief that one-down is "aria." Similarly, my belief that one-down is "aria" might be (partly) based on my belief that one-across is "aero." But it is hard to see how CTB can account for this: how could two beliefs cause each other? Consider an analogy: if your parents are the cause of your existence, then you cannot be the cause of your parents' existence!

The final problem for causal theories – and again, unrecognized – is the possibility of expunging a former basis of one's belief. Here is an example derived from Pollock's case of the widget factory (Pollock 1974). Smith is touring a widget factory. On a conveyor belt he sees what look to be some fine red widgets. On the basis of his visual experience, Smith believes that there are some fine red widgets on the conveyor belt. The factory owner approaches Smith and remarks, "Be careful, Smith: in this factory, looks can be deceiving. There are red lights shining over the conveyor belts. Those widgets you're looking at are the only actual red ones in the whole factory." When Smith hears this from the factory owner, he still believes that there are some fine red widgets. It's just that he now believes this on the basis of the factory owner's testimony and not on the basis of his experience; for he now knows that, in this factory, the fact that something looks red is no reason to think it is red. Smith's belief is no longer based on his visual experience, but it is still true that his visual experience caused his belief. Once again, the causal theorist gets the wrong result.[6]

For these reasons, we are highly suspicious of the prospects of a causal theory of the basing relation. Theorists have proposed various solutions to the problem of deviant causal chains, but none have been able to overcome all the problems we have raised. Until a more adequate causal account is on offer, we do best to look elsewhere for a correct account of the basing relation.

5.5   Doxastic Theories of the Basing Relation

The only proposed alternatives to causal theories are so-called *doxastic theories* of the basing relation. The distinctive feature of doxastic theories is the requirement that an agent believes that the basis of her belief is a good reason for her belief. We can state this simply enough:

> DTB. *b* is a basis for *S*'s belief that *p* iff *S* regards *b* as a good reason for believing that *p*.

The primary flaw of these theories is that they are unable to account for the possibility that we are mistaken about the bases of our beliefs. Consider beliefs based on wishful thinking. When we believe something on the basis of a desire, we do not typically realize we are doing so – we confabulate some reasons and think that our belief is based on them. And even when we are aware that our belief is based on wishful thinking, we certainly don't think that desiring that *p* is a good reason for believing that *p*! The same point can be made with beliefs based on prejudice: imagine that Professor Brown's belief that Professor Johnson is unqualified is based solely on his belief that Johnson is a woman. But Professor Brown is also self-deceived: he believes that he harbors no sexist prejudices. In fact, he strongly believes that his belief is *not* based on Professor Johnson's gender, but on the quality of her work. Doxastic theories do not seem to be able to handle this sort of possibility.

5.6 Our Own View: The Dispositional Theory

We have argued that existing theories of the basing relation face serious problems. We'd like to briefly propose an alternative theory. The basing relation, it seems to us, is a dependence relation: for one belief to be based on another is for the one to *depend on* the other in the right way. We think the sort of dependence in question involves how one would respond were the basis of one's belief lost – this is why we say that a belief stands or falls with its basis. If *b* really is the basis of one's belief that *p*, and one loses *b*, one responds by revising one's belief that *p*. One way of understanding this dependence is via counterfactuals. This would yield the following theory:

> **CFTB.** *S*'s belief that *p* is based on *m* iff *S* would revise her belief that *p* were she to lose *m*.

But, as is the case with so many other philosophically interesting notions, the counterfactual dependence expressed by CFTB is much too crude to capture the basing relation. Often, one *wouldn't* revise one's belief that *p* upon losing one's belief that *q*, even though the former is based on the latter; one might, for example, suddenly go brain dead, or (less drastically) find one has additional reasons for believing *p*.

A more promising means of capturing the dependence is via dispositions. After all, one can be disposed to revise one's belief that *p* upon losing one's belief that *q* even if one wouldn't actually revise one's belief (given other factors). Just consider a crystal martini glass packed in styrofoam. Surely the glass is *fragile*: it is disposed to break when dropped. Because it is packed in styrofoam, however, were it dropped, it would not break. The above remarks suggest the *dispositional theory of the basing relation*:

> **DPTB.** *S*'s belief that *p* is based on *m* iff *S* is disposed to revise her belief that *p* when she loses *m*.

Recall the example of Professor Brown who unknowingly bases his belief that Professor Johnson is unqualified on the fact that Johnson is a woman. This was a problem for doxastic theories of the basing relation, since Brown does not believe that Johnson's gender is a reason for thinking she is unqualified. But the example is no problem for **DPTB**. Suppose Brown were to find out that Johnson was actually a man. It is eminently plausible that he would re-evaluate his belief, and probably come to believe that Johnson was qualified (we can suppose that Johnson has published many excellent papers in top journals and that Johnson's renowned PhD advisor speaks very highly of him). Brown is disposed to revise his belief that Johnson is unqualified if he loses his belief that Johnson is a female. So **DPTB** agrees with our intuition that Brown's belief is based on Johnson's gender.

Similarly, **DPTB** can account for the problems that afflicted causal theories and does not face the problem of deviant causal chains. So we are optimistic that **DPTB** is on the right track, even if future objections mandate some revision.

5.7 Conclusions about the Basing Relation, and Two New Challenges

We began with the complaint that the best of the existing theories of the basing relation did not pass muster. In their place, we have offered the dispositional theory of the basing relation and tried to show that it succeeds where others have failed. The theory we have offered is intuitive and accounts for the data. But now we must confront two new challenges that may show that all the work we have done on the basing relation is beside the point. One challenge is a puzzlement about what basing would even mean in a holistic coherentist framework; the other derives from an interesting case presented by Keith Lehrer. We will now discuss these in order.

5.8 Holistic Coherentism and the Basing Relation

We have suggested that merely justifiable belief is not sufficient for warrant – justified belief is required. For warrant, it is not good enough that one has evidence, reasons, or justification that support one's belief; one's belief must be *based on* those reasons. On Pryor's version of dogmatism, to have a justified belief that one was looking at a red object, it is not enough that one has an experience as of a red object – one's belief that there is a red object must also be based on that experience. More generally, dogmatist theories of justification tell us which individual beliefs and experiences are reasons for further beliefs. The dogmatist can then say that for a particular belief to be justified, the agent must have the reasons dogmatism specifies and also must base her belief on that reason. It is easy to see how the basing relation fits into a dogmatist picture of justification.

We, however, have argued that dogmatism is an incorrect view of justification. Instead, we suggest that holistic coherentism is the better view. According to holistic coherentism, what justifies your belief is not some other particular belief or experience, but the fact that you have a sufficiently broad and coherent system of beliefs and that the belief in question coheres well with this system. But surely that only guarantees justifiable belief – the holistic coherentist must give some account of what the belief must be based on for it to be justified. Perhaps the holistic coherentist should say that the belief must be based on the fact that the belief system is sufficiently broad and coherent and that the belief in question coheres well with the system. But that can't be right. The basing relation is a *psychological* relation – it holds between beliefs and other mental states. Facts about the coherence of one's belief system are not mental states.

Perhaps, then, the coherentist should say that, to be justified, a belief *B* must be based on the following meta-belief:

> **MC.** My belief system is sufficiently broad and coherent and *B* coheres well with this system.

One problem with this suggestion is that **MC** seems to generate an infinite meta-regress. For in order for the belief that **MC** to be justified, it will have to be based on the following meta-meta belief:

> **MMC.** My belief system is sufficiently broad and coherent and **MC** coheres well with this system.

And so on. A further problem is that most of us are in no position to survey our belief system and check for coherence. We can at best check for local coherence in small subsets of our belief system, but whether all those localized bits of coherence cohere is something beyond our ken.

Feldman and Conee (1985) once faced a similar challenge in defending a view of justification they call *evidentialism*. On the evidentialist view, a belief is justifiable for *S* if and only if it fits *S*'s total evidence. Feldman and Conee recognized that they also needed an account of *justified* belief (what they called "well-founded" belief) and that the following wouldn't do:

> **TE.** *S*'s belief is justified if and only if it fits *S*'s total evidence and is based on *S*'s total evidence.

The problem is that the totality of *S*'s evidence is far too much for *S* to survey in forming a belief. Feldman and Conee weaken their condition as follows (24):

> **TE*.** *S*'s belief is justified if and only if it fits *S*'s total evidence and there is some subset *E* of *S*'s total evidence such that (i) the belief fits and *E* and (ii) the belief is based on *E*.[7]

The idea is that though your belief must in fact fit your total evidence, it need only be *based on* a small and survey-able portion of your evidence that it fits. This means that although a belief cannot be justified unless your total evidence supports it, you need only consider a reasonably small subset of your evidence. (How much evidence need you consider? Enough to make the belief reasonable, presumably.)

Perhaps the holistic coherentist can make a similar move. The coherentist might require that S's belief be based on a reasonably small but coherent subset S's "web of beliefs." For example, consider Smith's belief that the table is red. Suppose it is justifiable according to holistic coherentism: it coheres well with the rest of Smith's beliefs, which themselves form a large and coherent system. Still, in order to be justified, it does not seem that Smith's belief that the table is red must be partly based on his belief that Mars is red (though the two beliefs do cohere). It is presumably enough that his belief be based on his visual experience (or a belief about his visual experience), his belief that he is not in any sort of strange lighting conditions, his belief that color vision is quite reliable, and perhaps some beliefs about the improbability of a fake table in the room. In saying that Smith's belief needs to be based on these other beliefs, we are *not* saying that these other beliefs *caused* Smith to believe that the table is red or that he consciously (or even unconsciously) *considered* them in forming his belief. All that we are saying is that in order for his belief to be justified, he must be disposed to revise it if he loses any of these other beliefs.

This seems like something a holistic coherentist could sensibly say. The beliefs on which we have suggested Smith's belief is based are very directly relevant to how well Smith's belief coheres with the rest of the system. If it coheres with these beliefs, then it coheres with the rest. Requiring that Smith's belief be based on them, then, guarantees that Smith's belief is to some degree *sensitive* to facts about coherence. That seems enough to transform a justifiable belief to a justified belief. We tentatively propose the following condition:

S's belief that p is justified if and only if:
(i) p coheres with S's belief system B, and B is adequately large and coherent;

(ii) *S*'s belief that *p* is based on each member of a subset *B'* of *B*.

As it stands, however, this definition is inadequate. *S* cannot simply base his belief on any old subset of his belief system. In the example, above, it seemed that *S* did not need to base his belief on his belief that Mars is red; but he *did* need to base it on his belief that color vision is reliable. How, then, are we to specify the relevant subset? We won't here propose an answer to that question, though we suspect that there is a good answer to be had. For now, we'll be content with the above account of justification, even though we recognize more specification and elucidation is required for a completely adequate account.

With this account of justification in hand, we are presently considering the following theory of warrant:

S's belief that *p* is warranted if and only if:
(i)   *S*'s belief that *p* is justified;
(ii) *S*'s justification for *p* is undefeated.

The challenge we turn to next threatens this account of warrant. Initially, it seems that it threatens our account of justified belief, for it seems to suggest that basing is not required. This is to suggest that one of our conditions on warrant is not necessary. But we will conclude that, if there is a threat, it is to the *joint sufficiency* of conditions (i) and (ii).

5.9 Lehrer's Challenge to a Basing Requirement

We began this section with the intuition that for a belief to be justified by some reasons, it must be based on them. We then noted that this seems to cause trouble for holistic coherentism and made a proposal regarding what coherentists should demand as the bases of our beliefs. Keith Lehrer, however, has challenged the connection between justified belief and the basing relation.

In *Theory of Knowledge*, Lehrer asks us to imagine a man named Raco, a racist who believes that members of a certain race are susceptible to a particular disease while members of his own race are not susceptible (Lehrer 2000a: 196–7). This belief is entirely caused by Raco's prejudices. Not only is it the case that if Raco did not have this set of prejudices, he would not have the belief, but it is precisely *because* Raco has these prejudices that he believes that members of the other race are susceptible to the disease. However, later in life, Raco becomes a doctor and, after a considerable amount of research, discovers a great deal of evidence supporting his belief. He both understands and appreciates this evidence, and once he has become aware of this evidence, it is this evidence that Raco would cite if asked for what justifies his belief. The medical evidence Raco acquires is *independent* of the process by which he comes to hold his belief – but Lehrer builds the case in such a way that Raco would also continue to hold his racist belief even if it was disconfirmed by subsequent medical studies. So Raco's belief is not based on the evidence, and yet that evidence (and Raco's recognition of it *as evidence*) seems to be what justifies Raco's belief.[8]

Lehrer offered the Raco case in order to dispute the connection some have made between justification and the basing relation, but it is worthwhile for us to consider the cases in the light of the dispositional view of basing we have provided in this chapter. Before we continue, however, one thing needs to be stipulated: our analysis of the basing relation does not have to amount to a condition of justification. We have tried, so far, only to show what it means for a belief to be based on the evidence. We have not yet had anything to say about whether a belief's being based on the evidence is (or is not) a proper condition of justification. Lehrer's challenge, thus, is not a direct challenge to our (or anyone else's) analysis of the basing relation itself. Rather, it is a challenge to those who think that having one's belief based on the evidence is a requirement for justification.

Lehrer's case is supposed to be one in which Raco's belief is justified by the evidence and yet is not based *on* the evidence. But Lehrer's case seems to presuppose some version of a causal theory of basing. So, Raco has beliefs that were not caused by the evidence according to a causal theory of the basing relation, and he would not cease to believe what he does if the evidence were to be removed or changed. The question is whether Raco provides a case of belief based on the evidence in our own dispositional analysis of the basing relation. We are inclined to think that our own analysis would actually regard Raco as a case in which the belief is based on the evidence after all.

Recall that our analysis does not require that one actually change one's belief if the evidence changes or is defeated. We require only that one be *disposed* to change one's belief in such cases, though we also were clear in saying that such dispositions might be masked by other factors. So the question our own analysis requires is this: would Raco have any disposition to change his beliefs, if the evidence were removed or defeated – even granting that other factors would ensure that he did actually continue to hold his racist beliefs? Would the change in the status of the evidence make *any difference* to Raco and, if so, how should we understand that difference?

Plainly, one difference such a change would make is that Raco would cease to be inclined to cite the evidence in support of his belief, if that evidence were defeated. This alone seems to us to be an indication of the sort of disposition to change beliefs that our own analysis of the basing relation requires. All other things equal, then, we would expect to see Raco change his beliefs, once he recognized that the evidence is defeated. Such an expectation would not be realized, however, but only because we recognize other factors in each case that would defeat the disposition to change beliefs – in Raco's case, his unceasing racism. But these other factors do not *at all* provide grounds for thinking that the disposition to change beliefs that our analysis requires is *absent altogether*. They only provide grounds for thinking that the disposition we require is itself defeated by the other factors, but continues to be indicated by other changes in Raco's behavior (e.g., when presenting evidence for their beliefs to those who challenge them).

It is a feature of our account that it accommodates cases in which the predicted behavior (change of belief) is not displayed – for that is how dispositional traits actually work in the real world. So it is enough for us to say that we *think*

our account can defend the intuition with which we began
this section – namely, that in order to be justified, one's belief
must be based upon the evidence – but also to grant that even
if there are cases of justification where the basing relation, as
we have understood it, does not apply, our account of the
basing relation itself will be unaffected. We leave it to our
readers, then, to decide whether justification requires having
one's belief based on the evidence.

5.10   Conclusion, and a Worry about Justification as Warrant

One of the things we like best about Lehrer's Raco case is
that it really does appear to be a case in which the relevant
belief is justified, and yet, there still seems to be something
very wrong going on. What is wrong is the underlying toxin
of his racism, which explains not only how he came to hold
his belief, but also explains why he would continue to hold
that belief even if the evidence that justifies it were defeated.
  If the account of warrant (as justification) we are considering is correct, however, then once Raco appreciates the
medical evidence, his belief is warranted. Since the belief is
also true, the present account of warrant implies that Raco
knows. And yet, we expect that at least some of our readers
would not want to grant such a knowledge claim. Something
is still *very wrong* with the way Raco does things, cognitively.
Once we have a closer look at a very different approach to
warrant – the externalist approach – we will be in a much
better position to see why some epistemologists would be
inclined to say that Raco does not have knowledge. So, let
us turn now to externalist notions of warrant and keep Lehrer's Raco case in mind.

Current Trends

Unfortunately, the basing relation has been largely neglected
over the past 20 years. A useful survey of work up until the
mid-1990s can be found in Korcz (1997). Encouragingly, two

papers have recently been published on the basing relation and, in our opinion, they advance the discussion in interesting ways: one by Kevin McCain (forthcoming) and another by Turri (2011). One of the authors of this book, Ian Evans, also has a forthcoming paper on the basing relation, in which he gives a more thorough argument for the dispositional theory given herein. The other co-author, Nicholas Smith, also has a forthcoming paper, co-authored with Hannah Tierney, on Lehrer's and others' arguments about basing.

Hardly a year goes by without the publication of some new paper on the Gettier problem, though few attempts are made these days to try to solve it. There is still no wide consensus as to why attempted solutions seem inevitably to fail.[9] We mentioned Williamson's view: knowledge is unanalyzable. Another interesting thread has emerged in the literature: that unless one's analysis of warrant entails truth, one will be vulnerable to Gettier problems. Too many papers have been published on this question to cite here, but a good overview can be found in Huemer (2005).

6

Externalist Theories
of Warrant

I have always said that a belief was knowledge if it was
(i) true, (ii) certain, (iii) obtained by a reliable process.

Frank P. Ramsey 1990: 110

6.1 Introduction to Externalism

We said at the end of the last chapter that Lehrer's interesting
case of the racist doctor might seem to some as if it does not
qualify as knowledge, *even though the case looks like one in
which the doctor is completely justified in what he believes
about the disease.* In this chapter, we will not attempt to
adjudicate this issue, but we will consider the kinds of theories that might help to explain such a reaction, because the
theories we consider here conceive of warrant in terms that
are very different from what we have discussed so far. The
theories we consider in this chapter do not think of warrant
in terms of justification, or the internal conditions of or relations within one's cognitive system at all. Instead, they look
at cognitive processes and the relations that obtain between
the knower and the known. As such, they are what have come
to be known as "externalist" theories. As we said in chapter
1, an externalist is one who believes that warrant derives
from facts about the cognition in question that are external
to the epistemic agent's awareness. We do not need to be

aware of what warrants our knowledge in order to be warranted, for an externalist.

But before we review these, and to make the rest of our discussion of externalism and internalism clearer, we should first address a proposal made by Alvin Goldman, in his famous paper "What is Justified Belief?" (Goldman 1979). In this paper, Goldman provides a thoroughly externalist account of *justification*, according to which a belief is justified just in case it results from a cognitive process that reliably produces true beliefs. As we have been understanding the term "justification," it is a matter of an agent's having awareness of reasons for belief. We accordingly view accounts of warrant that include a justification condition as internalist. Goldman, however, argues against this. What makes a belief justified is the fact that the belief is the result of a reliable belief-forming process – a fact of which the agent may be wholly unaware. This view is known as reliabilism.

Reliabilism is an attractive account of warrant and, as an account of warrant, it will receive close attention in this chapter. As an account of *justification*, however, we think reliabilism is a non-starter. The appeal of reliabilism is that it secures what epistemologists call *the truth connection*: justification and truth are connected in some way – a justified belief must be a belief that is in some way likely to be true. Theories of justification often struggle to explain why this connection obtains.[1] Reliabilism is in a good position to explain the connection: if a belief was produced by a mechanism that reliably produces true beliefs, then that belief is probably a true one.

The problem with reliabilism about justification is that it seems to make justification and truth *too* connected. This is the *New Evil Demon Problem* (Cohen 1984). Imagine a subject that has all of the same experiences and beliefs as you – they are your internal duplicate. Surely, this subject is as justified in her beliefs as you are in yours. But suppose this subject's beliefs are systematically false: unlike you, she is being massively deceived by an evil demon. Her belief-forming processes, then, are wholly unreliable. According to Goldman's reliabilism about justification, then, none of her beliefs are justified. But this seems like the wrong thing to say. Your deceived duplicate may not know as much as you because her beliefs are mostly false, but her beliefs are surely as reasonable or justified as yours, for her reasons or evidence or justification are just the same as yours.[2] Goldman and others have, of course, tried to respond to this challenge, but we find the responses unconvincing. In the "Current Trends" section, motivated readers will find references to reliabilist attempts to solve this problem and can decide for themselves if they are successful.

Reliabilism does, however, have some appeal as an account of warrant. Recall that we defended a view of justification that says that perceptual beliefs are only justified for agents who have justified beliefs that perception is reliable. Forming such justified beliefs about the reliability of perception is a fairly sophisticated cognitive task. As we noted at the end of chapter 4, it does not seem to be a task of which most non-human knowers are capable. This creates trouble for an account of warrant that requires justification. Reliabilist accounts of warrant, on the other hand, do not require knowers to be aware of or have justified beliefs about the reliability of their cognitive mechanims. Reliabilist accounts of warrant require only that knowers *use* reliable cognitive mechanisms. Wooj the cat's ability to find his litter box seems to indicate that non-humans are perfectly capable of meeting the reliabilist standard of warrant.

The three externalist accounts of warrant that we will consider share this feature. The *causal theory* says that a belief that p is warranted just in case it is caused by the fact that p. Wooj's belief that his litter box is in the laundry room certainly seems to have been caused by his litter box's being in the laundry room (that's how he saw it there). The *tracking theory* says, roughly, that S's belief that p is warranted just in case the belief tracks the truth: S wouldn't believe p if it were false, and would believe p if it were true. If we had put Wooj's litter box in the basement instead of the laundry room, he wouldn't have believed it was in the laundry room and would have believed it was in the basement; Wooj can track the truth. The *reliabilist theory* says that S's belief that p is warranted just in case it was produced by a reliable belief-forming process. We have seen that Wooj has reliable belief-forming processes – at least with respect to the whereabouts of his litter box.

To recapitulate, internalists are those who think that warrant consists in justification. Externalists will be those who think of warrant in terms of the processes by which we come to hold our beliefs. What we have seen is that externalist theories seem to have an advantage over internalist theories in that they are better poised to explain the possibility of non-human knowers. Given our starting point, we regard this as an important advantage. We now turn to a detailed examination of the three externalist accounts of warrant mentioned above.

6.2 The Causal Theory of Warrant

Perhaps the simplest theory of warrant to have been offered by externalists is what is called the "causal theory." A well-known version of such a theory was advanced by Alvin Goldman (1967):

CK1. *S* knows that *p* if and only if the fact that *p* is causally connected in an "appropriate way" with *S*'s believing that *p*.

The "appropriate ways" Goldman recognizes are: perception, memory, a causal chain of inferences from true propositions, and combinations of these three.

At first glance, it may be unclear how CK_1 counts an an externalist theory of warrant. Each of Goldman's appropriate ways of being causally connected with *p* seem to secure internal justification for believing *p*. If you perceive that *p*, then it seems to you that *p*, and it's seeming to you that *p* is an internally accessible reason for believing *p*. If you remember that *p*, then you seem to remember that *p*; this too is an internally accessible reason for *p*. And, of course, if you conclude that *p* via a chain of inferences, those inferences serve as internally accessible reasons for *p*. Isn't this just a complicated way of requiring justification for belief?

While CK_1 *might* entail that an agent has justification for her warranted beliefs, it maintains that such justification is not sufficient. It is not enough that one *seems* to see, remember, or have an argument for, *p*. Recall your duplicate who is being deceived by an evil demon. She has access to the same reasons you do, but according to CK_1 she is not warranted in any of her beliefs: she does not actually perceive or remember anything and all of her inferences involve false propositions (unbeknownst to her, of course). CK_1 says that justification is not sufficient for warrant. It's not enough that it seems that you're causally connected to p; in order to have a warranted belief, you have to *actually be* causally connected to p. And that's not something that is internally accessible. It is in this sense that CK_1 is an externalist theory.

Goldman devised CK_1 in part as a solution to the Gettier problem. Rather than taking the more traditional approach involving internalist justification, Goldman proposed dropping justification altogether and replacing it with a causal connection. It's easy to see that CK_1 can handle Gettier's original cases. Recall Smith the jobseeker. Let p in this case stand for the proposition that the man who will get the job has 10 coins in his pocket. Smith's belief that p was not warranted, we decided. Can CK_1 account for this? This amounts to asking whether Smith's belief that p was causally connected to p in an appropriate way. It's clear that Smith did not *perceive* that p: all he perceived was that Jones had 10 coins in his pocket. It's also clear that Smith did not *remember* that p – no one had yet gotten the job. Smith reached p via an inference like the following:

1. Jones has 10 coins in his pocket.
2. Jones will get the job.
3. The man who will get the job has 10 coins in his pocket.

The second premise in Smith's inference is false. So CK_1 says that Smith's belief that p is not causally connected to p in an appropriate way and is therefore not warranted. This is the right result.

Unfortunately, Goldman's causal theory cannot handle all Gettier cases. As Goldman himself recognized, the following sort of case is a Gettier-style counterexample to CK_1:

Fake Barn Country
Suppose that [. . .] unknown to Henry, the district he has just entered is full of papier-mâché facsimiles of barns. These facsimiles look from the road exactly like barns, but

are really just façades, without back walls or interiors, quite incapable of being used as barns. They are so cleverly constructed that travelers invariably mistake them for barns. Having just entered the district, Henry has not encountered any facsimiles; the object he sees is a genuine barn. But if the object on that site were a facsimile, Henry would mistake it for a barn. Given this [. . .] information, we would be strongly inclined to withdraw the claim that Henry knows the object is a barn. (Goldman 1978: 122)

It seems clear that Henry doesn't know that there is a barn on the side of the road. Nevertheless, his belief that there is one is causally connected to the fact that there is one in one of Goldman's "appropriate ways": he *sees* the barn. This counterexample caused Goldman to abandon causal theories in favor of reliabilism. We will examine reliabilism shortly, but Fred Dretske (1981) has offered a different causal theory that may be able to handle *Fake Barn Country*:

CK$_2$. *S* knows that *p* if and only if *S*'s belief that *p* was caused or is causally sustained by the information that *p*.

Here we need to say something about Dretske's notion of information. The information that *p* is not the fact that *p*. The information that *p* is something that *informs us* of the fact that *p*. The fact that *p* generates information, and that information can be carried by a "signal." Carla's saying "It's hot in Tucson" is a signal that can carry the information that it is hot in Tucson: if Carla says it to you on the phone, you can receive the information (provided Carla is reliable, and the phone lines are working, etc.). Dretske gives us the following precise account of information:

I. A signal *s* carries the information that *p* iff the probability of *p* given *s* (and one's background knowledge) is 1. (1981: 65)[3]

So, in order for *S*'s belief to be caused by the information that *p*, *S* must *have* the information that *p*, and *S* must have received this information from some signal (words on a page, perceptual experience) that carries the information that *p*.

And, for that signal to carry the information that p, it must make the probability of p for S equal to 1 – there must be no chance that, given the signal, p could be false.

That is a strong requirement on knowledge. We might worry that it can never be satisfied – that no signal ever carries information in Dretske's strong sense. But setting that worry aside, it seems clear that Henry in *Fake Barn Country* has not received the information that there is a barn. For, in *Fake Barn Country*, seeming to see a barn does not make it at all likely that one is seeing a barn; there are too many barn façades around. This means that though there is some sense in which Henry's belief is caused by the fact that p, Henry has not received the information that p. So CK_2 says that Henry doesn't know, as desired.

Much more could be said about Dretske's causal theory. But we must stop the discussion short as there are other versions of externalism to consider. The major trouble with causal theories is that they seem unable to explain what we might generally call "abstract knowledge," which would include virtually all examples of mathematical knowledge, knowledge of the theorems of formal logic, and all of the other examples of knowledge *a priori* – that is, knowledge that is independent of (or logically prior to) experience. Such abstract facts don't *cause* anything (nor, on Dretske's account, do they generate any information).[4] Goldman thought that a traditional "justified true belief" account was adequate for abstract knowledge, but it is clear that the Gettier problem applies just as much to abstract knowledge. It is our contention that an adequate theory of knowledge be *general*: it should explain experiential and abstract knowledge, as well as human and non-human knowledge. Surely, these are all various types of the same thing: *knowledge*. We can hope that a truly adequate theory of knowledge will explain what all types of knowledge have in common. For that reason, we must look beyond causal theories.

6.3   Tracking Theories

Robert Nozick's tracking theory (Nozick 1981) is able to account for abstract knowledge and also gets the right answer in *Fake Barn Country*. The basic idea of the tracking theory is that knowledge requires that *S* tracks truth – roughly, *S*'s belief that *p* tracks truth regarding *p* just in case *S* believes *p* when it is true and doesn't believe *p* when it isn't. This provides a very simple and intuitive analysis of knowledge:

TT. *S* knows that *p* iff:
  (i) *p* is true;
  (ii) *S* believes that *p* is true;
  (iii) If *p* were not true, *S* wouldn't believe it;
  (iv) If *p* were true, *S* would believe it.

Condition (iii) provides what has come to be known as the *sensitivity condition*. The idea behind sensitivity is intuitive enough: if you know that *p*, then your belief isn't true as a matter of luck. It would seem that one way to rule out luck is to require that you wouldn't have believed that *p* had *p* been false. Many prominent theories of knowledge have involved versions of the sensitivity condition – Dretske (1981), Nozick (1981), DeRose (1995), and Sosa (2007) have all offered theories of knowledge that impose sensitivity requirements.[5]

Though many cases of knowledge involve sensitive beliefs, we will soon see that some cases of knowledge are not sensitive. But, first, we should clear up a potential confusion about sensitivity (condition (iii), remember). Sensitivity does not say that *S couldn't* falsely believe *p*. It simply says that *S wouldn't*. You could falsely believe that you have hands, but you wouldn't. If you didn't have hands, it wouldn't *look* like you did, and so you wouldn't falsely believe that you had hands. This is because if you didn't have hands, it would be because you (say) got in a car accident and lost them, not because an evil demon is deceiving you. It is important to understand the difference between "would" and "could." Nozick's theory is about what *would* have happened were *p* false, not what *could* have happened.[6]

Properly understood, then, the tracking theory (TT) explains why many ordinary cases of knowledge are, in fact, knowledge. Another benefit of TT is that it gets the right answers in standard Gettier cases. In the jobseeker case, we know that even if it were false that the man who will get the job has 10 coins in his pocket – if Smith had, say, *11* coins in his pocket – Smith would still believe it. Smith's belief is not sensitive.

Better still, the tracking theory gets the right answer in *Fake Barn Country*. Had Henry not gotten lucky and looked at the one real barn in the field, he would have been looking at one of the fake barns. But were he to see a fake barn, he would still believe it was a real barn. So Henry's belief is not sensitive. According to TT, Henry does not know that he is looking at a barn, according to Nozick's theory. This is the intuitively correct result.

These advantages of TT, however, are offset by some problems.

To see how these other problems arise, consider the case of *Lucky Knowledge* (Feldman 2003: 87–8):

> Black is hard at work in her office. From time to time she looks up from her desk and computer out the window toward the street. On one such occasion she happens to glance out the window toward the street. Just at that moment she sees a mugging on the street. She has a clear view of the event. She is a witness. In this case, Black knows that a mugging has occurred.

It would certainly seem as if Black knows that a mugging has occurred, but condition (iv) of TT is not satisfied: It could easily happen that Black does not glance out the window at the crucial moment, in which case the mugging occurs but she does not believe it. Consider another case, the case of the *Lottery Loser* (Hawthorne 2004):

> The Lottery Loser thinks lotteries are a waste of money and so never buys a ticket. Winners are announced in his local paper every Wednesday. The Lottery Loser is addicted to checking the winning numbers every Wednesday, even though he never buys a ticket. And every Wednesday, before checking the numbers, the Lottery Loser thinks to himself, "Once again, I'm not the winner of the week's lottery."

Intuitively, the Lottery Loser knows that is not the winner. After all, you can't win if you don't have a ticket, and the Lottery Loser is well aware that he never buys a ticket. If he *were* the winner, he would have had a ticket. But, as a pessimist, he still would have believed that he would not win. So, even if it were false that he won't win this week, he still would have believed that he wouldn't win. TT thus generates the absurd result that the Lottery Loser doesn't know he will lose!

Nozick himself recognized the problem such cases create for TT, and so he proposed an amended version, call it TT*:

TT*. *S* knows that *p* iff:
  (i) *p* is true;
  (ii) *S* believes that *p* is true on the basis of method *M*;
  (iii) Were *p* false, *S* would not believe that *p* on the basis of *M*;
  (iv) Were *p* true, *S* would believe that *p* on the basis of *M*.

This raises difficult questions about how to specify methods of belief formation, but let us set such worries aside.[7] Black's method of belief formation is "inference" from a perceptual experience as of *p* to *p*. The Lottery Loser's method is inference from the belief that he doesn't have a ticket. If Black hadn't looked up to see the murder, or if the murder had occurred away from view, she wouldn't have believed that a murder had occurred *on the basis of seeing a murder*. If the Lottery Loser were to win, he would know he had a ticket and would not believe he would lose *on the basis of not having a ticket*. So TT* says that Black and the Lottery Loser know, as we desired.

Unfortunately, problems remain:

The Wealth and Privilege Tournament
Sixty golfers are entered in the Wealth and Privilege Invitational Tournament. The course has a short but difficult hole, known as the "Heartbreaker." Before the round begins, you think to yourself that, surely, not all sixty players will get a hole-in-one on the "Heartbreaker."[8]

Intuitively, you know that not all 60 players will get a hole-in-one on the Heartbreaker. But if all 60 players were about to get a hole-in-one on that hole, you would still believe they weren't for exactly the same reasons (or using the same "method"). The case is a standard example of inductive experience. Based on your knowledge of the difficulty of the hole (arrived at by knowledge of how many people go over par on the hole) and your knowledge that even the best golfers rarely get a hole-in-one on shots of that difficulty, you make an inductive inference: that not every one of these 60 golfers will pull off the highly unlikely shot. But if, against all odds, that is exactly what was about to transpire, you would still believe as you do.

The trouble is perfectly general. In any inductive inference, if your conclusion were in fact false, you would have the same inductive evidence that you do and so would believe your conclusion all the same. Nozick's tracking theory absurdly claims that knowledge by inductive inference is impossible. We say this is absurd because one of the paradigms of human knowledge – scientific knowledge – depends almost completely upon induction. This, we think, is ample reason to reject the tracking theory of knowledge, its many benefits aside.

6.4   Tracking Theory and Skepticism

Nozick argued that one of the major benefits of the tracking theory was that it provided a response to the skeptic that nevertheless respected the intuitive pull of skepticism. Consider the following skeptical argument:

1. If I know that I have two hands, then I know that I am not being deceived into thinking I have two hands by Descartes' Demon.
2. I don't know that I am not being deceived by Descartes' Demon.

Therefore,

3. I don't know that I have hands.

The truth of the first premise depends on a principle called "closure under known logical implication," or "**Closure**" for short:

Closure. If *S* knows that *p*, and knows that *p* entails *q*, then if *S* competently infers *q* from *p*, *S* comes to know *q*.

Closure, in effect, says that we can expand our knowledge by deductive inference. Since I know that my having hands entails my not being deceived about this, **Closure** says that if I know I have hands, I can come to know I am not being deceived. The skeptic claims this is silly: how could know you are not being deceived? If you were, everything would seem the same to you.

What does Nozick's theory say about all of this? Well, first consider the claim that I don't know that I have hands. We have already seen that this belief is sensitive: if I didn't have hands, I wouldn't believe that I did. So Nozick's theory of knowledge says that the skeptic's conclusion is mistaken. But then it must say that one of the skeptic's premises is false. Which one?

Apparently not premise 2. Suppose, like the authors of this book, you believe that you are not being deceived by Descartes' Demon. What if that belief were false – what if you *were* being deceived by the Demon? Well, it seems that you would still believe that you weren't being deceived and for exactly the same reasons. Your belief that you are not being deceived is not sensitive, and so condition (iii) of **TT*** is not met. According to **TT***, then, you do *not* know that you are not being deceived. **TT*** agrees with the skeptic about premise 2.

This means that **Closure** is false, according to **TT***. Suppose that your belief that *p* is sensitive, and that *p* entails *q*. It can happen that you infer *q* from *p*, but your belief that *q* is not sensitive. Then you will know *p* but not *q*, which is the opposite of what **Closure** predicts. According to Nozick, then, the skeptic goes wrong in thinking that **Closure** is true. We are right in thinking that we know we have hands and the skeptic is right in thinking we don't know we're not being deceived. On Nozick's theory, since **Closure** is false, there is no tension between these two claims.

Much has been, and continues to be, written about **Closure**. Dretske is famous for arguing that **Closure** fails in a number of ordinary cases.[9] This is a topic that we cannot hope to address adequately here. But regardless of whether **Closure** is in general true, Nozick's theory seems to generate failures of closure that are quite absurd. One good case was provided by Saul Kripke in an unpublished lecture given to the American Philosophical Association in the early 1980s:

> *Fake Barn Country II*
> Henry is unwittingly driving through *Fake Barn Country II*. As in *Fake Barn Country*, *Fake Barn Country II* is filled with very realistic looking fake barns and a single real barn. However, in *Fake Barn Country II* the fake barns are all blue and the real barn is red (Henry is unfortunately ignorant of this fact). Henry sees the real red barn and believes that he is looking at a red barn. He then infers that he is looking at a barn.

What should we say about this case? It seems that we should say that Henry neither knows that he is looking at a red barn nor that he is looking at a barn. What can Nozick say? Notice that the former belief is sensitive but the latter is not. If Henry weren't looking at a red barn, he'd be looking at a blue barn and so would not believe that he was looking at a red barn (on the basis of seeming to see a red barn). But if Henry weren't looking at a barn, he would still infer that he was looking at a barn (using the same method). On Nozick's theory, Henry knows that he is looking at a red barn, but not that he is looking at a barn!

If it seems intuitive to some readers to say that Henry *does* know that he sees a red barn, surely it will also seem intuitive to say that Henry knows he sees a barn. To say that someone could know the former without being in any position to know the latter is absurd.

A further issue here is that the strong skeptical argument we posed in chapter 2 does not seem to turn on **Closure** at all. Nozick's theory has no special diagnosis of that argument, and that argument, we submit, represents the real skeptical challenge. Having seen the many problems confronting the tracking theory of knowledge, let us examine a different theory.

6.5   Reliabilism

A different, and widely influential, externalist account of warrant is *process reliabilism*, originally developed in

Goldman (1979). His new idea was that in assessing a belief, we should look at the *cognitive process* that formed the belief. Specifically, we should look at whether the cognitive process in question is *reliable* – whether it tends to produce true beliefs. Roughly, process reliabilism says that a belief is warranted just in case it was produced by a reliable cognitive process. The view has a great deal of intuitive appeal. Consider some belief-forming processes that yield warrant: perception, memory, mathematical proof, etc. One thing all these processes seem to have in common is that they are *reliable*. Conversely, consider some belief-forming processes that do not yield warrant: wishful thinking, guessing, palm-reading, etc. What all these processes seem to have in common is that they are *unreliable*. More often that not, wishful thinking leads to false beliefs.

So, roughly, reliabilism is captured by the following thesis:

RK. *S* knows that *p* if and only if *S*'s true belief that *p* was the product of or is sustained by one or more cognitive processes that reliably produce true beliefs.

On this view, *all there is* to warrant is reliability. And note well: **RK** does not require that *S* is *aware* that her belief results from a reliable cognitive process – so long as the process is, in fact, reliable, the belief is warranted. Nor need *S* have access to arguments or evidence for her beliefs. To quote Goldman:

> It is often assumed that when a person has a justified belief, he knows that it is justified and knows what the justification is. It is further assumed that the person can state or explain what the justification is. On this view, a justification is argument, defense, or set of reasons that can be given in support of a belief. . . . I make none of these assumptions here. . . . I do assume that a justified belief gets its status of being justified from some processes or properties that make it justified. *But this does not imply that there must be an argument, or reason, or anything else 'posessed' at the time of belief by the believer.* (1979: 2; emphasis added)[10]

Reliabilism is, then, a radically externalist theory of knowledge. Let us first examine the advantages of reliabilism.

Aside from its intuitive appeal, one clear advantage of reliabilism is its ability to explain abstract or *a priori* knowledge. Though abstract facts can't cause beliefs in us, there's no obvious problem with the view that certain belief-forming processes might reliably produce true beliefs *about* such facts. Indeed, the leading contemporary account of *a priori* knowledge is a reliabilist one (Casullo 2003). This, along with its obvious ability to explain animal knowledge and its satisfactory explanation of the truth connection, have made it an attractive option for many contemporary epistemologists.[11] Nevertheless, there are some difficulties.

The first problem is, interestingly enough, Goldman's own *Fake Barn Country*.[12] Henry is generally pretty good at recognizing barns. Usually, when he sees a barn, he can tell it's a barn and when he sees a non-barn, he can tell it's a non-barn. One is tempted to conclude that Henry's barn-detection mechanism is reliable.[13] But if Henry's barn-detection mechanism is reliable, **RK** says that he knows he sees a barn, which is the wrong result.

The trouble seems to be that Henry's belief-forming mechanism is reliable in "normal" environments, but not in *Fake Barn Country*. The reliabilist, then, needs to say in which environments belief-forming processes need to be reliable. There are two obvious, but different, ways the reliabilist could go here:

1. The process must be reliable in *normal* or *typical* environments.
2. The process must be reliable in the *actual* environment in which the belief is formed.

Certainly, *Fake Barn Country* supplies a very abnormal and atypical circumstance. If the reliabilist were to take option 1, this would generate the result that Henry's belief is warranted, which is wrong. *However*, it's important to notice that *Fake Barn Country* is really just another Gettier case. It's pretty clear that standard Gettier cases are counterexamples to **RK**;[14] reliabilists are going to need an additional condition on warrant that rules out Gettier cases *anyway*. So the reliabilist who requires reliability in normal circumstances need not regard *Fake Barn Country* as a *special* problem. She can refine her theory as follows:

RKNC. *S* knows that *p* if and only if *S*'s true belief that *p* is
(i) the product of (or sustained by) one or more cognitive
processes that reliably produce true beliefs *in normal
circumstances*; and
(ii) GETTIER BLOCKER.

The reliabilist may not have anything special to say about the
correct Gettier condition, but she can hope that some adequate condition is forthcoming from the Gettier literature.

If the reliabilist instead takes option 2, she can say that
Henry's belief-forming process is not reliable in *Fake Barn
Country*, and so Henry doesn't know that he sees a barn.
This is the correct result. This might motivate a reliabilist to
adopt the following theory:

RKAC. *S* knows that *p* if and only if *S*'s true belief that *p*
is the product of (or sustained by) one or more cognitive
processes that reliably produce true beliefs *in the actual
circumstances in which S's belief that p was formed (or is
sustained)*.

There is a problem with this view, however. Processes that
are generally unreliable and do not seem to produce warrant
can luckily be deployed in circumstances in which they are
reliable. Imagine a man named Red whose (very strange)
barn-recognition mechanism counts as a fake barn any barn-
looking object that is blue and counts as a real barn any barn-
looking object that is red. This mechanism, of course, is quite
unreliable and has gotten Smith into trouble more than once.
Suppose, however, that one day Red happens to enter *Fake
Barn Country II* (unbeknownst to him, of course). He sees a
red barn which happens to be the one real barn. Here in *Fake
Barn Country II*, Red's barn-recognition mechanism is quite
reliable: all of the blue barn-looking objects are fake and all
of the red barn-looking objects are real. According to **RKAC**,
Smith knows he is seeing a real barn. But that seems wrong.
Red got lucky by being in *Fake Barn Country II* without
knowing at all that he was in very unusual circumstances.

To really specify a reliabilist account of warrant along the
lines of **RKNC** or **RKAC**, more would need to be said about
what normal or actual circumstances are. "Normal" is a

relative term – what's normal for one person might not be normal for another. Further, the places where we test, say, vision for reliability seem *abnormal*: it's an unusual circumstance to be asked to identify rows of random letters, with one eye closed, by a person in a white coat! And what about "the actual environment in which the belief is formed"? What is the actual environment in which Henry forms his belief? Is it the planet Earth? Then his process is reliable in the relevant environment. Or perhaps it is the narrow region of space where the one real barn exists? Again, this is an environment in which Henry's process would seem to be reliable.

An analogous difficulty arises if we challenge the reliabilist to specify belief-forming processes. We've often referred to Henry's "barn-detection mechanism." But processes can be described in different levels of detail. A more detailed description of the process would be "forming the belief that there is a barn when presented with a visual experience of a red barn." This process is reliable in *Fake Barn Country II*. A less detailed description of the process would be "vision." This process, too, is generally reliable in *Fake Barn Country*. This is called the *generality problem*, and it is one of the greatest obstacles to developing a reliabilist theory.[15]

But before we even think about whether it is worthwhile to try to see if the theory could be completed in these ways, it is worthwhile considering two sorts of objections against reliabilism that have been made by internalists. The first sort of objection has been made in various ways, but we will consider only two relevant examples. The first was given by Laurence BonJour:

Norman the Clairvoyant
Norman, under certain conditions which usually obtain, is a completely reliable clairvoyant with respect to certain kinds of subject matter. He possesses no evidence or reasons of any kind for or against the general possibility of such a cognitive power or for or against the thesis that he possesses it. One day Norman comes to believe that the President is in New York City, though he has no evidence either for or against this belief. In fact the belief is true and results from his clairvoyant power under circumstances in which it is completely reliable. (BonJour 1985: 41)

The problem here is obvious – Norman can be in possession of completely reliable processes and yet have no reason to think that he is, and thus can come to have beliefs as a result of those processes, where he has absolutely no reason to think that such beliefs are true. The fact that such beliefs are true and the product of reliable cognitive processes does not seem to be enough for Norman to know that they are true. The other case was provided by Keith Lehrer:

The Human Thermometer
Suppose a person, Mr Truetemp, undergoes brain surgery by an experimental surgeon who invents a small device that is both a very accurate thermometer and a computational device capable of generating thoughts. The device, call it a tempucomp, is implanted in Truetemp's head so that the very tip of the device, no larger than the head of a pin, sits unnoticed on his scalp and acts as a sensor to transmit information about the temperature to the computational system in his brain. This device, in turn, sends a message to his brain causing him to think of the temperature recorded by the external sensor. Assume that the tempucomp is very reliable, and so his thoughts are correct temperature thoughts. All told, this is a reliable belief-forming process and a properly functioning cognitive faculty.

Now imagine, finally, that Mr Truetemp has no idea that the tempucomp has been inserted in his brain and is only slightly puzzled about why he thinks so obsessively about the temperature; but he never checks a thermometer to determine whether these thoughts about the temperature are correct. He accepts them unreflectively, another effect of the tempucomp. Thus, he thinks and accepts that the temperature is 104 degrees. It is. Does he know it? Surely not. (Lehrer 2000a: 187)

Again, the problem in this case is obvious: Without any evidence in support of his temperature beliefs (and, indeed, with some evidence that people are not reliable temperature-sensors generally), Mr Truetemp cannot know what the temperature is even though he comes to have true beliefs as a result of reliable cognitive processes.

Both of these cases raise what has come to be known as the "opacity objection." It is called this because in both cases the reliability of the relevant processes (because it is external to the cognitions themselves) is opaque (as opposed to transparent) to the ones in possession of the reliable processes. The point of both cases is the same: unless we are in a position to recognize that our cognitive processes are reliable, their reliability is not sufficient for warrant. But a recognition that our processes are reliable amounts to being justified in our beliefs. Accordingly, both are general objections to all forms of externalism, and both seek to push us back to an internalist account of warrant.

6.6   A Call for Caution about Opacity Objection

We agree with BonJour and Lehrer that Norman and True-temp should not be counted as knowing what they believe. But we would also urge considerable caution with respect to our thinking about these examples. Two things in particular strike us about such examples that seem to mandate a certain degree of hesitation. First, notice just how very far from ordinary cases these really are. We do not generally think of ourselves as living in a world in which we are called upon to make assured and expert judgments about cases of clairvoyance or people with temperature sensors implanted in their heads without knowing it. Even if we do have some reason to trust our intuitions when it comes to judging fairly common cases, involving cognitive processes with which we are more famil-iar, we think our intuitions much less likely to be reliable when applied to cases that are further from those we are more accus-tomed to judging. And having said this much, we should then also point out that certain elements of these cases actually do make them much more familiar than they seem at first, and when we focus on the more familiar examples that are like these cases, we will find our intuitions reversing themselves.

To see this, let us return to the case of Wooj the cat, who is very good at finding and using his litter box when he needs it. We are inclined to think that Wooj knows where his litter box is. But now notice that the way Wooj goes about his cognitive business is essentially just like the way Norman does in BonJour's case, and also just like the way Truetemp does in Lehrer's case. Wooj does not think about whether his cognitive capacities are reliable or trustworthy – indeed, he is incapable of such meta-cognitive self-assessment. He has certain cognitive equipment, and he uses it quite effectively. But the operations of these capacities are completely opaque to Wooj. Norman and Truetemp do things the same way. Each has some reliable cognitive equipment that generates beliefs in them, but whose operation is completely opaque. If we want to say that Wooj knows, why should we deny that Norman and TrueTemp know?

BonJour and Lehrer would like us to conclude from their cases that mere reliability is not enough for something to count as knowledge, and the cases of Norman and Truetemp do seem to most of us not to qualify as knowledge. But then, when we think about what animals do and how they do it, it seems to many of us that what they do does sometimes count as knowledge – even though what they do looks like it is essentially the same sort of thing that Norman and Truetemp do. This is why externalists often respond to the cases of Norman and Truetemp by simply denying the intuitions that BonJour and Lehrer say we should have. If it counts for knowledge when Wooj functions this way, the externalist might argue, then it should also count for knowledge when Norman and Truetemp function this way. This is sometimes called the "bottom-up" approach to the analysis of knowledge, whereas those who begin with paradigms that seem suited mainly to human beings, and then disqualify animals because they do not meet the conditions thus proposed, are said to take a "top-down" approach.[16] Either approach seems to get us into some trouble with our intuitions at some point: either top-downers are right to say that Norman and Truetemp do not know – and so also Wooj does not know – or bottom-uppers are right to say that Wooj knows – and so also Norman and Truetemp know.

Some epistemologists have felt the pressure of this conundrum and have proposed that "knowledge" is actually an equivocal concept: it is one thing when applied to human beings and another when applied to non-human animals.[17] In chapters 8 and 9, however, we will propose a way out of this conundrum, according to which a univocal general account of knowledge can be provided, which, when applied to cases like Norman and Truetemp, will count them as not knowing, and yet, when applied to the case of Wooj, will count him as knowing where his litter box is. But for now, it is enough that we have identified some ground for caution in regard to what we should conclude from cases such as BonJour's Norman and Lehrer's Truetemp.

Current Trends

The internalism/externalism debate is another topic in epistemology that has fallen on hard times. In 2006, however, Michael Bergmann published *Justification without Awareness*. This book represents one of the most careful treatments of the internalism/externalism divide ever produced and presents trenchant criticisms of internalism. It is, in our opinion, essential reading for aspiring epistemologists. Markie (2009), Rogers and Matheson (forthcoming), and Hasan (2011) all offer interesting responses.

On the topic of epistemic closure, too much has been written over the years to offer anything like a survey here. But we will note an interesting trend. Many epistemologists have begun to doubt "multi-premise closure": if you assign probability less than 1 to each premise in an argument, then the probability calculus tells us that if you have enough premises, your conclusion should have probability less than 0.5, which is not strong enough for knowledge. Most of us thought, however, that "single-premise closure" remained safe from such considerations. Schechter (forthcoming) and Lasonen-Aarnio (2008) have each offered compelling arguments against even single-premise closure. No doubt, these arguments will receive a great deal of attention from epistemologists.

7
Epistemic Evaluation

Naturalization of epistemology does not jettison the normative and settle for the indiscriminate description of ongoing
processes. For me normative epistemology is a branch of
engineering. It is the technology of truth-seeking or, in more
cautiously epistemic terms, prediction . . . There is no question of ultimate value, as in morals; it is a matter of efficacy
for an ulterior end, truth or prediction.

Quine 1986: 664–6

7.1   Do Attributions of Knowledge Imply Value Judgments?

As Jaegwon Kim (1988) has shown, in his famous reply to
W. V. O. Quine's early advocacy of an externalist approach
to warrant (Quine 1969b), externalists have generally made
no attempt to explain the evaluative nature of justification,
or to explain how or why the satisfaction of certain epistemic
norms might be required for knowledge. Lying behind the
externalist's uneasiness about the inclusion of norms within
the analysis of knowledge are a number of concerns about
both the epistemology and the metaphysics of evaluation. The
application of norms requires a recognition that some practices (in this case epistemic practices) are *better* than others.
Philosophers have struggled with evaluation for many reasons,

and not only with the question of how we should make our value judgments, but also especially with how we can *justify* or *defend* such judgments, rationally, and what such judgments show us about truth and reality. Are value judgments *objective* or simply *subjective* in nature? If the former, in what *sense* are they objective? If the latter, why would anyone think such judgments have a place in the analysis of knowledge – isn't the question of whether someone knows something or not simply a matter of *fact*? Why suppose that the attribution of knowledge involves (even implicitly) a *value judgment*?

The sorts of worries that such questions express are important questions in the philosophical area known as "value theory," and the moral or ethical versions of these questions are the special focus of much of the sub-field within value theory known as "meta-ethics." This, accordingly, is not the place to attempt to answer such fundamental questions about values. Instead, then, we will seek in this chapter only to consider the different kinds of evaluation that epistemologists have discussed in relation to the analysis of knowledge.

7.2 Evaluation by Epistemic Norms

Norms are value judgments that take the form of prescriptions – they tell us "do this" or "don't do that." Some norms – *practical norms* – tell us how to act. These include rules of morality and rational action. We're concerned here not with practical norms, but with *epistemic norms*. It's not easy to say just what makes a norm epistemic. A glib definition would be, "norms that epistemologists are interested in." A more helpful account says that epistemic norms are the norms governing belief. Epistemic norms, in this sense, tell us what to believe. This will be a useful working definition, but we'll want to keep in mind the possibility that there could be epistemic norms governing our reasoning and evidence-gathering practices and habits.

There are different kinds of norms, and there may be several kinds of norms that apply in epistemology. The first distinction between kinds of norms is between instrumental and categorical norms. An example of an instrumental norm is the advice you might give to a friend: "If you want to pass the test, you should do the reading." In this case, the norm expressed is "You should do the reading," but the norm only governs those who want to pass the test. If your friend has no interest in passing the test, she cannot be criticized under the instrumental norm for not doing the reading. Categorical norms, on the other hand, govern everyone, regardless of their desires and goals. Moral norms typically have this character. Many moral norms tell us how to do good (or avoid doing bad). Consider the plausible norm that says you should not kill people just for fun. This norm isn't contingent on whether you care about doing good (or avoiding bad). Anyone who kills just for fun is violating this norm, and is subject to criticism, regardless of whether they care about doing good.

Are epistemic norms instrumental or categorical? To get a fix on the question, consider that epistemic norms often seem to be advice about how to get true beliefs (though this does not, as we will see, exhaust the nature of epistemic normativity). We could think of this as a goal that many of us have: the goal of "believing the truth and only the truth."[1] We could then think of epistemic norms as instrumental. In other words, epistemic norms tell us to form beliefs *insofar as we want to form true beliefs*. If this account of epistemic normativity is correct, then a belief is only subject to epistemic evaluation if the agent *wanted* to form a true belief.[2]

On the other hand, we might suppose that epistemic norms apply to everyone, even those who don't care about truth. To understand things this way is to suppose that the norm expressed is not simply an instrumental norm, but, rather, a *categorical* one. Under this heading, we find, naturally enough, the consequentialist account, which conceives of norms as rules to maximize true beliefs and minimize false beliefs. But we also find the deontological approach, which conceives of norms as *duties, responsibilities*, or *obligations*; and the procedural account, which takes them to be procedures that tell us how to reason correctly (in the way that a manual tells you how to, say, operate a machine correctly). A different approach to epistemic evaluation is the aretaic, or virtue-theoretic account, which understands epistemic values as character traits disposing us to go about our epistemic business in certain ways. In this chapter, we will compare the strengths and weaknesses of each understanding of epistemic evaluation, and show how each one might inform our analysis of knowledge.

7.3 Instrumental versus Categorical Formulations of Norms

The epistemic norms relevant to the analysis of knowledge seem to be categorical. Let us continue with the helpful idea that epistemic norms aim at promoting true belief. The question we confront is whether these norms apply even to people who don't care about forming true beliefs. Perhaps the best way to think about this question is to ask ourselves whether we can legitimately find the beliefs of such people *inappropriate, blameworthy,* or otherwise *defective.* It seems that we can. Some people don't care whether they have false beliefs about ghosts – they just think it's fun to believe in ghosts. Still, we can (and do) evaluate such beliefs with epistemic norms: we might think that, in some sense, people shouldn't believe that ghosts exist because there is overwhelming reason to think ghosts don't exist. Or consider the plausible norm that demands that beliefs be true. Someone who believes in ghosts has a false belief, and this is grounds for criticizing the belief – a false belief is at least partially defective *as a belief.* And that is true even if the person with the false belief *doesn't care.*[3] Accordingly, we conclude that believing truly and believing in accord with the evidence are norms that an analysis of knowledge will likely have to take into account, and both of these norms seem to be categorical in nature.

7.4 Deontological Norms and Doxastic Voluntarism

Do we have *duties* or *obligations* with respect to our beliefs? Does it make sense to say that someone either has a *right* to hold a certain belief, or *no right* to hold some other belief? The question is ambiguous: it might be asking whether we have *moral* duties or obligations to believe in certain ways. This is a plausible way of understanding Clifford's famous dictum that, *"[I]t is wrong everywhere and for anyone, to believe anything upon insufficient evidence"* (Clifford 1947: 77; emphasis in original). Clifford seems to be saying here that we have a strong moral obligation not to believe anything without adequate evidence. This position began a very important debate on what has come to be called the "ethics of belief." Some view epistemic evaluation as a special sort of moral evaluation: it is the moral evaluation of beliefs. This position seems to us misguided. Certainly, it does seem to us that some beliefs are morally wrong – the beliefs that lie behind racism, for example. But there may be beliefs that are *morally* wrong, but *epistemically* right (and vice versa):

1. If someone threatens to murder an innocent person if you believe that a rainstorm is coming, you are morally wrong to believe that a rainstorm is coming, even if all of the evidence points in favor of rain.
2. If someone threatens to murder an innocent person unless you believe that a rainstorm is coming, you are morally wrong to believe that a rainstorm is not coming, even if there is no evidence in favor of rain.

The examples are silly and one might disagree with our assessment of them. But that is besides the point. The point is simply that we can *understand* a belief being morally right but epistemically wrong (and vice versa). Further, some epistemically wrong beliefs seem morally neutral. Suppose you believe, for obviously bad reasons, that a friendly ghost haunts your house. This has almost no impact on your behavior, aside from your occasional tendency to think to yourself things like, "I wonder what sorts of trouble that old ghost will get into today!" From the epistemic perspective, this belief leaves something to be desired. But is there anything morally right or wrong about it? We must admit that it doesn't seem so to us. Ethical evaluation and epistemic evaluation are independent, though there may of course be overlap.

There is another way of thinking about the question whether we have duties or obligations with respect to our beliefs. We can think of this as the question whether we have *epistemic* duties or obligations. Even if we think epistemic evaluation is independent from ethical evaluation, we can ask whether epistemic norms are deontological in nature. We saw that some think epistemic norms have the following form:

If you want the truth, then you should believe *p* iff. . . .

Deontologists think epistemic norms have the following different form:

In circumstances *C*, you are obligated (have a duty) to believe *p*.

The idea of holding people responsible for their beliefs creates an immediate concern. This concern derives from Kant's plausible principle that "ought" implies "can": it makes no sense to say that someone *ought* to do *x* unless that person *can* do *x*. But belief doesn't seem to be the sort of thing over which we exercise voluntary control. As William Alston puts it, "When I see a car coming down the street I am not capable of believing or disbelieving this at will."[4] If we do not have voluntary control over what we believe, then we might suppose that it makes no sense to think of epistemic evaluation as telling us what we *ought* to believe, or informing us of our deontological *duties* in epistemic matters. The thesis that we have direct voluntary control over our beliefs is called *doxastic voluntarism*. It has seemed plainly false to many (the present authors included).

Matthias Steup has argued that even if doxastic voluntarism is false, we may still have epistemic obligations. For even if we have no *direct* control over what we believe, it does seem that we have *indirect* control. We tend to believe what we think our evidence supports, and we can control the degree to which we reflect on our evidence (and the time we spend seeking new evidence). This suggests that we can control what we believe by reflection on our evidence:

[I]f I believe upon having read a La Rouche pamphlet that the Queen of the United Kingdom is involved in a world-wide conspiracy, I believe something for which I should, epistemically speaking, be blamed. After all, it was within my power to give a little thought to the matter, to weigh the evidence, and thereby to figure out that I had better withhold this belief. (Steup 1988: 72–3)

For a belief to violate an epistemic obligation, one need not be capable of *directly choosing* not to hold that belief. It is enough, Steup contends, that one could do something that would result in one not having the belief (such as giving careful thought to the matter or weighing all the evidence). This is all that the ought-implies-can principle requires.[5]

Unfortunately, we think even this modest understanding of the control we have over our beliefs is unrealistic. Suppose I reflect on the evidence and see that it clearly indicates that the Queen is not involved in a worldwide conspiracy. Is this any guarantee that I will refrain from believing that the Queen is party to conspiracy? It doesn't seem so. Psychological forces beyond my control may compel me to a belief that I know is irrational. So suppose that careful reflection on the evidence does not prevent me from believing that the Queen is involved in conspiracy. There doesn't seem to be anything I could do to avoid having the belief. So on Steup's account, the belief is not a proper object of epistemic evaluation. But that seems wrong – we evaluate the belief as irrational, unjustified, not warranted, etc.

It has also been argued that epistemic oughts need not imply doxastic cans. All of us, in an important sense, play the role of believers. One can play a role well or ill – one can play the roles as one *ought to* or as one *ought not to*. These "role oughts" do not seem to imply "cans," as Richard Feldman points out:

There are roles that result from one's playing a certain role or having a certain position. Teachers ought to explain things clearly. Parents ought to take care of their kids. Cyclists ought to move in certain ways. Incompetent teachers, incompetent parents, and untrained cyclists may be unable to do what they ought to do. Similarly, I'd say, forming beliefs is something people do. That is, we form beliefs in response to our experiences in the world. Anyone engaged in this activity ought to do it right. In my view, what they ought to do is to follow their evidence (rather than their wishes or fears). I suggest that epistemic oughts are of this sort – they describe the right way to play a certain role. (Feldman 2001: 87–8)

Feldman concludes that for epistemic evaluation to be deontological, it does not have to be committed to doxastic voluntarism (Feldman 2001: 90).[6] It is worth pointing out, we think, that role obligations seem different from traditional deontic obligations. An untrained cyclist is not to be *blamed* for his uneven cadence, even though he (role-) ought to have an even cadence. It's unclear whether, in changing his focus to role oughts, Feldman is still even talking about deontology.[7]

No doubt epistemologists will continue to debate deontological norms and their connection to doxastic voluntarism. We don't aim to settle such issues here, but we will suggest that *some* epistemic norms must be conceived as deontological in nature, at least in Feldman's sense.[8] This will become clear once we have considered consequentialist conceptions of epistemic norms.

7.5   Consequentialist Conceptions of Epistemic Norms

We began this chapter with some considerations that would seem strongly to indicate a consequentialist conception of epistemic norms, namely, that it seems to be an important feature of our epistemic life that it is *goal-oriented*, where at least one primary goal is, as we have now so often said, "getting it right" when we believe something. But if all epistemic norms are aimed at this goal, then we have very good reason to think that they are all consequentialist, such that "getting it right" is the consequence. For those creatures, such as human beings, for whom "getting it right" means having true beliefs instead of false beliefs, the goal could more narrowly be expressed (as it often is) as: "believing the truth and only the truth." In this way of construing epistemic norms, we would evaluate an epistemic practice or process on the sole basis of whether or not that practice or process was well-suited to the production and sustaining of true beliefs. And we would evaluate the products of epistemic practices or processes on the sole basis of whether or not the product was one that achieved the goal of getting it right (or, in our case, of being a true belief).

It seems to us simply obvious that at least many epistemic norms are properly conceived as consequentialist, with truth (or at least getting it right) as the targeted consequence. After all, virtually every attempt to analyze knowledge that epistemologists have offered has included a truth condition – so aiming at truth is simply *part of what we do* when we try to know something. But we are also inclined to think that consequentialist formulations of epistemic norms cannot exhaust the field.

First, it seems to us that some epistemic norms can be fully satisfied even when they cannot be explicated in terms of success at "believing the truth and only the truth" or getting it right. To see why, we need only remember the *New Evil Demon Problem* from chapter 6. There, we considered an agent who always does her best to carefully weigh all of her evidence before coming to form beliefs. Because of the interference of the evil demon, however, her belief-forming processes always lead her astray. No doubt, the machinations of this demon prevent her from achieving a certain sort of epistemic success: getting it right. And this, of course, prevents her from obtaining knowledge. Still, she has done all that can be asked of her as an epistemic agent – she has formed her beliefs exactly as she ought to have. This suggests that some epistemic norms are deontological. Only this could explain why we do not fault the person in the demon world: we regard such a person as having done her epistemic *duty* or fulfilled her epistemic *obligations*, despite her failure to *get it right* in her beliefs.[9]

Still, the *New Evil Demon Problem* also suggests that knowledge requires satisfying consequentialist norms. We can suppose that the agent in the *New Evil Demon Problem* occasionally happens upon true beliefs – perhaps it amuses the demon occasionally to make this agent's beliefs true. In those situations, we will have an agent with a true belief who has done her epistemic duty (she'll be *justified*, presumably). But will she *know*? It doesn't seem so. The reason, it seems, is that the way she forms beliefs is not (in her unfortunate situation) a good way of discovering the truth. This suggests a consequentialist norm: use the belief-forming method that will most likely generate a true belief. Satisfaction of some norm like this is required for knowledge.

As the *New Evil Demon Problem* shows, there are the methods of belief formation that we have an intellectual duty to use and there are the methods of belief formation that are most likely to yield the truth. It is only when these coincide that knowledge is possible. The result seems to be that the domain of epistemic norms is more complicated than one in which all applicable norms could be reduced to a single form. In fact, in the next section, we will argue that there is yet a third type of epistemic norm, satisfaction of which is required for knowledge.

7.6　The Aretaic or Virtue-Theoretic Conception of Epistemic Evaluation

The sorts of epistemic evaluation we have discussed so far are focused upon what might be called the "dos and don'ts of epistemic agency" – they tell us what to believe. Virtue-theoretic norms shift the locus of judgment from epistemic *beliefs* to traits of the epistemic agent's *character* – they tell us what sorts of cognitive traits and habits to develop. If we look at epistemic evaluation very generally, we will recognize a number of traits that are specifically *epistemic* virtues. One of the pioneers in virtue epistemology offers a list of such virtues:

> Examples include intellectual carefulness, perseverance, humility, vigor, flexibility, courage, and thoroughness, as well as open-mindedness, fair-mindedness, insightfulness, and the virtues opposed to wishful thinking, obtuseness, and conformity. One of the most important virtues, I believe, is intellectual integrity. (Zagzebski 1996: 155)

Our analysis of knowledge will likely include both consequentialist and deontic epistemic norms. What's more, we see reason to think that it will include another sort of norm: aretaic, or virtue-theoretic, norms. To see this, consider a rather fanciful case (and, again, we warn our readers that what follows is an unabashed appeal to intuitions!). Suppose two people wanted to find out the specific gravity of a particular batch of wort, the liquid extracted from the mashing process in the production of beer. The first person (call him Brewmaster), a dedicated beer-maker, determines this by using a well-designed hydrometer and carefully measuring the temperature of the wort twice (to be sure he has a reliable reading), and then applying the standard formula in his calculations – again, doing the calculations twice, just to be sure.[10] The second (call him Lazy) simply picks up Brewmaster's notes and copies the numbers. Let us also assume that Lazy has no interest in and no clue as to how actually to measure specific gravity, and also has no particular reason to think that the numbers he gets from Brewmaster are correct. Instead, he just wants to do the task he has been assigned to do (maybe just for the paycheck), and he finds this way of doing it much easier than trying to figure anything out or learn how to perform the task for himself. Lazy is, however, a flawless copy-cat: he never errs in copying the exact numbers Brewmaster puts in his notes. Let us also stipulate that Brewmaster always reports his results in his notes precisely as he discovers them. Whether or not he knows (or cares) about Lazy's copying, Brewmaster would never think to write down his results differently from the way he actually discovers them. The result is, obviously, that Lazy and Brewmaster would have completely equal success in discerning the specific gravity of the wort, and would have the same success every time they tried.[11] Our question is this: do they both achieve that success in *equally good ways*?

Plainly not; and this seems to have effects on whether or not we would regard Lazy as *knowing* what the specific gravity of his wort is. We think Brewmaster does, but Lazy does not. It's true that Lazy used a process that is reliable. But for all he knows, he's gotten it all wrong. The problem, we're tempted to conclude, is that Lazy did not use a reliable method *because of* some epistemic virtues he possessed. Instead, his epistemic vices happened to lead him to a reliable method and the right result. That doesn't look like knowledge.

It seems, then, that knowledge requires satisfying a virtue-theoretic norm: be virtuous in the way you form beliefs. In this vein, many epistemologists have tried to somehow make virtue central to knowledge. There have been several such attempts,[12] each with interesting and provocative nuances. Here we focus on two of the most influential: those offered by Ernest Sosa and Alvin Plantinga.

7.7 | Sosa's Virtue Epistemology

Sosa believes that a complete analysis of knowledge can be offered in aretaic terms. He begins by understanding belief as a *performance*, like that of an archer who takes aim and shoots an arrow (Sosa 2007: 22). Sosa says that the archer's performance can be evaluated in three distinct ways: accuracy (whether it hits the target or not), adroitness (whether it manifests a skill on the part of the archer), and aptness (whether or not the accuracy is *because* of the archer's adroitness, whether or not it is *creditable* to the archer[13] (and not, for example, a freak of wind, which could either defeat a skilled archer, or actually freakishly assist the archer in a given case). Sosa calls these the three "A's" of performance, and then applies them to knowledge, with the result that knowledge is belief that is accurate (true), adroit (virtuous), and apt (the result of the believer's virtue) (Sosa 2007: 23–4).

The key provision for our current discussion is the adroitness condition, which is where Sosa finds a place for virtue in the analysis. He goes on to characterize epistemic virtue in terms of our cognitive capacities or powers, and how these are rightly or wrongly exercised. But he also recognizes that our cognitive capacities are not those of omniscience; instead, their reliability is conditioned upon certain environmental factors. Our color perception, for example, is reliable only when we are in an environment of white light. Hence, one cannot exercise virtuous (adroit) color perception in conditions other than where the ambient light is white (Sosa 2007: 31–4). Sosa formulates this into what he calls "principle C":

C. For any correct belief that *p*, the correctness of that belief is attributable to a competence only if it derives from the exercise of that competence in appropriate conditions for its exercise, and that exercise in those conditions would not then too easily have issued a false belief. (Sosa 2007: 33)

But because the "three A's" of epistemic assessment are supposed to be distinct, it follows that a belief could be adroit (the product of a cognitive capacity or competence), but not accurate or apt. We have already mentioned a case of the latter, where a skilled archer might hit the target because of a freakish wind. Cases of the former would be like those in which the skilled archer *misses* the target because of a freakish wind. This, however, raises a critical question of the condition-sensitive nature of our capacities: it would seem the archer's skills do not extend into circumstances in which there are freakish winds. So are the adroitness and accuracy conditions truly distinct, or does the former actually entail the latter? Precisely because the adroitness condition is itself *conditional* upon environmental factors, it is not clear that there really are cases in which an epistemic agent exercises virtue in the sense Sosa's account requires but fails to achieve the right results – for the relevant factor in the failure to achieve those results might reasonably be taken as the result of the limitations of the applicability of the virtue in question.

Obviously, this is not what we think of when we discuss epistemic virtues in the way we found in the Zagzebski quotation we gave above. One who has and exercises intellectual integrity does not always get it right, which, presumably, is at least one reason why epistemic humility is also a virtue! What Sosa wants in an epistemic virtue most of all, however, is reliability. Notice that other epistemic virtues do not necessarily have reliability as requirements – epistemic humility, for example, which may be correct about the epistemic agent's prospects, does not seem to have any entailments about how reliably the agent succeeds in believing what is true. After all, one may be properly humble precisely because one *does not* get it right very often! Sosa's account of virtue epistemology, accordingly, is focused entirely upon whatever virtue(s) we may possess and exercise that promote reliability in terms of accuracy of belief. The problem we have noted is whether or not, properly understood, they require something even greater than reliability, as it remains open to question whether cases in which the agent fails to be accurate aren't also cases that are outside of the scope of the agent's epistemic adroitness, properly understood. It would at least be helpful to have our theory clear on this issue. This is hardly a refutation of Sosa's view, but is reason enough to continue our search.[14]

7.8 Plantinga's Proper Functioning Account

Alvin Plantinga has given a very different account of epistemic evaluation, avoiding the term "virtue" for "proper functioning." Like other virtue theories, what functioning counts as "proper" is not assessed strictly in terms of *results* or specific epistemic *acts*, but in terms of characteristics associated with our cognitive capacities themselves. Here is how Plantinga puts his account:

> [A] belief has warrant for me only if (1) it has been produced in me by cognitive faculties that are working properly (functioning as they ought to, subject to no cognitive dysfunction) in a cognitive environment that is appropriate for my kinds of cognitive faculties, (2) the segment of the design plan governing the production of that belief is aimed at the production of true beliefs, and (3) there is a high statistical probability that a belief produced under those conditions will be true. Under those conditions, furthermore, the degree of warrant is an increasing function of degree of belief. (Plantinga 1993b: 46–7)

To see exactly how Plantinga's account works, we will do well to look very carefully at each of its components, and to do this, it may be easiest if we work backwards, taking the three conditions in the reverse order of their appearance in his statement of them. The simplest of these to understand, given what we have already discussed in this book, is condition (3), which is the simple requirement that the operation of the properly functioning capacity is *reliable*. So, Plantinga's account is, at heart, also a version of an externalist, reliabilist account.

But mere reliability is not enough for Plantinga, and so his account also avoids the simpler versions of reliabilism that we discussed in the last chapter. In addition to *reliable* cognitive capacities, Plantinga also includes a condition (2) that the cognitive capacities in question operate within a design plan that is aimed at the production of true beliefs. Plantinga includes this stipulation because he can imagine cases in which the fact that a capacity reliably produces true beliefs turns out to be an accidental feature of that capacity's role in the cognitive life of the cognitive being. One example of this that Plantinga gives is our predilection to various kinds of wishful thinking: for example, the lover who is convinced well beyond the support of the actual evidence that his beloved is faithful to him (Plantinga 1993b: 12). His wishful thinking may well turn out to be a reliable source of true beliefs – after all, just because the evidence does not adequately support the lover's convictions, they may still turn out to be true: perhaps his lover really does have a wandering eye, contrary to her lover's convictions, but never actually manages to attract a rival to her current lover. What we should conclude from such cases, according to Plantinga, is that our cognitive capacities may not all have truth as their aim, and so only those that do should be included among the capacities whose proper functioning will yield candidates for knowledge.

Finally, Plantinga also includes a condition – much like Sosa's account of epistemic adroitness (Sosa's own version of epistemic virtue) that requires a capacity to be working "as it ought to," which (given condition (2)) means that it is a cognitive capacity that aims primarily at truth and it is functioning in such a way as (per condition (3)) to produce truth reliably. Moreover, just as Sosa's conception of adroitness does, Plantinga recognizes the limitations of our capacities and stipulates that the capacity must be operating within an appropriate cognitive environment.

The main novelty of Plantinga's account is his second condition, according to which we must recognize the existence and operations of cognitive capacities whose "design plan" aims at the production of true beliefs. But this feature of his account is the one that we believe leads to the most implausible aspect of his analysis – namely, that the proper analysis of knowledge could not be regarded as cogent without the addition of theism: Plantinga thinks that our possession of cognitive capacities with the design plan that aims them at truth makes no sense from an evolutionary perspective.[15] We will have more to say about this feature of

Plantinga's analysis in the next chapter; for our own analysis of knowledge that we supply there is a version of a proper functional account, only ours does not require proper functioning to be supplied or supported by an intelligent designer.

For now, however, it is worthwhile to note other potential problems for Plantinga's account. One such problem has to do with important ambiguities in the notion of a "design plan." Plantinga thinks that the best – and indeed the only plausible – way to think of a design plan, when it comes to a cognitive capacity, is in terms of the intentions of a *designer*. But this is not the only way to think of a design plan – one might also think of a design plan as a description of the precise way that something works, when operating normally. Imagine a cruel scientist, call him Tempevil, who designs a device (the tempucomp) intended to engender spontaneous temperature beliefs in the one in whose brain the device is implanted. Tempevil intends the device to be highly inaccurate, but irresistible, so that the one in whose brain the device is implanted will be driven crazy by irresistible, but false, temperature beliefs. Tempevil has a grudge against someone else, Truetemp, and implants the device in Truetemp's brain. However, it turns out, as a result of no intention by Tempevil in the designing process, that the device would spontaneously implant temperature beliefs that were very accurate to conditions in Beijing, China. This peculiarity might not have defeated Tempevil's cruel intentions because Truetemp lives in Tucson, Arizona. But, as fortune would have it, as soon as Tempevil implants the device, Truetemp receives a job offer in Beijing, meets the love of his life there, and settles down for a happy ever after – one in which he is at first surprised to discover that he has acquired a peculiar new source of beliefs, but soon comes to recognize that these beliefs are actually completely reliable.

In this case, the feature of the tempucomp that makes Truetemp's beliefs highly reliable is *not* a part of the designer's intentions – it is not part of the design plan *in Plantinga's sense*. However, if we had a full description of what the device does when operating normally, we would see that getting the temperature right in Beijing is perfectly normal for the Tempucomp. In this sense, forming true temperature beliefs in Beijing *is* part of the Tempucomp's design plan.

We think of cognitive capacities as better understood in terms of what they do, and what environments they are suited to, rather than in terms of how or why they may serve the intentions of an intelligent designer – a notion that we find extremely problematical in any case, when applied to things like human beings and other animals. We find nothing mysterious (or requiring supernatural explanation) in the idea that we actually have cognitive capacities that are reliable in some environments and not reliable in others, and therefore nothing mysterious (or requiring supernatural explanation) in understanding the operations of these capacities in terms of norms, such as those we find in Feldman's "role oughts," or in terms of their success in producing correct beliefs, or in terms like Sosa's adroitness (virtue), or, for that matter, in terms of functioning properly and not suffering from dysfunction. It is this non-mysterious and natural sense of proper functioning, accordingly, that we will use in the analysis of knowledge we provide in the next chapter.[16]

7.9 Concluding Remarks

In this chapter, we have surveyed a number of different conceptions of epistemic evaluation, and found that all of the forms epistemologists have discussed have some place in a completely adequate theory of knowledge. In other words, we accept that a complete theory of knowledge will accommodate deontological claims about what we ought to believe, consequentialist claims about success in achieving certain goals, procedural claims about which epistemic practices should be followed, and also claims about what does and what does not count as epistemically virtuous. We also found that none of these exhausted the field of epistemic evaluation, and found some forms of epistemic evaluation (some epistemic virtues) that were independent of knowledge (e.g., intellectual integrity and humility). It might seem as if this result is a fragmented and extremely untidy one, such that no unified account of knowledge and warrant can possibly include all of the many forms of evaluation that now seem to apply. But we will try to show in the next chapter that this is not at all what we should conclude, though we do recognize that the field of epistemic evaluation has proven to be much more complex and varied than epistemologists have generally supposed.

At any rate, the very existence of epistemic virtues makes it unlikely that all epistemic evaluation will be able to be reduced to a single form. In the other sections of this chapter, we have resisted claims that epistemic evaluation must be understood in just one form, and the result now seems to be that *all* of the forms of evaluation we have discussed have some role to play in epistemology. This is, we admit, not the sort of tidy result that theorists try to provide, but it also underscores the very complicated nature of our subject matter.

Current Trends

The literature on virtue epistemology has exploded over the past decade. Once again, we regret to say that an exhaustive survey would not be possible here. Battaly (2008) offers a useful survey. Additionally, John Greco has recently published a book on the topic (2010) that will be of interest to those thinking about intellectual virtues.

Doxastic voluntarism and deontology have been topics of active research recently. Matthias Steup has published an excellent volume of new essays on the topic (2001). Much of the recent literature on the topic has centered around the question whether belief essentially aims at the truth. For a sampling, see Setiya (2008), Shah and Velleman (2005), and Velleman (2000).

8

A New Theory of Knowledge, Part 1

The Desiderata and Non-Human Knowledge

> I have a cat named "Ginger." I know that her litter box is in the laundry room. I might tell my house sitters that Ginger knows that her litter box is in the laundry room, and so they should be sure to leave Ginger access to the laundry room. That is a perfectly natural discourse about Ginger, knowledge, and her litter box. So does Ginger have the same knowledge that I do that her litter box is in the laundry room? Don't be silly! Ginger does not know what a laundry room is, and she does not know what litter is, though she has, in her dear little brain, enough information to find her litter box in the laundry room and do what cats do in litter boxes in laundry rooms.
>
> Lehrer 1991: 31

8.1 Back to the Beginning

We promised at the beginning of this book to provide an analysis of knowledge, and it may seem that we are very far from this goal, having now gone through many disparate accounts of warrant and epistemic evaluation and having found a good deal of merit in mostly everything we have reviewed. So it may seem at this point that it will be an impossible task to pull together all of the different threads that have shown themselves to have value along the way. But, in fact, the actual theory of knowledge we will propose in this chapter will be remarkably simple in form – its simple form, however, will capture a great deal of complexity.

We began with what we called a "preliminary" theory of knowledge, which we named "**WTB***" and which went as follows:

WTB*: S knows that p just in case
1. p.
2. S believes that p.
3. S is warranted in believing that p.

Since we have not encountered any reason along the way for thinking that any feature of **WTB*** is mistaken, we conclude that at least the first two conditions of **WTB*** belong in our final theory. But the third condition needed to be spelled out further, and now that we have reviewed what epistemologists have had to say about warrant, it looks as if this part is going to be quite complicated. So let us review the desiderata of the theory we must present, as these have presented themselves along the way, and then we can begin the process of weaving these into a full theory.

8.2 Five Desiderata for an Adequate Theory of Knowledge

Early on, we raised the possibility of non-human animals having knowledge, and we have returned to this issue periodically in our discussions of several topics. The very question of non-human knowledge is more complex than we think epistemologists generally have recognized, as it brings with it the possibility of cases of knowledge and belief that may not have propositional content. This is why we began by characterizing knowledge as being *informational* rather than *propositional*, and we have not yet found anything in our other topics that would clearly rule out the possibility of non-human knowledge. Accordingly, our first desideratum is that our account will at least leave open the possibility of non-human animal knowledge:

(D1) Some beings that may not represent information *propositionally* may achieve knowledge.

Whether there are such beings, and precisely how we may characterize their knowledge or their manner of representing things would have to be a matter of case-by-case debate among epistemologists, ethologists, and others with expertise about the ways in which such beings engage in cognition. Our goal should not be to settle all such debates in advance, but only to leave open the very possibility of such debates, by not simply defining possible outcomes away.

Our second desideratum cuts in the opposite direction, as it were. When we talked about justification as warrant, it seemed that being justified required, among other things, being able to recognize the appropriate evidence *as evidence*. But this achievement cannot be reached without considerable cognitive sophistication. Going back to the cat in all of our examples, would it be reasonable to think that Wooj recognizes the evidence of where his litter box is *as evidence*? There *is* evidence regarding the whereabouts of Wooj's litter box, of course, and Wooj's good eyesight, memory, and excellent sense of smell all enable Wooj to employ that evidence as he heads for his litter box. But it seems unlikely, at best, that Wooj has the level of cognitive sophistication required to assess evidence *as evidence*, even if it seems obvious that he is cognitively responsive to that evidence. If so, Wooj cannot accomplish the feat of being justified, at least in the sophisticated sense we required in chapter 5. But it would seem to follow, then, either that we cannot include a justification condition as one of our desiderata, or else that we can do so only at the cost of failing to satisfy our first desideratum, D1.

These options should strike us as too extreme, however. Even if Wooj cannot accomplish the sophisticated maneuvers required for justification, normal, adult human beings *can*. And not just that, but when we are asked whether an adult human being has knowledge, we are (at least in most cases) strongly inclined to answer in the negative if she is not adequately justified. What this seems to show us is that, even if adequate justification is not required for Wooj to know something, it *is at least sometimes* required for any normal adult human being to know something. This allows us to include a second desideratum that does not conflict with the first, but which accommodates the need for justification, where we find such a need:

(D2) Adequate justification is *at least sometimes* a necessary condition of knowledge.

What is tricky about D1 and D2 together is that they seem to require a theory in which no justification is required in many of the cases D1 requires, and yet justification is still required in the cases D2 requires. But we hope to show that this apparent tension in our first two desiderata is easily resolved.

Our third desideratum was introduced in the first section of chapter 5, when we discussed the Gettier problem. Given all that we have already had to say about that problem, we believe the third desideratum can be stated directly and without further comment here:

(D3) Where justification is required for knowledge, that justification must be *undefeated.*

Later in that chapter, we discussed the basing relation, and considered how we might best conceive of our strong intuitions that one cannot have knowledge unless one's belief is based on the evidence. We ended up defending what we called a "dispositional" theory of the basing relation (DPTB),

DPTB: *S*'s belief that *p* is based on *m* iff *S* is disposed to revise her belief that *p* when she loses *m*.

Given this understanding, we can now state our fourth desideratum:

(D4) For a belief to be warranted (and thus to be a case of knowledge), it must be based on the evidence.

At the end of that chapter, we reviewed a case that Keith Lehrer, a famous critic of the basing requirement, has offered for thinking that the desideratum we just specified should *not* be included in our account of knowledge. But we found that even if we granted that his cases showed that one could be *justified* even when one's beliefs were not based on the evidence, we found we could not concede that one could have *knowledge* where the belief was not based on the evidence. The reason we gave there, and which we were able to explore much more completely in chapter 6, was that some kind of *external* condition was also required, for warrant. We reviewed the various externalist accounts of warrant that epistemologists have offered in chapter 6, and showed why we were disinclined to accept some of these. But one did allow us to say plainly what was wrong in Lehrer's Raco case.

Raco, recall, had evidence and recognized the evidence *as evidence*. So it seemed reasonable to suppose he could be counted as being justified – even though Raco's belief derived from a different source than what justified his belief. But as we said at the very end of chapter 5, there still seemed to be something terribly *wrong* with the way Raco went about his epistemic business. By the time we got to chapter 6, we could articulate better what exactly was wrong in Raco's case: highly *unreliable* cognitive processes were at work, so that even though Raco did actually get things right in his belief, the way in which the belief in question came into being and was sustained might incline us to deny that Raco had knowledge. We can accordingly now identify yet another desideratum for our theory of knowledge:

(D5) For a belief to qualify as knowledge, it must be generated or sustained by cognitive processes that reliably produce accurate cognitions – cognitions that accurately represent the world.

We should pause and compare what D5 requires with what our other desiderata mandate. Let us return to Wooj the cat: in his case, as we said, D2 does not seem to be engaged. But what about D3? Well, the way we formulated D3 would make it seem that it would not apply, either, as long as D2 does not apply. But recall that *not just* justification can be defeated by Gettier-style examples; as we said in section 6.5, reliabilism is also susceptible to these sorts of problems. So, we should either add yet another desideratum to make the same qualification for reliability that **D3** makes for justification, or (as we prefer), we should now amend **D3** to cover both justification and reliability, as follows:

> (**D3***) ~~Justification and reliable~~ processes must be *undefeated*, for knowledge.

But now, what about reliable processing and the basing relation? The epistemological literature mostly discusses basing in relation to justification. But we needn't think of it as limited in this way. Let us return to Wooj the cat. Is Wooj's belief about the whereabouts of his litter box based on the evidence? We think it is. The ways in which Wooj responds to the evidence are different from the ways we do it. For example, probably memory is more important in our own processing than it is in Wooj's case, whereas the sense of smell is probably more important in Wooj's case than in ours. We go to some effort to clean our cat's litter boxes regularly just to be sure that our own sense of smell becomes *less* reliable as a way to locate the smelly thing! Not so with Wooj – even when the litter box is freshly cleaned, there is enough odor left for him to sniff his way to it very reliably. Wooj can also process the visual evidence in different ways than we do – Wooj is much better than we are when there is very little ambient light (for example, at night with the lights turned off). But Wooj doesn't come to have the beliefs he has just by magic or randomly – his beliefs are based on his own cognitive responses to the available evidence. So Wooj seems to us to satisfy **D4** very nicely. Indeed, we might even say that he satisfies **D5** – the reliability condition – precisely because he does such a good job at satisfying **D4**. Were his cognitive capacities such that he only poorly satisfied **D4**, or failed to satisfy that condition at all, we would expect Wooj also to fail to satisfy **D5**; we would expect him to be *unreliable* in the way he represents the world. So we see a tight connection between being reliable, as per **D5**, and having one's belief based on the evidence, as per **D4**. To put it somewhat crudely, the ability to be reliable seems to be anchored by having cognitive capacities that respond to the evidence in such a way as to be able to base one's beliefs on the evidence.

8.3 Desiderata Deriving from Epistemic Evaluation

D1 through **D5** do not exhaust our desiderata, however, because we have yet to address the most complicated issue of all: epistemic evaluation. In chapter 7, we offered only a very brief review of how this topic may influence our conception of warrant, and what we found was an array of epistemic norms and evaluations, some of which seemed connected to warrant (such as the norm implicitly expressed in **D2**: "Consider the evidence *as evidence!*") and some of which do not (e.g., the virtues of epistemic integrity and humility). But particularly in the area of epistemic evaluation, we should again be alert to possible conflicts between the theoretical desiderata we have already stated. To see this, consider **D2** again. Do the same epistemic evaluations apply to Wooj as to us – fully functioning adult human beings? If a fully functioning adult human being fails to consider the evidence *as evidence* we regard him as epistemically *blameworthy*, as having perhaps failed to satisfy a deontological rule of some kind – or maybe even several of these: it may be that one fails to consider evidence *as evidence* because one has also failed to pay attention to the evidence at all! Now Wooj pays attention to the evidence in his own ways, as we have said. But we have also said that he is probably not capable of paying attention to the evidence *as evidence*. In his case, the connections between evidence and belief are not at all *reflective*, but we would fault a fully functioning adult human being for being *unreflective* at times when we think reflection is appropriate. But we *never* think reflection is appropriate for Wooj, because that would be a foolish requirement in his case. So we would fault one another for some things that we would not fault in Wooj's case. Moreover, we don't even have to go outside our own species to see a high degree of variability in the ways we apply epistemic norms and other evaluations: for example, we think that blind people can know things about their environment, but we don't regard them as epistemically *blameworthy* for not using visual perception as at least part of their evidence for their beliefs about the world.

For the sighted, the use of eyesight might be included among our epistemic duties or obligations, with regard to discerning what is present in our environment. But for the blind, we dispense with such duties or obligations.

Such examples show us that the ways in which we apply epistemic norms and other forms of epistemic evaluation depend upon what we regard as the applicable cognitive capacities of the target of such evaluations. If Wooj can't engage in reflective reasoning, we do not normatively require him to do so, but then we also restrict the areas in which he might be a candidate for knowledge to those that do not absolutely require reflective reasoning. Because a blind person cannot use visual perception, we do not normatively require him to use vision, in order to know something. However, we also limit that person's ability to know to areas where vision is not absolutely necessary. In brief, the appropriate application of epistemic evaluation will depend upon our assessment of what the epistemic being's cognitive capacities actually are.

But that's not all. We will also limit our evaluations to cases in which the epistemic being's relevant capacities are appropriately suited – for example, normal vision in the conditions of white light. If we put a fully functioning normal adult human being in conditions where the light is other than white, we do not fault the human being for the false color beliefs she comes to have in that environment – unless, of course, we have given her reasons to believe that the lighting is altered, for example, by having a sign on the door to the room she is about to enter that says, "Caution: this room does not use white light. Colors in this room will appear differently from how they do in normal daylight." If she reads this sign and then continues to make color judgments inside the room just as if she were in normal lighting, we would fault her for failing to give due consideration to the evidence she was provided by the sign on the door.

Epistemic evaluation, then, must be understood as highly sensitive to two factors: the cognitive capacities of the being whose beliefs or epistemic activities are under evaluation, and also the environment within which the capacities themselves are being applied. Important differences in the relevant capacities, and also important differences in the environments in which these capacities are exercised, will lead to important differences in the ways in which we apply epistemic evaluation, if we are going to evaluate appropriately.

This high degree of sensitivity to the relevant capacities and environments means that the rules for appropriate evaluation cannot be stated very specifically for all cases in a single formulation. To evaluate Wooj's cognitions and cognitive activities, we must first understand what Wooj can do, cognitively, and then see how that applies to the very specific situation in which we find Wooj going about his cognitive business. We do not hold him responsible, deontologically or procedurally, to perform things in ways that do not apply to beings like Wooj. Moreover, we also do not evaluate him even in accordance with the same consequentialist considerations: we expect human beings to form *true* beliefs, but, as we have said, it seems unlikely that Wooj can achieve truth. He can, perhaps, achieve correct or accurate beliefs in some other sense, but the point is that we would have to characterize even the targets of consequentialist norms for Wooj rather differently from the way we would characterize them for fully functional, adult human beings. And the same may obviously be said for aretaic norms – for what will count as epistemically virtuous for Wooj, and for us.

It follows from these considerations that we simply cannot reasonably hope for a theory of knowledge that will satisfy all five of the desiderata we have given thus far in such a way as to be *very specific* with respect to *how these desiderata get satisfied*. When Wooj knows something, he will be achieving that accomplishment in very different ways from how we do, such that *doing it right* for Wooj, evaluatively, will be constituted by different capacities working in different ways from what we would require of fully functioning adult human beings. And the way that Wooj does his epistemic business will be different from the way that bats do theirs – especially those species of bat that primarily use echolocation to represent the world. That is *not* how we do it, and that is *not* how Wooj does it – and yet perhaps bats can know things, too.

But if we cannot expect anything very specific to capture this highly variable range of conditions for proper epistemic evaluation, with respect to warrant, is there at least some *generic* way in which to articulate our final desideratum (or desiderata)? One way we might try is simply to refuse to take the question any further than we have taken it to this point. We can see that there will be applicable evaluations, such that having these be positive and not negative will be required for warrant. So perhaps we might just stop now, and state:

(**D6**) All applicable epistemic evaluations must be positive, for knowledge.

But this is way too broad because, as we have seen, not all epistemic evaluations are applicable to warrant – recall the cases of epistemic integrity and humility. As we said in chapter 7, one can manifest these virtues without knowing, and one can know without manifesting these virtues. To see, then, how we might improve upon (**D6**), let us return to the idea of epistemic agency, where the cognitive being has certain goals. So let us think a little more about Wooj and see if we can say a little more about epistemic evaluation in his case.

8.4   Epistemic Evaluation and Non-Human Animals

Wooj feels the familiar urge and heads for the laundry room, where he finds and uses his litter box. Stop! Back up!

Wooj feels the familiar urge and then . . . what happens? Wooj's cognitive capacities become activated on a mission to find his litter box. His goal: find the litter box. He's very good at this, because he remembers where it was last time, and his nose confirms that it is likely to be in the same place this time. So, he heads for the laundry room. Of course, we could trick Wooj and put the litter box somewhere else, but once he has checked the laundry room, he will deploy his cognitive capacities again to find where we put his litter box this time. He sniffs the air, and heads for the guest bathroom. There it is! This cat is hard to fool for long! Now it is time for a snack. Wooj heads for the kitchen and lowers his head into his bowl of kibble, munching away.

Pat the bat flutters quickly through the evening sky, echolocating with a voice so high that human beings cannot even hear her singing.[1] She "sees" a large juicy bug just 10 feet ahead of her and slightly below. She swoops and devours it. So good! Pat does not go about her business in anything very like the way Wooj does. Wooj does not use echolocation, whereas this is mostly how Pat goes about her business. Pat's eyesight is actually just *terrible*, compared to Wooj's. Wooj navigates his spaces on four legs, and is extremely good at judging distances for when he needs to jump. Pat has wings instead of forelegs and flies to things, instead of jumping. But she, too, manages to go where she needs to go, almost always without mishap – just like Wooj. Pat is doing things right, for a bat.

Fred was about to cook dinner when he realized that he had run out of onions. He can't make the recipe he was planning without onions. So, he gets on his bicycle and rides to the nearby store, where he picks up two large Walla Wallas, has the cashier weigh them, pays, and leaves. Home again in minutes, he goes back to his dinner plan. Fred's a great cook, and those onions are perfect in this recipe!

As Fred plans his menu, notes the lack of onions, rides his bike, and all the other things he does, he does not use echolocation, and he only uses his sense of smell in any way that is important to him as he is actually cooking the meal. Of course, he can smell some things in the air as he rides his bike, but these things are not important to him, and he pays no attention to them. Unlike Wooj and Pat, Fred uses quite a bit of *calculation* and *thoughtful deliberation* along the way. He thinks about how many onions he will need, and what size. He considers using his car, but decides the store is close enough, he can use the exercise, and besides, using the bike is better for the environment. He counts out the money to pay at the store. And so on. How very *unlike* Pat and Wooj Fred is! But Fred is doing things right, for a human being.

Wooj is doing things right – for a cat; Pat is doing things right, for a bat; Fred is doing things right for a human. But is there something more to say than this? We think there is: a *generic account* of "doing things right, for a _____." More specifically, there is the generic evaluation "forming beliefs in the right way, for a _____."

As we said earlier, these sorts of cases show that "doing things right, for a _____" will be heavily conditioned by how we fill in the blank. We do not expect Fred to maneuver his bike around by using echolocation. We do not expect Wooj to deliberate. If Pat relies on her eyesight, she'll starve. We don't fault any of these for failing to use capacities they do not have, but we do evaluate their performance in terms of the capacities they do have. Each one is a being *of a certain kind*, and each one has cognitive capacities that allow beings of that kind to function in the world.

Now in some cases, we are inclined to think that beings like Fred – and maybe also Wooj and Pat – know things. Part of the reason we think that they know is that they formed their beliefs in the right way, for beings of their kind. But that is not all that matters. There is also the question of how reliable beings of their kind are when forming beliefs in the way they do.

Consider Stinger the wasp, who eats spiders.[2] She is as good at this as any of her fellow wasps, so let us be respectful about how well adapted she is. But the truth is, when she attacks, she misses much more often than she hits. This is because the spiders on which Stinger preys have adapted their own defense-system: They decorate their webs with decoys that confuse Stinger into attacking the decoy instead of the spider. But, as we said, Stinger is as good at this as any of her peers. So she persists, and, as we study her behavior, we find that Stinger will attack webs that are highly decorated with decoys as much as 40 percent more often than she attacks undecorated webs. This makes it more likely that she will eventually attack a real spider, instead of a decoy, even on a highly decorated web. Her attacks are unreliable, but that's OK. By the end of the day, she has eaten enough real spiders to thrive.

As well adapted as Stinger is, we do not think Stinger knows that what she is about to attack is a spider. The problem is that Stinger is unreliable in forming accurate representations regarding her prey. Stinger is good enough at finding and killing spiders to thrive, but she makes lots and lots of mistakes along the way. So the obvious criterion we seem to be using in counting Wooj, Pat, and Fred among the beings that know something, and not counting Stinger as knowing that what she is about to attack is a spider, is the familiar criterion of reliability.

So one way we apply epistemic evaluation takes into account the *kind* of being under evaluation, and, in attending to this condition, what we focus on are the distinct cognitive capacities of beings of that kind. Another kind of epistemic evaluation takes into account whether beings of that kind have cognitive capacities that are reliable. We can think of the former kind of evaluation as the "proper functioning" that Plantinga talks about. Is there a way to link proper functioning and reliability? Indeed, there is.

Proper functioning suggests the notion of a function – something can't function properly unless it has a *function*. What is the function of echolocation in bats, abstract reasoning in humans, or sight and smell in cats? The answer, it seems to us, is that the function of these cognitive capacities is to form accurate beliefs. Insofar as their function is to form accurate beliefs, then when these processes are functioning *properly* we can expect that they will reliably form true beliefs (but more on this in the next chapter).

But that's not all: these processes evolved in certain environments. We shouldn't expect Wooj's sense of smell to work under water, Pat's echolocation to work in an "echo room" with sound-reflecting walls, or Fred's reasoning to work in a world run by Descartes' demon. We can only expect such processes to work in *normal environments*, where what is normal depends on the sorts of environments the processes evolved in. Fred might get lucky and form a true belief in a demon world, but we wouldn't count him as knowing. Warrant requires operating in normal environments, with the understanding that what's a normal environment for Pat's echolocation might not be a normal environment for Wooj's sense of smell.

So let us add this to our list of considerations:

An environment (*E*) will be a **normal environment** for the cognitive capacities of a cognitive being (*S*), just in case that environment is the sort of environment within which *S*'s cognitive capacities function properly.

To sum up, then, warrant requires forming beliefs in the right way, for a being of your kind. Forming beliefs in the right way, for a being of your kind, amounts to using the properly functioning cognitive processes available to you as a being of that kind. Furthermore, warrant requires that the function of these cognitive processes is *forming accurate beliefs*, that these cognitive processes reliably form accurate beliefs in normal environments, and that they are being used in a normal environment. Schematically:

> *S* (a being of kind *K*) is warranted in her belief that *p* just in case:
> - *S*'s belief that *p* was generated and sustained using all relevant cognitive processes available to *S* as a being of kind *K*.
> - These processes' function is the formation and sustaining of accurate beliefs.
> - These processes reliably generate and sustain accurate beliefs (in normal environments for these processes).
> - *S* generated and sustains the belief that *p* in a normal environment for these processes.

8.5   Proper Functioning and Other Dimensions of Evaluation

To say that an agent's belief issues from and is sustained by reliable, properly functioning processes in a normal environment is one way of evaluating the agent's belief. But is this just one form of evaluation among others? After all, we've seen many other forms of epistemic evaluation that seem relevant to warrant. Our claim in this section is that the many other forms of evaluation can be regarded as the many forms and faces of reliable proper functioning in normal environments.

First, let us consider the consequentialist norms aimed at the formation or sustaining of true (or accurate) belief. Part of being warranted, it seemed, is forming and sustaining your belief in a way likely to provide you with accurate beliefs. When Wooj feels the urge, and relies on his sense of smell to locate the litter box, he's relying on a process that, when properly functioning in an appropriate environment, is highly reliable. That just means that it is very likely to generate and sustain an accurate belief about where the litter box is. So when Wooj uses his reliable, properly functioning processes in appropriate environments, we can evaluate his beliefs positively from the consequentialist perspective.

Second, we can consider the deontic norms. Insofar as we are considering an agent, like Fred, who has some degree of control over how he reasons, we will be able to ask whether Fred reasoned as he ought to have reasoned. Suppose Fred used the relevant cognitive processes available to him as an adult human being. Then surely we will want to say that Fred has done his duty, forming and sustaining a belief as he ought to have. And this will be true even if, unbeknownst to Fred, his cognitive processes are unreliable or are being used in unfavorable circumstances. Those kinds of being who have some control over their epistemic lives, then, will be evaluated positively from the deontic perspective when they use the relevant cognitive processes available to them.

What about beings – like Pat, perhaps – who don't exercise this kind of epistemic agency? Pat can't decide to suppress *other* cognitive processes (such as wishful thinking) and instead trust her echolocation. Pat *automatically* uses her echolocation. Insofar as we think that epistemic "oughts" imply doxastic "cans," Pat won't count as doing her duty, even though she is doing things right, for a being of her sort. But this is no problem, for Pat doesn't have epistemic duties. For beings that have epistemic duties, using the relevant cognitive processes available to them will result in satisfying their duties. Our account of warrant only indirectly requires duty satisfaction. So, on our account, warrant requires the satisfaction of epistemic duties by agents that have duties and does not require this of agents that do not. This is a happy result.

Finally, we consider the aretaic, or virtue-theoretic, norms that warrant seemed to require. A virtuous epistemic agent, we think, is one who properly uses the reliable cognitive processes available to him, in the environment for which they are suited. Clearly, one could, on a singular occasion, properly use a reliable process in the right environment. Such an agent might still not be virtuous, for they might normally misuse their cognitive equipment, or fail to use relevant processes. We leave it an open question whether only virtuous agents can attain knowledge, though we have our doubts. Still, we think our account will at least require the exercise of certain virtues. For an agent's reliable cognitive processes are a sort of virtue, if not of the agent, then at least of her cognitive system. Since our account of warrant requires the exercise of such processes, it requires the exercise of cognitive virtues. Just which virtues, of course, will depend on the kind of being in question. Pat needs to echolocate (among other things); we human beings need to avoid our biases (among other things).

We think, then, that the positive evaluation associated with using the appropriate reliable processes available to you, in the right environment, encompasses all other forms of evaluation that warrant requires. Accordingly, we can now formulate a revised version of our sixth desideratum for knowledge, which we think covers all of the necessary modes of epistemic evaluation:

(D6*) For S to know that *p*, *S*'s belief must be generated and sustained by reliable, properly functioning processes in a normal environment for these processes.

8.6   Other Desiderata

We are now considering the following analysis of knowledge:

PFTK: *S* knows that *p* just in case
1. *p*.
2. *S* believes that *p*.
3. *S*'s belief that *p* was generated and sustained by using all relevant cognitive processes available to *S* as a being of kind *K*.
4. These processes' function is the formation and sustaining of accurate beliefs.
5. These processes reliably generate and sustain accurate beliefs (in normal environments for these processes).
6. *S* generated and sustains the belief that *p* in a normal environment for these processes.

It should be clear enough, then, just how PFTK satisfies most of our desiderata. D1 is satisfied by the fact that nothing in this analysis requires that knowers represent information propositionally. D2 says that justification is sometimes required for knowledge. We discuss justification in more detail in the next chapter, and so won't address this desideratum fully here. But we can say that the kinds of cognitive processes available to adult humans – those required for warrant – are just the sort that generate what we traditionally think of as justification. So, for adult human beings in at least many cases, forming beliefs using the properly functioning processes available to them will be tantamount to forming justified beliefs. **PFTK** requires justification for humans in many cases, but does not for cats or bats.

Our third desideratum (**D3***) tries to rule out the Gettier cases by requiring that one's justification or reliable processes must be undefeated (with the proviso that the notion of undefeated justification has been left unanalyzed). We have seen that our analysis only requires justification of some knowers. But the Gettier problem isn't limited to such knowers – even Wooj can be "Gettiered"! Imagine Wooj looks out into the yard, and his keen eyesight detects what he takes to be a tasty bird. He then creeps outside because he judges there is a bird to be captured. In fact, what Wooj is seeing is not a bird at all, but a cleverly designed robot. Nevertheless, in the bushes where Wooj did not look, there is a nice plump bird. Wooj has been Gettiered! He does not know that there is a bird in the yard, even though there is, he believes it, and he believes it as the result of using relevant, reliable, properly functioning processes available to him in a normal environment.

"Not so fast!" you might say. "Wooj is in very *abnormal* circumstances – there were no cleverly designed robotic 'birds' in the environment in which feline eyesight evolved." So, it might be argued that all Gettier-style problems are removed in **PFTK** by conditions 5 and 6 of the analysis. Perhaps this is the right diagnosis of the case, but we doubt it. The robot in our case surely does make the relevant environment *abnormal*, but this is just an artifact of our particular example. It seems likely that in the environments in which feline eyesight evolved, there were always some objects that from a slight distance looked exactly like birds to the cats eyeing them. These doppelgängers could then be used to construct Gettier cases that don't violate the "normal circumstances" requirement.

What should we say, then, about the Gettier problem?[3] We fear that we don't have any better answer than any of the many other theories of knowledge epistemologists have offered, for which an additional condition to rule out Gettier problems is simply added on. So we will supplement our account with the following condition, just to be safe:

>   7. The processes that generated and sustain S's belief that p are not defeated.

This addition will always appear to some readers as simply ad hoc. However, as we said, it is a condition that is quite familiar among theories of knowledge, and nearly always as the sort of add-on that we supply here. Some epistemologists have contended that Gettier problems can never be ruled out. If so, then our condition 7 is a requirement that cannot be met. However, if that is so, then we contend that a complete analysis of knowledge cannot in principle be given, since we do not think that defeated processes could ever warrant knowledge.

Let us move on to the fourth desideratum, that one's beliefs be based on one's evidence. As we said before, it looks as if Wooj (and therefore also Pat, and certainly fully functioning adult human beings) can satisfy this condition in virtue of satisfying condition 3–6 in our analysis. No process could count as functioning properly in our sense, if the cognition it produced or sustained in us was not based on the evidence.

So that leaves desiderata five and six. D5 says that warranted beliefs are generated and sustained by reliable cognitive processes. This is guaranteed by condition five of PFTB. We argued that D6* ensures that all epistemic evaluations that are required for warrant are positive. We showed in the previous section that our account of warrant guarantees this result as well, and how the positive outcome was actually a direct result of proper functioning.

So, contingent upon our discussion of justification in the next chapter, we conclude that the combined seven conditions in PFTB satisfy all of the desiderata required for an adequate analysis of knowledge.

Current Trends

As we have said all along, one of the significant advantages of externalist conceptions of warrant is that they can accommodate knowledge in non-human animals. Our own account is no different in this respect, while adding to the externalist general approach a way also to include the requirement that appropriate epistemic evaluations also be satisfied, for knowledge. Our account thus fits best, we contend, with all of the important recent work being done in the field of animal cognitive ethology, which studies the cognitive and communicative behavior of animals – in many cases revealing striking cognitive abilities. Those interested in examples of what ethologists regard as advanced cognitive capacities among animals should have a look at Seyfarth, Cheney, and Marler (1980), who discovered that vervet monkeys use different calls to communicate threats by different sorts of predators; Schusterman, Southall, Kastak, and Kastak (2001), on the vocal communcations among pinniped populations (e.g., California sea lions); Allen and Bekoff (2007), who have shown remarkable memory abilities in scrub jays; and Watanabe and Huber (2006), who have studied the ability of non-linguistic animals to perform feats of abstract reasoning. Good general studies in this field include Bekoff (2006), Hurley and Nudds (2006), Ristau (1991a), and Shuker (2001). Although his own view is a form of reliabilism, the one epistemologist who has paid more attention to evidence from cognitive ethology than any other is Hilary Kornblith. See especially his 2002.

9

A New Theory of Knowledge, Part 2

Human Knowledge

9.1 Human Beings and the Justification Requirement

We have talked about cats and bats, and wasps and spiders. But what about *us*? Is it enough to say about us that knowing is nothing other than the proper functioning of our reliable cognitive capacities? It would be, if it weren't for the unusual fact about human beings that we also at least sometimes require human beings to be *justified* in what they believe. But the addition of justification looks like a joker in the deck from which we have been dealing our theory. Up until this point, everything we have said could be characterized as an *externalist* theory of warrant, because everything we have said has been based on the operations of cognitive capacities and reliable processing, none of which need to be present to the conscious scrutiny of the cognitive being. But as soon as we included the stipulation that justification is at least sometimes a necessary condition of knowledge – and, with it, the requirement that evidence be recognized and employed by the epistemic agent *as evidence,* we assured that our account could not be one that is given in purely externalist terms. What we intend to dispute, however, is not the claim that our account includes an element of internalism – it does – but rather that by having this inclusion, we fail to offer a "naturalistic" account of knowledge.

When Quine proposed "naturalizing epistemology," he sought to rid epistemology of the two elements that he regarded as "unnatural," or as failing to qualify for description and analysis within the realm of science. One of these elements was justification, which Quine wished to jettison precisely because the very notion of justification includes the *other* element Quine regarded as not susceptible to naturalistic analysis, namely, evaluation. Subsequent epistemologies have been too quick to embrace Quine's prejudices. These prejudices are at least two in number. First, we think that Quine is wrong to believe that evaluation cannot be "naturalistic." And, second, we also think that the requirement of justification for at least some instances of human cognition to qualify as knowledge, is as *natural* a fact as a fact can be. We think the requirement for justification grows out of and is the direct result of the kinds of cognitive capacities that human beings have *as a matter of their very nature as human beings.*

To put it somewhat differently, we require justification for knowledge in some cases, because that is what is required for the cognitive capacities that are our *natural endowment* to function properly. But finally, and in this case *contra* Plantinga, who articulated an earlier version of proper functionalism, we also contend that we will best understand the very fact that we have the cognitive capacities that we do as a *natural endowment*, if we explain their presence in us not, as Plantinga would have it, by an appeal to some supernatural designer, but rather as the product of natural selection. We conclude that the account we provide, including, as it does, elements of internalism, justification, and epistemic evaluation, is naturalistic through and through. Accordingly, we will call upon our colleagues in epistemology to cease and desist, once and for all, from making the false claim that only externalist theories qualify as "naturalistic" ones. Let us discuss each of these three claims – the two we make against Quine, and the one we make against Plantinga, in order.

9.2   Naturalistic Evaluation

In the last chapter, we applied our conception of proper functioning to cases that seemed like they might be good candidates for non-human knowledge: Wooj the cat's cognitions in regard to the whereabouts of his litter box or food dish, and perhaps Pat the bat's cognitions in regard to the location of an insect within her field of echolocation. As we discussed these matters, we unreservedly and unqualifiedly employed the language of evaluation – cognitive proper functioning, for Wooj, was none other than doing things *right*, for a cat. In fact, we think the application of evaluation in epistemology is not at all unlike its perfectly natural inclusion in other scientific enterprises, such as veterinary or human medicine, environmental science, or any of a number of other areas in the life sciences.

The veterinarian at the city zoo has been watching Shiva, the lioness. She has not been eating well lately, and she has lost some weight. She seems listless, uninterested in the toys she used to enjoy mauling in her carefully constructed habitat, and the vet notices that Shiva's fur is thinning in patches, with her skin patchy and somewhat reddened underneath. He says to his assistant, "There's something wrong with Shiva." If we are to regard all evaluation as "unnatural," then what the vet says to his assistant in this case is either no better than a sloppy and unnatural way of saying something *else*, that he could and perhaps should say using only non-evaluative language, or else he has said something that does not fall within his scientific expertise. But the latter is obviously false – who could be *better* than a highly trained veterinarian to read the signs and discern that there is something wrong with Shiva? So perhaps, to be fully *"naturalistic,"* we should find a way to rephrase what the vet said to his assistant that will remove the *unnatural* stain from his actual words. How might we do this? Well, we might simply list the symptoms the vet had marked in the big cat. But to do this is not at all to make the point the vet sought to make. He wanted to tell his assistant that there was an evaluation to be made *on the basis of these symptoms*. Simply listing the symptoms would not make this point – unless, of course, the vet's assistant can and does make the same inference the vet made himself: when Shiva has these symptoms, there is something *wrong* with her. But just because the vet may not need actually to state the evaluation out loud, it does not follow that the evaluation is thereby removed. In such a case, it is simply made in silence as the vet and his assistant consider Shiva's condition.

The vet and his assistant are evaluating Shiva's health. She is either in *good* health, or else she is in some condition that falls short of good health. What qualifies as good health for a lioness will be different from what qualifies as good health for a sea lion – a lion's body temperature, for example, will normally be 1–3 degrees higher (Fahrenheit) than a sea lion's. Moreover, what qualifies as *good* health will be a natural fact about that kind of animal, and will depend upon the sort of animal that it is. To put it in a way that is obviously convenient for our own purposes, an animal will qualify as being in good health and psychological condition if that animal's physical and psychological capacities are *functioning properly*. Part of what it means to understand and know what a lioness is, scientifically, is to know what is *good* for such an animal, and what it means for an animal of that sort to be in a good or less-than-good, condition. And precisely because veterinarians are in a position to make such evaluations, we regard them as knowing more than ordinary people what there is to know about lions. Accordingly, we simply reject what we have called "Quine's prejudice" about evaluation being non-natural. It seems to us, on the contrary, that part of what we learn when we study natural science is how to make more expertly the sorts of evaluations we expect from well-trained veterinarians and physicians. In such cases, and also in the case of epistemic evaluation, the bases for evaluation derive from the natures of the things under evaluation.

9.3   Justification as a Natural Process

In chapter 5, we defended a holistic coherentist account of justification. On this account, a belief is justifiable for an agent just in case it coheres with the agent's background system of beliefs (and experiences) and this background system itself is sufficiently broad and coherent. The problem of easy knowledge compelled us to accept the following requirement:

> **KR.** A belief source K can produce justified beliefs for S only if S is justified in believing that K is reliable.

In that chapter we sketched how justified beliefs about the reliability of our cognitive processes can arise. The achievement of this sort of justification requires a high degree of cognitive sophistication. For example, checking for coherence among our beliefs, extending our system of beliefs by inference, and justifying our beliefs to others all require the ability to engage in *abstract reasoning.* Furthermore, assessing the reliability of our cognitive processes (and checking the quality of our evidence) requires the ability to engage in *meta-cognition.*

We concluded that chapter with a dilemma: either rule out relatively unsophisticated animals from the class of knowers, or allow that adult humans need not exercise these capacities in order to know. Neither option was intuitively satisfying. Surely Pat the bat can know where the bugs are, even though she can't sit down and reflect on the reliability of her use of echolocation. And surely an adult human cannot know what the temperature is, if he forms his temperature beliefs using a thermometer in complete ignorance of its reliability. Fortunately, we think our account of warrant can avoid this dilemma.

In chapter 8, we explained how our account of warrant allows unsophisticated animals to know things. What warrant requires is that these animals employ properly functioning reliable cognitive processes available to them as beings of their kind. Insofar as they cannot engage in metacognition or abstract reasoning, they need not employ such processes. Does that mean an adult human can know that p even if her belief that p is unjustified? We think it does not, for adult humans *can* engage in meta-cognition and abstract reasoning. Indeed, the ancient Greek philosopher, Aristotle, thought that the defining attribute of human beings was our *rationality* – our ability to *reason.* In all other ways, Aristotle thought we functioned like other animals and were simply within that genus. We're not sure we can completely agree with Aristotle on this point, as we are inclined to think that at least some members of different animal species have more sophisticated cognitive capacities than Aristotle seemed to suspect. But we do agree with this much of what Aristotle thought: human beings are at least among those species that can engage in reasoning and meta-cognition. We are somewhat like Wooj, because we can also achieve and sustain knowledge via sense perceptions, especially vision, though we're not as good as Wooj when it comes to night vision. But, unlike Wooj, we can form justified beliefs about the reliability of our vision and we can also make complicated inferences from what we see ("Huh . . . When white light passes through a prism, a rainbow of colored light comes out. It must be that white light is actually composed of colored light of various wavelengths!").

We think that abstract reasoning and meta-cognition are as natural for adult humans as echolocation is to Pat the bat or night vision is to Wooj the cat. For an adult human, part of cognitive proper functioning is the correct exercise of these capacities. When these capacities function properly, they generate justification – that is, they result in large and coherent systems of belief. So it is that justification is at least *sometimes* a necessary condition of knowledge, as we said in the last chapter. It is a necessary condition of knowledge when the knowledge involved is *human* knowledge. This is not to say that every instance of even human knowledge will involve complicated reasoning or meta-cognition – clearly, we often form beliefs immediately on the basis of perception without reasoning getting involved. But, as humans who have the capability to reason and reflect on our own cognition, perception can only produce warrant for us insofar as we have justified background beliefs about its reliability and the perceptual beliefs cohere with everything else we believe. For if they didn't cohere – or we didn't have background beliefs about our reliability – then some reasoning and reflection *would* be required to figure out why the belief doesn't cohere or whether it is to be trusted. So, even when reasoning is not required, justification still is.

Two things follow from these observations. First, the fact that justification is only *sometimes* a necessary condition of knowledge is to be explained by the natural fact that human beings have the cognitive capacity of reasoning. So, attention to human cognitive capacities produces an account in which the specific case of *human* knowledge requires justification. But this is no more an *unnatural fact* than the requirement that at least sometimes the use of echolocation will be a necessary condition of such knowledge.[1]

Second, though human knowledge is very different from bat knowledge, it does not at all follow that knowledge is in some sense an equivocal term – actually *meaning* different things in the different cases.[2] Knowledge is something *generic*, in our account, so that what will count as knowledge in specific cases will have to be sensitive to the reliable cognitive capacities that apply to that specific case, whether cat, bat, or human. But the generic form of the account is the same in every case, and that form reduces to a relatively simple formula (the same we gave last chapter):

PFTK: *S* knows that *p* just in case
1. *p*.
2. *S* believes that *p*.
3. *S*'s belief that *p* was generated and sustained by using all relevant cognitive processes available to *S* as a being of kind *K*.
4. These processes' function is the formation and sustaining of accurate beliefs.
5. These processes reliably generate and sustain accurate beliefs (in normal environments for these processes).
6. *S* generated and sustains the belief that *p* in a normal environment for these processes.
7. The processes that generated and sustain *S*'s belief that *p* are not defeated.

There are different kinds of knowledge, of course. Some kinds are available to some cognitive beings and not others. And there are very different ways of attaining or sustaining knowledge. Most beings that know anything have several ways of achieving or sustaining knowledge. Some beings have more ways of knowing than others; and some have highly unusual ways of knowing. But none of this shows that "knowledge" must actually have different meanings or refer to fundamentally different sorts of achievements. Rather, knowledge is a generic term that we apply to all cases that accord with the general analysis given above. As we have seen, this captures a great deal of complexity, but, in the end, the analysis itself is actually quite simple in form.

9.4 Naturalism vs Supernaturalism[3]

In this chapter so far, we have attempted to show why "naturalistic" attempts to remove the proper functions of certain human cognitive capacities from epistemology are deeply wrong-headed. But now we face a different challenge, and it comes from the author of the account that is in many ways the most like the one we have given, Alvin Plantinga. Plantinga thinks that naturalism in epistemology cannot succeed,[4] on the ground that reliabilism and other forms of naturalized epistemology face a special kind of skeptical challenge: why should we suppose that we really do have reliable cognitive equipment? The answer most naturalist epistemologists have given to this question is that human evolution, via the process of natural selection, has supplied us with the sort of cognitive equipment that allows us to know many things – that is, that allows us to believe many true things as a result of belief-forming systems that reliably produce true belief. This claim, however, has been challenged on the ground that natural selection only supports survival, but is neutral with regard to getting things right when we judge our environment.[5]

In this section, we do not take up Plantinga's positive probabilistic argument for preferring supernaturalism to naturalism.[6] Instead, we will only try to show that the skeptical challenge by which Plantinga motivates his supernaturalism can be met by naturalists. By doing so, we avoid the main problem Plantinga sees for the sort of naturalistic account of knowledge that we offer in this book. *Contra* Plantinga and other skeptics about the reliability of our cognitive capacities, we will show that there are good reasons to think that at least *some* of our capacities are veridically reliable, and that their reliability is an artifact of natural selection.[7]

9.5   The Challenge

Seemingly anticipating our evolutionary defense of human cognitive reliability, Darwin himself at one point seemed to warn against making the very inference we seek to defend, in a famous passage in a letter to William Graham:

> the horrid doubt always arises whether the convictions of man's mind, which has been developed from the mind of the lower animals, are of any value or at all trustworthy. Would any one trust in the convictions of a monkey's mind, if there are any convictions in such a mind? (Darwin 1881: 315–16)

The doubt Darwin expresses here has come to be known in the epistemological literature on this topic as "Darwin's doubt."[8] A more recent expression of the same doubt has been given by Patricia Churchland, who puts the doubt rather more forcefully:

> Boiled down to essentials, a nervous system enables the organism to succeed in the four F's: feeding, fleeing, fighting and reproducing. The principle chore of nervous systems is to get the body parts where they should be in order that the organism may survive. [. . .] Improvements in sensorimotor control confer an evolutionary advantage: a fancier style of representing is advantageous *so long as it is geared in the organism's way of life and enhances the organism's chances of survival.* Truth, whatever that is, definitely takes the hindmost. (Churchland 1987: 548)

Now, we do not at all deny that fitness may not *always* require veridical reliability. As Churchland points out, in any number of ways human fitness might actually be increased by traits that are veridically *unreliable*[9] – for example, recent studies have shown that human beings experience greater sexual satisfaction to the extent that they have a positive physical self-image. The accuracy of the self-image, however, is not a factor.[10] Some have even argued that evidence shows massive irrationality among human beings, of a sort that is likely to conflict with any degree of epistemic reliability.[11]

Many thinkers have seen a good deal more reason for hope from evolutionary theory. So, for example, we get the following assessment by W. V. Q. Quine, as it relates fitness in human beings to veridical reliability in making inductive inferences:

> What does make clear sense is this other part of the problem of induction: why does our innate subjective spacing of qualities accord so well with the functionally relevant groupings in nature as to make our inductions tend to come out right? Why should our subjective spacing of qualities have a special purchase on nature and a lien on the future?
>
> There is some encouragement in Darwin. If people's innate spacing of qualities is a gene-linked trait, then the spacing that has made for the most successful inductions will have tended to predominate through natural selection. Creatures inveterately wrong in their inductions have a pathetic but praiseworthy tendency to die before reproducing their kind. (Quine 1969c: 126)[12]

Many philosophers have found more solace from Darwin's theory, regarding the veridical reliability of our cognitive capacities, than Darwin himself seemed to find, at least in the moment of his doubt. But philosophers are not the only ones who have argued that natural selection grounds veridical reliability. So we find developmental psychologists Alison Gopnik and Andrew Melzoff also making claims like Quine's: "Science gets things right because it uses psychological devices that were designed by evolution precisely to get things right" (Gopnik and Melzoff 1997: 17).

Among philosophers, reliabilists and other externalists have been quick to embrace such reasoning – particularly because they have conceived of their approach as fulfilling Quine's call for "naturalism" in epistemology. Some have found the whole idea of animal knowledge strong support for such "naturalism," but also for the idea that veridically reliable cognition would be supported by evolutionary theory. A very clear example of this approach may be found in Hilary Kornblith (1999), who cites an example taken from animal ethology for the claim that knowledge is a "natural kind."

Kornblith quotes from Carolyn Ristau's (1991b) work on the piping plover:

On some approaches of an intruder, the bird may do a grada-
tion of broken-wing displays, which may perhaps begin with
a fanning tail and gradually increase the awkwardness of walk
until it has one and then both wings widely arched, fluttering,
and dragging. It may then vocalize loud raucous squawks as
well. The broken-wing display is usually made while the bird
is moving forward along the ground, although stationary
displays are also made. . . . The bird presents a convincing
case for being injured, and the observer often trudges hundreds of meters after the bird only to see it suddenly fly away
with agility. At that point one is far from the nest or young.
(Ristau 1991b: 94, quoted in Kornblith 1999: 328)

Kornblith concludes that knowledge attributions may be
made when such successful behaviors are traits associated
with the entire species:

It is the focus on the fitness of the species to the environment
which forces us to explain the possibility of successful behavior, and it is the explanation of successful behavior which
requires the notion of knowledge rather than mere belief.
Knowledge explains the possibility of successful behavior in
an environment, which in turn explains species fitness. (Kornblith 1999: 331)

The problem with Kornblith's assessment in this case,
however, is that it applies to a case in which the behavior is
not veridically reliable:[13] Plainly, in the case Ristau gives, the
plover puts on her display for the human observer, who we
can assume posed no threat to the bird or her offspring in
the nest!

9.6 Constructing a Better Response
to the Challenge

Quine and Kornblith and others, we contend, have perhaps
been a bit too quick in assuming that evolutionary theory
would ground veridical reliability in our cognitive processes.
But we believe skeptics have also been too quick to assume
that evolution does not support such reliability. In fact, we
believe that skeptics and naturalistic epistemologists have

been mostly talking past one another. To see why, it would help a great deal at this point if we paid a little closer attention to what evolutionary theory actually does and does not require. This attention, we claim, will help to clarify the grounds for the kind of skepticism about human veridical reliability that we find presented by Churchland and others, but also to see why this ground is insufficient for the skepticism they think it entails.

To begin, then, let us remind ourselves of what evolutionary theory requires. Here is how Mourenza and Smith put it:

> Natural selection provides the means for evolutionary change by virtue of three conditions: phenotypic variation between individuals or groups of individuals, differential reproductive success resulting from such variation, and heritability of the traits in question. Accordingly, those traits that provide advantage to the organism in terms of survival in its physical environment will conduce to fitness, as they make it more likely that the organism will reproduce. (Forthcoming: 3)

But what does this show us about our epistemic goal of "getting it right"? To get an answer to this question, we will do well to remind ourselves, first, that reliability can come in different forms. As Peter J. Graham notes, "For sperm, success *once in a while* is success often enough. [. . . But] [f]or the heart, succeeding rarely will not suffice; hearts need to pump blood reliably" (Graham forthcoming: 12). In these cases, Graham is talking about the reliability of certain functions that operate at the purely physical level. Should we expect there to be similar degrees of reliability at the *cognitive* level – and, most importantly, should we expect at least some of these to contribute to fitness when and only when (like the heart in performing its non-veridical function) they achieve very high degrees of *veridical* reliability?

The question we need answered, let us be clear, is not whether evolutionary forces would *directly* support veridical reliability. They do not; nor should we expect them to do so. As Patricia Churchland rather colorfully puts it, natural selection is only concerned with what she calls "the four F's: feeding, fleeing, fighting and reproducing" (quoted above). But that does not at all show that evolutionary forces could not or would not support veridical reliability *indirectly*.

Although he explicitly "puts aside" all considerations of knowledge (Graham forthcoming: 2), Graham offers a conception of what he calls "epistemic entitlement" that aligns very well with our account of knowledge. In his view, it is important to notice that some of the ways in which human beings function are cognitive, and some of these can only be supposed to function properly if they reliably produce true beliefs. He uses visual perception as a particularly clear example of this fact. Moreover, because these are the product of our evolutionary history, he counts them as *etiological functions* – that is, they have been selected in our evolution precisely because the effects of these functions (e.g., perceiving accurately) contributes to fitness. He makes the analogy between visual perception, whose etiological function is accurate representation of the world around us, with the etiological function of our hearts:

> The heart is for pumping blood; that is its function. Why? Because ancestors of our hearts pumped blood, and by pumping blood contributed to fitness, and did so better than alternatives. (Graham forthcoming: 9)

We can compare this etiology with that involving visual perception. Paraphrasing from the above quotation: visual perception is for creating and sustaining true beliefs about our environment. Why? Because our ancestors visually perceived the world, and their doing so contributed to fitness, and did so better than alternatives (e.g., by using echolocation). So Graham concludes that "a belief forming process [will confer epistemic entitlement] iff functioning normally, where the process has forming true beliefs reliably as an etiological function and so is reliable in normal conditions when functioning normally" (Graham forthcoming: 15).

Accounts such as Graham's (and ours) do not at all violate the restriction, as it is so colorfully put by Patricia Churchland, that fitness is only concerned with "the four F's." But the way in which it is compatible with this restriction is by recognizing that, as a matter of fact, *some* cognitive capacities and processes happen to help us (and other animals) as they engage with the world in their evolutionarily mandated quest to succeed in "the four F's." These capacities and processes thus display an etiological function that contributes to the account of knowledge we have provided, and in a way that obviously avoids the sort of skepticism associated with "Darwin's doubt."

9.7 Sexual and Social Fitness

One of the authors of this book has recently advanced further reasons for thinking that natural selection and evolutionary fitness support veridical reliability for at least some cognitive capacities in human beings and other animals. After all, fitness does not simply consist in avoiding predators in order to live another day. To remind ourselves again of Patricia Churchland's phrase, selection is the result of success in "the four F's," and obviously one cannot succeed in *all* of the F's simply by surviving over time. In the cases of human beings and other social animals, success in "the four F's" will also be the product of *social* success – we are not likely to succeed in *any* of "the four F's" unless we can successfully achieve a secure place in the sort of social group that human beings tend to live in.

Now, some elements of such success do not seem to be heritable in the way that evolutionary fitness requires. So, the relative social and sexual success enjoyed currently by those amply adorned with body piercings and tattoos is not likely to last even a generation. Even if there is some evolutionary account to be made for why human beings engage in such displays, the specific forms of display that work at any given time plainly do not always maintain the same value for attracting mates over several generations.

Other traits, however, may reasonably be thought to have inter-generational advantages, and thus be reasonably supposed to be the sorts of functions that do provide selective advantages. Examples of such traits include[14] reliable capacities for judging the states of mind of potential partners with respect to sexual availability, interest, and readiness. Plainly, those who function less reliably on these sorts of judgments will spend more time pursuing potential partners who are not available, not interested, or not ready. Those who are more reliable in these judgments can expect to achieve a higher ratio of success to failure. Now, it is also certainly possible that a certain level of wishful thinking (obviously, an unreliable cognitive process) would be advantageous here, since human beings may also *become* more available, interested, and ready when confronted with expressions of interest from a potential partner. Even so, there are predictable limits to the degree to which we are tolerant of misperception of these issues, and one is not likely to be advantaged by too high a degree of unreliability as one pursues such goals.

The negative argument seems to work as well: those who are perceived as suffering from defects in reliable cognitive functioning (think of those with severe cognitive developmental disabilities) – and those who combine such defects with *social* deficits (e.g., in cases like severe autism) – are not generally perceived as promising partners in our joint pursuits of "the four F's." We are not claiming that no one could ever find ones with such conditions appealing or consider partnering with them; rather, we are saying that such things are not *merely* cognitive challenges to those in such conditions. Such conditions also create social and sexual challenges, and these challenges are generally not conducive to fitness in "the four F's."

In their paper, Mourenza and Smith survey an array of evidence, from children's social development in what is called "pretence play" (the kinds of games in which children "make believe") to the highly regular features of play among canids (domestic dogs, coyotes, wolves, etc.) where veridical reliability is not merely an advantage, but actually a prerequisite for engaging in such play at all.[15] The examples they offer from the animal kingdom are especially useful here, since engaging in such forms of play is a requirement of social inclusion in canid groups. Animals who cannot or will not engage in such play will be excluded from the pack, and the negative effects of such exclusion for their pursuit of "the four F's" are obvious. In these and the many other cases they provide, the case that veridically reliable cognitive functioning is an artifact of natural selection is thus well supported.

Our argument in this section has been that social animals gain significant benefits from veridically reliable cognitive functions in terms of membership (and presumably also status) within the sorts of social groups that in turn provide significant advantages for selection. Again, our argument in the last section also applies here: we do not claim that natural selection *directly* supports social inclusion or the sort of veridically reliable cognitive processes that provide advantages within social environments. Rather, we claim that social inclusion is itself selected among some animals, including human beings, because social inclusion provides clear advantages in the pursuit of "the four F's." And, for the purposes of social inclusion, veridical cognitive processing of some kinds and in some sorts of cases is itself a requirement.

9.8 A Survey of Some Advantages of Our Account

We are now at last in a position where we can consider several ways in which our account of warrant provides advantages over other accounts that are in various ways similar to it. To begin, let us remind our readers that the account we have offered is what epistemologists have called an "externalist" account, insofar as it rests ultimately upon a feature of the way in which the knower goes about the process of coming or continuing to know. We have characterized this feature in terms of "proper functioning."

The first advantage to our theory is that it avoids one of the most common objections to externalism. Recall (as we discussed in chapter 6) that internalists have sometimes argued against externalism with the "opacity objection." Giving examples such as Norman the clairvoyant and Truetemp, internalist critics have argued that a reliably formed belief may not amount to knowledge if the would-be knower has no idea whether the belief was reliably formed. This is not an objection that can be raised to our account of warrant. For, on our account, Norman and Truetemp do not know, just as internalists intuit. On our account of justification, a belief is only justified if we have reason to think that it was reliably formed. Since Norman has no reason to think that his clairvoyance is reliable, none of his clairvoyant beliefs will be justified. But we argued that where an agent's belief is unjustified, it must not have been formed as the result of properly functioning cognitive processes. So Norman's clairvoyant beliefs are not warranted, according to us, however reliable they may be.

There is yet another reason why these cases do not provide any difficulty for our account.[16] Recall Graham's stipulation that proper functioning required an *etiological* account, and argued that such an account comes from our evolutionary history. Recall, too, that part of what we found problematic in the cases provided in framing the opacity objection was their unfamiliarity – we worried when we introduced those objections that the intuitions on which they relied were not as well supported by our ability to judge cases that were more familiar in our experience. But their unfamiliarity is the result of their coming from *outside* of the etiological ground for our conception of proper functioning – Norman's clairvoyance and Truetemp's bizarre new ability to tell what the temperature is are not grounded in their evolutionary ancestors enjoying the advantages of using such cognitive capacities, and Norman's and Truetemp's own possession of such capacities cannot at all be explained in terms of evolutionary fitness. So, even if their remarkable capacities are highly reliable and have the right causal connections to the way things are in the world, neither example can count as proper cognitive functioning for this reason, as well. The same may be said of any case in which some new reliable cognitive capacity were enjoyed by an individual – but none of these will satisfy the account of knowledge we have given.

But now this might itself be counted as a defect of our theory: why, indeed, could not some new cognitive capacity *become* a source of knowledge? For example, what if Norman were to test his spontaneously formed beliefs about the location of the President against news reports and other (known to be) reliable sources, and find that he did, indeed, have clairvoyance? Or what if Truetemp tested his temperature beliefs against a number of thermometers and discovered that he really was able to tell what the temperature is, just by thinking about it? And so on. We agree that we humans can learn new cognitive processes and acquire knowledge through their exercise. But this is only possible when we form justified beliefs that the new process in question is reliable. Once we have done that, the new process will form justified beliefs, and forming justified beliefs is functioning properly for humans. So our account handles our impressive ability to expand our cognitive repertoire.

Another advantage of our account is that it has more explanatory power than purely *internalist* accounts of warrant. To see this, let us return to the brain-in-a-vat skeptical scenario.[17] Poor Philip is a brain in a vat. His cognitive system has all of the same features and internal connections as ours have. Hence, from the point of view of justification, Philip enjoys the same justification for any and all of his beliefs as we have. But Philip plainly does *not* know much of what we *do* know. Some of what Philip believes might still be true – for example, Philip also believes that two plus two is equal to four. However, he believes this because the mad scientist who maintains Philip's brain in the vat "programs" that belief into Philip's brain. That is why Philip does not know what he believes truly. How do we diagnose what is wrong with Philip? It is obvious that what is wrong is with Philip's *external* relations. The way we account for this wrongness in our theory is to note that Philip, although using appropriate cognitive processes that are functioning properly, is most certainly *not* in a normal environment. His cognitive processes *would* be reliable, and *would* generate warrant for him only when used in environments relevantly similar to the ancestral environments in which they conferred selective fitness.

A final case to consider will reveal both a similarity of a sort with Plantinga's version of proper functionalism, and a significant difference. So let us take the case of Adam, who has just been created only a moment ago by God in the Garden of Eden. Like us, Adam has a pretty sophisticated cognitive system. Unlike us, Adam's cognitive system is not the result of eons of natural selection; it is the result of God's *design*. We have emphasized the role for cognitive capacities whose veridical reliability constitutes an etiological function. In our account, the explanation of this function is given in terms of natural selection. Plainly, although Adam enjoys veridically reliable cognitive capacities, the explanation of these capacities does not derive from evolution. But this does not show that Adam's veridical cognitive processes do not have etiological functions. They do, because these functions were given to Adam *for a reason*: Adam has them because God wanted Adam to be able to function in a veridically reliable way as he sought to comprehend his new environment. So the etiological requirement of our account is satisfied in Plantinga's supernaturalist explanation of veridical human cognitive reliability. This, then, is both a similarity and also a difference in Plantinga's and our accounts: Although the specific etiology provided in each account is quite different, both supply etiological functions of the required sort.

But this similarity should not mask an important difference between our view and Plantinga's, and this difference may be seen in the way we evaluate the case of Adam. Plantinga, like us, can avoid standard versions of the opacity objection involving cases like Norman the clairvoyant and Truetemp. Unreflectively using clairvoyance or tempucomps is not part of human proper functioning. We appealed more specifically to justification to explain why that sort of use of strange processes does not generate warrant, but since Plantinga does not think that justification is necessary for human warrant he simply notes that clairvoyance and tempucomps are not part of the human "design plan."

But appeal to the design plan will not, we think, help Plantinga deal with the opacity worry in general – or with the specific applicability of that problem to the case of Adam. Internalists have focused on examples like Norman the clairvoyant because it is easy to imagine someone having a clairvoyant power but having no idea whether it is reliable. This is different from our ordinary perceptual processes, the reliability of which we all know quite a bit. But precisely because Adam was just created only a moment ago, it seems obvious to us that Adam has not (yet) had the opportunity to reflect on his perceptual faculties, and thus has not (yet) had the opportunity to make any judgments about their reliability. Accordingly, our theory would hold that, at least until he has spent some time using and coming to appreciate the reliability of his (God-given) cognitive capacities, Adam will not (yet) have justified beliefs resulting from their use and so would not be warranted. Plantinga, however, does not have the resources to make this assessment. For Adam's beliefs would be formed as the result of properly functioning processes in his "design plan." Adam, in other words, would achieve the *easiest* of "easy knowledge." His knowledge would be instant and immediate, from the very first moment of his creation. This implausibility, it seems to us, represents a real weakness in Plantinga's account and a comparative strength in our own.

9.9 Conclusion

In his chapter on this topic, Alvin Plantinga argued that the veridical reliability of human cognitive capacities could not be supported without linking our capacities to a benevolent and intelligent designer. If our argument in this chapter is correct, however, we do not seem to require an intelligent designer in order to explain how good we are at achieving accurate, and not just useful, cognitions. Our evolutionary history – and not just our own, but also the histories of many non-human animals – are such as to have supplied us with highly reliable and veridical cognitive capacities. We worried at the outset of this discussion that the operations of natural selection might not be adequate in themselves to explain the development of veridically reliable cognitive capacities. But we have shown how these, together with some of the operations of sexual selection and also social selection (conceived as subsystems operating within natural selection), are more than enough to explain why human beings and other animals engage in reliably veridical cognitive proper functioning.

In this book, we began with a rather unusual consideration. It seemed to us reasonable to think that non-linguistic animals might know things. Certainly, the cognitive ethologists who study non-human animals seem convinced that many animals know many things. But once we granted that, we also noticed that making an allowance for non-human knowers required considerable changes to standard theories of knowledge, which typically require both truth and belief conditions. We found, however, that in the way they are usually understood such conditions simply beg the question against non-human animals, and so needed to be significantly modified.

We then turned to the question of warrant (and the challenges of skepticism, which seem to show that we cannot achieve warrant). Like most epistemologists, we settled on a version of fallibilism – leaving open the possibility of knowledge even in cases in which our warrant *might have been defeated* (but, of course, never in cases in which it actually *is* defeated). We reviewed many different approaches to warrant – both internalist and externalist – and also considered some of the many dimensions of epistemic evaluation. Many of these seemed to provide valuable insights into our subject, but all of the ones we reviewed also seemed to us to be either flawed or incomplete in some ways.

In our own theory, we brought together many of the features we found useful in other theories. Our theory is broadly externalist in the sense that it relies on ways in which cognitions are formed that are opaque to the knower, such as whether they are functioning properly and whether they are functioning in the sort of environment to which they are suited. But our theory ended up having two very distinctive features, which externalist theories of the past have often either overlooked or rejected outright:

1. We acknowledge a primary role for epistemic evaluation, which is reflected in our conception of "proper functioning." Most naturalist theories of the past sought to avoid any inclusion of normative or evaluative elements in their accounts. We argued, on the contrary, that recognition of appropriate evaluative elements is essential to the concept of knowledge, but also entirely natural. Indeed, our own conception of proper functioning is taken right from evolutionary theory, and the concept of fitness within a natural environment. Of course, another "proper functionalist" account of knowledge has been given (Plantinga 1993b), and, as such, it also recognized a role for an evaluative component. But that other account was certainly not a *naturalist* account, as we have seen.
2. But, unlike *any* other externalist account of knowledge that has ever been offered, ours supplies a profoundly

internalist element, when we apply the concept of "proper functioning" to human knowers. The very same proper functional account that we offer, which recognizes non-human knowers in the animal kingdom, also requires that knowers make use of the cognitive capacities that are part of their evolutionary heritage, and by which they have achieved fitness in the environments they inhabit. These capacities, in human beings, include the capacity to justify, and to create the kinds of *internal relations* between cognitions that are usually the main focus of internalist accounts of warrant. We also showed, however, why these sorts of relations and their place in an account of knowledge are best understood by holistic coherence theory. We showed why this approach gives the most plausible answer to the problem of the criterion, especially when we think about testimony as a source of knowledge. As we said at the end of chapter 4, holistic coherence theory has not received much support in recent years, and so the support we give it here will probably be controversial. But, more broadly speaking, we certainly know of no other accounts in which holistic coherence theory plays such a central role in a theory of knowledge that is *externalist* in form. On that basis alone, our theory is quite novel, even if we have helped ourselves to a number of features of previous theories.

In brief, then, knowledge is what is produced by a cognizer when that cognizer uses veridically reliable cognitive processes that are functioning properly in an environment to which they are suited. That is what Wooj achieves when he uses his excellent sense of smell and sight to find his litter box. In our own case, the reliability of our cognitive functioning is greatest when we do our very best to use the cognitive mechanisms which human beings enjoy most of all – our ability to reason. When we employ this capacity and perform it properly, it is only natural that we engender reliable and veridical results. Accordingly, knowledge for human beings is the same in kind as knowledge for other sorts of animals: it is what is achieved when our veridically reliable cognitive capacities function properly.

Current Trends

Plantinga's supernaturalism has been the focus of a great deal of recent debate. The best collection of articles devoted to this topic is Beilby (2002). A good defense of evolutionary explanation in psychology (of which our own account would be obviously a part) may be found in Cosmides and Tooby (1997). Critics of our sort of defense of veridical cognitive reliability as an artifact of natural selection include Downes (2000), Fodor (1998 and 2007). An interesting argument to the effect that natural selection actually supports false belief may be found in Stich (1990) and McKay and Dennett (2009). But powerful and cogent replies to such objections may be found in Griffiths and Wilkins (2010), and especially Graham (forthcoming). A clear general explanation of Darwinian theory may be found in Ruse (1986).

Notes

1 Introduction to the Theory of Knowledge

1   The corner-quotes we use here (also known as Quine corners) are an opportunity for a brief lesson in technical philosophy. In presenting our theory of knowledge, we use two variables, "*S*" and "*p*." "*S*" is a variable that ranges over potential knowers and "*p*" is a variable that ranges over sentences (or propositions). Now, suppose we plug in "Tom" for "*S*" and "The keys are on the night stand" for "*p*." Suppose condition 1 of our theory didn't have corner-quotes around "*p*." Then our theory would say that Tom knows that the keys are on the night stand just in case *the keys are on the night stand is true.* The clause in italics doesn't make any sense! We want it to say that Tom knows the keys are on the night stand just in case "the keys are on the night stand" is true (i.e., is a true sentence). But it won't do to just put quotes around "*p*" in condition 1. To see why, reflect on what quotation marks do: putting quote marks around a word generates a name for that word (a way of referring to the word): cats are animals, "cats" is a four-letter word, and " "cats" " is a name of a four-letter word! (Got it?) So "*p*" is a variable and " "*p*" " is the name of that variable. If the first condition of our theory reads "(1) "*p*" is true," then our theory will say that Tom knows that the keys are on the night stand just in case "*p*" is true; that's not what we wanted. This is where corner-quotes come in. They say, in effect, to take whatever we substitute for the variable and put quotes around that. So, with corner-quotes, our theory says

that Tom knows the keys are on the night stand just in case "the keys are on the night stand" is true (i.e., is a true sentence). That's just what we wanted.

2 This observation has recently been taken as a crucial feature of knowledge in theorizing that falls under the rubric "anti-luck epistemology." An overview of and contribution to this research trend may be found in Pritchard (2005).

3 By characterizing the "something else" needed as "warrant," we follow Plantinga (1993a). As we will see, there are importantly different conceptions of what this "something else" should consist in, and the term "warrant" seems to us to be appropriately neutral between these different conceptions.

4 Contrastive knowledge has seen much discussion by epistemologists in recent years. For an important discussion, see Schaffer (2005).

5 For a recent influential argument that knowledge how is just a form of knowledge that, see Stanley and Williamson (2001).

6 That is, Goldman (1979).

2 The Challenge of Skepticism

1 For an interesting recent treatment of the dreaming scenario, see Sosa (2007). Sosa argues for an "imagination model" of dreaming: just as we don't *believe* what we merely imagine, we don't believe what we merely dream. On the imagination model, then, it's *not* possible that your beliefs are the result of a vivid dream – if you were merely dreaming that, for example, you're reading this book, you wouldn't actually believe it. But, of course, while dreaming, it does *seem to us* as though we believe, for example, that we are James Bond. So on the imagination model dreaming threatens not just our ability to know who we are and what we are doing – it also threatens our ability to know *what we think*, to know what is going on in our own minds! This possibility is alarming, indeed. For criticism of Sosa's solution to this new form of skepticism, see Ballantyne and Evans (2010).

2 Other skeptical scenarios are obviously possible to create. Hilary Putnam (1992) imagines that we are all brains in a vat, fed with artificial stimulations by a mad scientist who controls everything we experience thereby, quite artificially and falsely. Another such scenario that has more recently appeared in popular culture is created in *The Matrix*, where people live whole lives under artificial stimulation by those who control the Matrix.

3   We owe this way of putting the point to Pryor (2000).

4   For an impressive received account of *a priori* knowledge, see Laurence BonJour's *In Defense of Pure Reason* (1997). Casullo (2003) offers an excellent survey of theories of the *a priori* and offers his own.

5   Some philosophers have thought that there are also *contingent* a priori *truths*. Consider, for example, that the original meter stick is one meter long. This seems *a priori*, but notice that the original meter stick (*that very stick*) could have been longer than it is. This is a difficult issue, but if there are contingent *a priori* truths like this, then the skeptical argument of the preceding section will also obviously apply to them.

6   We might then go on to define epistemic impossibility and necessity: p is epistemically impossible for S = df. p is not epistemically possible for S; p is epistemically necessary for S = df. not-p is epistemically impossible for S. Believe it or not, defining epistemic impossibility and necessity in this way is controversial. See Huemer (2005) for discussion.

7   This version of the skeptical argument is inspired by Pryor's presentation (2000, 527–8).

8   The term "epistemic peer" is due to Gutting (1982).

9   We borrow this formulation from Kelly (2010: 112).

10 At least, where we're understanding disagreement as one party believing p and the other party believing not-p. A broader (and more complicated) notion of disagreement includes cases, for example, in which one peer is highly confident about p and the other is only somewhat confident – that is, cases in which peers differ in their degree of belief. For treatments of peer disagreement in these terms, see Christensen (2007), Elga (2007), and Kelly (2010).

11 Indeed, for many of your controversial beliefs you have *superiors* who disagree: people who are smarter, and have access to better evidence, than you. Surely, reflecting that a superior disagrees with you about p should drastically reduce your confidence in p. Honest readers will no doubt discover that they are unwarrantedly confident about many matters because of the existence of disagreeing superiors.

12 Roger White (2005) uses this sort of consideration to argue, in great detail, against extreme permissivism. We think, however, that his arguments only cut against what we might call "revealed permissivism" which is the denial of revealed uniqueness. Thanks to Stewart Cohen for pointing this out in conversation. For more on uniqueness, see Ballantyne and Coffman (forthcoming).

13 Christensen (2007) makes a similar point, but in greater detail.

14   Of course, this block to skepticism only lasts as long as we don't know much about the reasoning of those who disagree with us. But once we find out how they reached their views – and we see no reason for thinking our own view is more reliable than theirs – the skeptical threat re-emerges. For another attempt to embrace the equal weight view without serious skeptical consequence, see Elga 2007 and 2010. See also Kornblith (2010) for criticism.

3   Contextualism

1   The move here, found in Cohen's (1999: 60), is to argue that even though "knows" is not itself a gradable adjective, since its component "warrant" is, "knows" inherits context-sensitivity. For an interesting objection to this inference, see Stanley's (2004: 131–4).

2   Not all contextualists are internalists. Another version of contextualism that has rightly received considerable attention is that given by Keith DeRose (see DeRose 1992, 1995, 2005, and 2006), and that version is fully externalist. But because it shares all of the basic features that make it a contextualist view, we have elected not to represent DeRose's version in detail herein.

3   A final strategy would take us too far into linguistics to pursue here, but is worth mentioning. The invariantist might roll up her sleeves, dust off her linguistics books, and check to see whether "knows" really behaves like other context-sensitive terms. If it does not, then we will have some reason to think that in explaining our intuitions about **LOW** and **HIGH**, we should not appeal to context-sensitivity. For an impressive example of this strategy, see Stanley (2004).

4   This is just a special instance of a general psychological phenomenon called the *framing effect*. See Kahneman and Tversky (1984).

5   The first to have argued from something like **KPR** to subject-sensitive invariantism were Jeremy Fantl and Matthew McGrath in an impressive series of papers (2002, 2007, and 2009). Hawthorne (2004) tentatively defends a version of the view, and Jason Stanley (2005) defends what he calls *interest-relative* invariantism.

6   Actually, what is distinctive about the view is that how warranted *S* needs to be depends on some non-epistemic facts about *S*, but not necessarily pragmatic facts about how impor-

tant *p* is to *S*. We ignore this issue since all developed forms of the view concern themselves only with the practical importance of *p* for *S*. For further discussion, see Hawthorne (2004: ch. 4).

4   Warrant as Justification

1   Bergmann (see, e.g., his 2007) prefers to distinguish between *propositional justification* and *doxastic justification,* Feldman and Conee (1985: 24) distinguish between *justification* and *well-foundedness,* and Goldman (1979: 21) distinguishes between *ex-ante* and *ex-post* justification. The differences are terminological: "justifiable belief" = "propositionally justified belief" = "ex-ante justified belief" on the one hand, and "justified belief" = "doxastically justified belief" = "ex-post justified belief" on the other.

2   The example is a variant of one in Russell (2001: 36). The detail about tarot cards is an allusion to Lehrer (1971).

3   See, for examples, Norman (1997), Adam Leite's "localism," discussed in his 2005, and (for basic logical knowledge) Wright (2001).

4   We have in mind the view advanced in Peter Klein's 1999 (and refined in his 2000, 2005a and 2005b, 2007a and 2007b, and 2010). We do not think Klein really is an infinitist, but Klein himself does claim to advance this view. For further discussion of the issue of whether Klein really is an infinitist, see Bergmann (2007), Klein (2007b), and Ginet (2005).

5   For some additional criticism of Klein's view, see Cling (2004). For additional argument in favor of Klein's view, see Fantl (2003).

6   For an excellent, and thorough, discussion of the varieties of foundationalism, see Triplett (1990).

7   This is a variant of Pollock's definition of incorrigible justification (1974: 23).

8   Descartes, of course, is the *locus classicus* of this sort of view. In the twentieth century, it was defended by such distinguished philosophers as C. I. Lewis (1929 and 1946), and Roderick Chisholm (1966).

9   Here BonJour's argument hangs on a version of the access requirement: if a feature φ makes a belief *b* justified for *S*, then *S* is justified in believing that *b* has φ and that beliefs with φ are probable. This is an internalist principle and those who adhere to something like it are known as *access internalists*.

For a penetrating discussion of access requirements, internalism, and an argument that such principles generate a vicious regress, see Bergmann (2006: ch. 1).

10 Non-deductive inference rules include things like the principle of enumerative induction: F_1 was a G, F_2 was a G, F_3 was a G, . . ., F_n was a G; so, all Fs are Gs. Another non-deductive inference rule is: F looks C, so F is C, where C is some color.

11 Plantinga (1993a) is a notable example, as is Pollock and Cruz (1999).

12 In our view, Pryor's theory of justification is mostly a less detailed version of John Pollock's (1974) *defeasible reasons* theory. We present it instead of Pollock's because (a) it has recently received a lot of attention, and (b) the nuances of Pollock's view don't concern us here.

13 This is our own version of Lehrer's self-trust principle, modified to suit our specific needs. See Lehrer (2000a: 138).

14 Even the scientist who does some of the key experiments that establish a scientific belief relies on the testimony of others: inevitably, many (most?) of the data he uses will have come from the reports of his assistants or other scientists. So even the scientist who does the experiments that prove the existence of tectonic plates believes in those plates at least partly on the basis of testimony.

15 By "testimony," we obviously include non-verbal information as well, such as photographs, maps, etc.

16 Though extant work on testimony doesn't frame the issue in terms of the problem of the criterion, it is clear enough that that is what we are confronting here.

17 A classic statement of reductionism can be found in Hume's *Enquiry*, Part 1, para. 4–5. Adler (1994), Fricker (1994), and Lyons (1997) are more recent examples.

18 A classic statement of anti-reductionism can be found in Reid's *Inquiry*, chapter 6, sec. 24. Coady (1992) and Burge (1997) are important recent defenders of the view. See also Foley (1994) and Audi (2002).

19 Using the sort of reasoning we introduced in the previous chapter: the testifier told you that *p*, and you think that *p* is true, so you can infer that she was right about *p*!

5 Justification, Defeaters, and Basing

1 For a proposal of this sort, see Lehrer and Paxson (1969).

2 In Lehrer and Paxson (1969).

3 This example is given in Klein (1971).

4 This is the approach taken by Lehrer in Lehrer (2000a: ch. 7). Lehrer counts someone as being justified, just in case the person would continue to be justified when all falsehoods within that person's justification were removed (creating what Lehrer calls that person's "ultrasystem" of justification).

5 Our presentation of the problem is derived from Plantinga (1993a: 69 n.8).

6 Things are especially bad in this case. On the face of things, there is nothing irrational about Smith's belief: the evidence on which it was originally based is defeated, but Smith has other undefeated evidence that justifies his belief. However, the causal theorist must say that Smith's belief is still based on the defeated visual evidence. This would be irrational. So the causal theorist is committed to seeing irrationality where there isn't any.

7 Feldman and Conee add a third condition (1985: 24): (iii) there is no larger subset *E'* such that the belief doesn't fit *E'*. This is to guarantee that *S* takes into account all potentially defeating evidence he might have.

8 The Raco case is very similar to an earlier thought-experiment of Lehrer's (Lehrer 1971), involving a superstitious lawyer who initially comes to believe something on the basis of a reading of Tarot cards, but then because of this, comes to have good evidence for that belief. The similarity to the Raco case is sufficiently obvious that we will deal only with the Raco case here.

9 A recent argument for why all solutions fail is given in Zagzebski (1994).

6 Externalist Theories of Warrant

1 Coherence theories of justification, for example, have a notoriously difficult time explaining the truth connection. Plainly, one could have a fully coherent cognitive system in which much of what is included within it is false!

2 Against this, Timothy Williamson (2000) has argued that a subject's total evidence is just the set of propositions that she knows. He sums this up with the equation $E = K$. Unfortunately, considerations of space prevent us from a thorough assessment of Williamson's many ingenious epistemological views.

3 Dretske adds that the probability of *p* given only one's background knowledge (i.e., without *s*) must be less than 1. This is a complication we can ignore for present purposes.

4   This is because, as stipulated by the probability calculus, all necessary truths get probability 1. A signal can only carry information that *p* when the prior probability of *p* is less than 1.

5   Sosa actually imposes what he calls a *safety condition*: in nearby worlds where *S* believes that *p*, *p* is true (Sosa 2007). It is important to distinguish Sosa's condition from Nozick's, but both are variations on the same theme: that knowledge requires belief that wouldn't easily have been false. See Vogel (2007) for an excellent and extended criticism of this theme in recent epistemology.

6   Philosophers explain this in terms of "possible worlds." They say that "If it were the case that *p*, it would have been the case *q*" is true just in case in the "nearest" possible world(s) where *p* is true, *q* is also true. For the classic version of this view, see Lewis (1973).

7   See Feldman (2003) for discussion.

8   This case is found in Vogel (1999: 165).

9   See, for example, his 1970. For excellent criticism, see Vogel (1999).

10 Goldman, as we noted, offered reliabilism as a theory of justified belief. But his explanatory remarks here apply equally to a reliabilist account of warrant that rejects justification.

11 To name just a few: Alston (1995); Beebe (2004); Comesaña (2010); Henderson and Horgan (2007); Kornblith (1999).

12 It's worth noting that Goldman introduced *Fake Barn Country* in a 1976 paper (1978 in our bibliography) to motivate a *different* theory of knowledge: the *relevant alternatives* theory. On this theory, *S* knows that *p* if she can distinguish *p* from relevant alternatives. In *Fake Barn Country*, the possibility that something is a fake barn is a relevant alternative to its being a real barn. Since Henry is in no position to discriminate between real and fake barns, he does not know that he sees a fake barn. On the other hand, in places where fake barns are rare, the possibility that something is a fake barn is not a relevant alternative – if Henry were in one of those places, he *would* know that he sees a barn.

13 Since Goldman himself advocates process reliabilism as a theory of *justification*, he may be happy with this result: surely Henry is *justified* in believing that he sees a barn; he just doesn't *know*. Still, our concern here is with warrant, and many epistemologists have found a reliabilist account of warrant attractive.

14 We leave it to the reader to construct such a case. Those who want a little help can go to section 8.6, where we give such a case involving our favorite cat, Wooj.

15 See Plantinga (1993: ch. 9), for expressions of doubt that relia-bilism could ever provide these necessary elements for comple-tion. The most widely influential statement of the problem is due to Feldman and Conee (see, for example, their 1998). An earlier paper by Pollock (1984) develops a deeper version of the same problem. Some attempts at solutions can be found in Alston (1995), Beebe (2004), Comesaña (2010), and through-out Goldman's writings. A recent and interesting attempt to solve the environmental specification problem can be found in Bedke (2010).

16 These are the terms used by Dretske (1991).

17 See, for examples, Dretske (1991); Lehrer (2000a); Sosa (1997).

7 Epistemic Evaluation

1 Hess (2010: 35). Hess represents this goal as an epistemic ideal, rather than as a goal in the practical sense: "It is clear that the truth goal cannot be literally a goal as, for instance, a goal in a game, at which we aim in order to win" (Hess 2010: 35). We agree that truth is an important goal, epistemically; but we disagree that it is an ideal, rather than a practical goal. As Alan Millar puts it in his review of Hess's book, "[Truth] is a goal when I am looking for my keys. It is a goal attained when I find them" (Millar 2010: 1).

2 Richard Foley (1987) defends an influential account of epis-temic rationality that is instrumental in this sense.

3 Notice that the two norms "don't believe *p* if there is over-whelming reason to believe *not-p*" and "believe *p* only if *p* is true" can come into conflict: we might have overwhelming evidence for *p*, even though *p* is (unbeknownst to us) false. Here the one norm would tell us to believe *p* and the other to believe *not-p*. In this sort of case, however, the agent who believes according to the evidence has a good excuse for violat-ing the truth norm.

4 Alston (1989: 92). Epistemologists have discussed this question at some length. For examples of the range of positions on our voluntary control over belief, see Audi (2001), Feldman (2001), Ginet (2001), Steup (2000).

5 Heil (1983) draws a different conclusion from the falsity of doxastic voluntarism. He argues that our epistemic obligations concern not what we believe, but how we reason and gather evidence.

6   A different argument for denying that epistemic "oughts" imply voluntary control over our beliefs may be found in Chuard and Southwood (2009).

7   In fact, Feldman's account seems more like Pollock and Cruz's (1999) procedural account of epistemic normativity, which was conceived in opposition to deontological accounts. Unfortunately, we don't have the space here to discuss Pollock's account.

8   We give our argument for this in section 7.5, below

9   We are indebted to Alex von Stein for this observation.

10   For a description of this process, see "Dave's Dreaded Brewing Tools: The Homebrew Calculator" at <http://dd26943.com/davesdreaded/tools/convert.htm>.

11   The problem we pose here is sometimes called the "swamping problem," according to which, if we regard truth as the only epistemic goal, then knowledge is no better than other forms of true belief – the fact that true beliefs achieve the putatively sole epistemic goal "swamps" any supposed added value that knowledge would realize. For an excellent discussion of the swamping problem, see Pritchard (2010: 8–24).

12   See, for distinguished examples that we will not discuss further here: Greco (2003 and 2007), Neta and Rohrbaugh (2004), Riggs (2002), Zagzebski (1999 and 2003).

13   Some find the idea that a true belief is *creditable* to the epistemic agent the key to warrant, as the focal difference between knowledge and other forms of true belief. For examples of this idea from people other than Sosa, see note references in ch.2, n.14, above. Dissenting views are expressed in Lackey (2007 and 2009), and Pritchard (2010).

14   There is an additional interesting worry for virtue theories like Sosa's. It seems to many that knowledge can be acquired by testimony. Lackey has argued that when we acquire knowledge by testimony, our beliefs are due to *others'* intellectual virtues rather than our own (2007). This would be a problem for Sosa's adroitness and aptness conditions. It seems to us, however, that cases of testimonial knowledge still require considerable and virtuous applications of cognitive capacity in order to qualify as knowledge. Human beings have very sophisticated ways of detecting dishonest behavior, lack of conviction, lack of authority, and all of the other indicators of an unreliable source for testimony, and a failure to use any of these would in our minds prevent the receiver of testimony from acquiring knowledge. We discuss the acquisition of knowledge by testimony above (section 4.12).

15   Plantinga provides his argument for this in Plantinga (1993b: chs 11 and 12, 194–237).

16 This understanding of functioning properly is closely related to Pollock's account of a procedural norm. For discussion, see Pollock and Cruz (1999: ch. 5).

8 A New Theory of Knowledge, Part 1: The Desiderata and Non-Human Knowledge

1 We take the example from Smith (2002).
2 The following account derives from Reebs (2009).
3 For a history of the debates about this problem, see Shope (1980).

9 A New Theory of Knowledge Part 2: Human Knowledge

1 Precisely because we regard human reasoning as the effect of a natural cognitive capacity, we cannot help ourselves to one form of reply that has been made to Plantinga's challenge to epistemological naturalism (about which see next section), namely, that given in Paul Churchland (2009), who defends the reliability of scientific reasoning on the basis of what he regards as certain *artificial features* of such reasoning. But the very features Churchland cites strike us as features that reflect the proper functioning of our "native cognitive mechanisms," which Churchland contrasts to the "artificial mechanisms for theory creation and theory-evaluation" (Paul Churchland 2009: 136). Our own view is that the natural/artificial distinction Churchland makes here is itself artificial and does not give adequate respect to our natural endowment for reasoning. The fact that our "native cognitive mechanisms" are improvable via scientific education and practice is itself, in our view, a reflection of the very ways in which our native cognitive mechanisms work, when functioning properly. The same may be said for our increasing sophistication with and reliance on the ("artificial") technologies of scientific inquiry. The production and uses of these do not simply derive from artifice, but are rather the "artifacts" of our natural cognitive mechanisms working as they should. Birds (naturally) make nests; human beings (naturally) extend their "native capacities" through the making of tools. We suspect, however, that our dispute with Churchland here may be more semantic than philosophical

- he uses "natural" to mean only very narrowly the same thing as "natural-selection-shaped capacities of the biological brain alone" (Paul Churchland 2009: 138).

2   Contrast Sosa's bifurcation of "animal knowledge" and "reflective knowledge" (Sosa 2007). In our view, bat knowledge and dog knowledge and human (reflective) knowledge are all the same in general, but must be accounted for differently only because each species has different sorts of cognitive capacities. But the general account of knowledge covers all cases: knowledge is what occurs when a cognitive being uses its reliable cognitive capacities in such a way as to have them functioning properly. For an earlier version of this sort of account, see Smith (2002). The possibility that the verb "to know" might mean different things in different contexts is explored chapter 3.

3   This section owes much to Mourenza and Smith (forthcoming) and to Graham (forthcoming). Specific citations follow.

4   See Plantinga (1993b: ch. 11).

5   We will call reliability in "getting things right," "veridical reliability" herein. There can obviously be very different degrees of veridical reliability, and as we have already seen, what degree of reliability is required for knowledge may be a matter of considerably controversy. As we have already said, however, cases in which a cognitive being does not "get it right" will not count as cases in which the cognizer has functioned completely properly, epistemically, since one condition of proper functioning is "getting it right."

6   Others have criticized his argument, however: for several examples, see Beilby (2002).

7   What follows is admittedly what some critics will dismiss as nothing more than a "just so story" involving evolutionary theory, since we seek to give an account of the adaptability of a trait (the veridical reliability of human cognitive processes) that is itself denied by the skeptics we seek to answer. But note that the sort of account we provide is precisely the sort that the skeptical challenge we seek to address claims *cannot* be given. For a defense of the sort of explanation we provide herein, see Brandon (1990: 176–84).

8   As a matter of fact, Darwin is elsewhere much more optimistic about human veridical reliability than he seems to be in this passage. However, our object here is not to interpret Darwin, but rather to address the doubt he expresses here and that same skepticism as it has been expressed by others.

9   A very systematic study of just how unreliable our cognitive mechanisms – especially involving extremely common and fallacious forms of reasoning – can be in certain cases is given in

Stich (1990). Some reply is made to such cases, on behalf of evolutionary epistemology, in Fales (2002).

10 See, for example, Penhollow and Young (2008), who recommend not only improvements in physical fitness, but also "cognitive-behavioral therapy" for those who need help with their physical self-image.

11 So see Downes (2000): "Most people act successfully on the basis of false beliefs every day, for example, they derive all of their actions in one way or another from their various religious beliefs many of which, given that they flatly contradict one another, must be false" (441, n. 9). Other examples of such unreliability are given in Mourenza and Smith (forthcoming), though in the end they defend some human cognitive processes as reliable, and provide evolutionary explanations of this.

12 A similar argument is given in Popper (1972). See also Fodor (1981): "Darwinian selection guarantees that organisms either know the elements of logic or become posthumous" (121). More recently, Fodor has become more of a skeptic, however (see Fodor 1998 and 2007). According to Michael Ruse, "Human thought is moulded and constrained by the epigenetic rules. In the case of science, we use deductive and inductive methodologies because these have proven their adaptive worth in the struggle for existence" (Ruse 1986: 206). Daniel Dennett wholeheartedly concurs: "If an organism is the product of natural selection, we can assume that most of its beliefs will be true and most of its belief forming strategies will be rational" (Dennett 1987: 96). See also Cosmides and Tooby (1997) for a "crappy" version of the same argument: "Natural selection does not work 'for the good of the species,' as many people think. As we will discuss in more detail below, it is a process in which a phenotypic design feature *causes its own spread through a population* (which can happen even in cases where this leads to the extinction of the species). In the meantime [. . .] you can think of natural selection as the 'eat dung and die' principle. All animals need neural circuits that govern what they eat – knowing what is safe to eat is a problem that all animals must solve. For humans, feces are not safe to eat – they are a source of contagious diseases. Now imagine an ancestral human who had neural circuits that made dung smell sweet – that made him want to dig in whenever he passed a smelly pile of dung. This would increase his probability of contracting a disease. If he got sick as a result, he would be too tired to find much food, too exhausted to go looking for a mate, and he might even die an untimely death. In contrast, a person with different neural circuits – ones that made him

avoid feces – would get sick less often. He will therefore have more time to find food and mates and will live a longer life. The first person will eat dung and die; the second will avoid it and live. As a result, the dung-*eater* will have fewer children than the dung-*avoider*. Since the neural circuitry of children tends to resemble that of their parents, there will be fewer dung-eaters in the next generation, and more dung-avoiders. As this process continues, generation after generation, the dung-eaters will eventually disappear from the population. Why? They ate dung and died out. The only kind of people left in the population will be those like you and me – ones who are descended from the dung-avoiders. No one will be left who has neural circuits that make dung delicious" (all of these examples are cited in Mourenza and Smith forthcoming).

13 This critique comes directly from Mourenza and Smith (forthcoming), though it is worded differently.

14 All of the examples that follow are given and discussed in Mourenza and Smith (forthcoming).

15 Mourenza and Smith cite Rakoczy (2008) for the former, and Bekoff (2006) for the latter.

16 The following advantage is also explicated in Graham (forthcoming: section 5.1).

17 We take the following from Graham (forthcoming: sections 5.3 and 5.4).

References

Adler, J. 1994. "Testimony, Trust, Knowing." *Journal of Philosophy* 91: 264–75.

Allen, C. and Bekoff, M. 2007. "Animal Minds, Cognitive Ethology, and Ethics." *The Journal of Ethics* 11: 299–317.

Alston, W. 1989. *Epistemic Justification: Essays in the Theory of Knowledge*. Ithaca, NY: Cornell University Press.

Alston, W. 1995. "How to Think About Reliability." *Philosophical Topics* 23: 1–29.

Aristotle. 1962. *Nicomachean Ethics*. Trans. M. Ostwald. Basingstoke: Macmillan.

Audi, R. 2001. "Doxastic Voluntarism and the Ethics of Belief." In Steup, 2001: 93–111.

Audi, R. 2002. "The Sources of Knowledge." In Moser, 2002: 71–94.

Ballantyne, N. and Coffman, E. J. Forthcoming. "Uniqueness, Evidence, and Rationality." *Philosophers Imprint*.

Ballantyne, N. and Evans, I. 2010. "Sosa's Dream." *Philosophical Studies* 148: 249–52.

Battaly, H. 2008. "Virtue Epistemology." *Philosophy Compass* 3: 639–63.

Bedke, M. 2010. "Developmental Process Reliabilism: On Justification, Defeat, and Evidence." *Erkenntnis* 73: 1–17.

Beebe, J. R. 2004. "The Generality Problem, Statistical Relevance, and the Tri-Level Hypothesis." *Noûs* 38: 177–95.

Beilby, J. 2002. *Naturalism Defeated? Essays on Plantinga's Evolutionary Argument against Naturalism*. Ithaca, NY: Cornell University Press.

Bekoff, M. 2006. *Animal Passions and Beastly Virtues*. Philadelphia, PA: Temple University Press.

Bergmann, M. 2004. "Epistemic Circularity: Malignant and Benign." *Philosophy and Phenomenological Research* 69: 709–27.

Bergmann, M. 2006. *Justification without Awareness*. Oxford: Oxford University Press.

Bergmann, M. 2007. "Is Klein an Infinitist About Doxastic Justification?" *Philosophical Studies* 134: 19–24.

Bernecker S. and Pritchard, D., eds. 2010. *Routledge Companion to Epistemology*. London: Routledge.

Black, T. 2008. "Solving the Problem of Easy Knowledge." *The Philosophical Quarterly* 58: 597–617.

BonJour, L. 1978. "Can Empirical Knowledge Have a Foundation?" *American Philosophical Quarterly* 15: 1–14.

BonJour, L. 1985. *The Structure of Empirical Knowledge*. Cambridge, MA: Harvard University Press.

BonJour, L. 1997. *In Defense of Pure Reason*. Cambridge: Cambridge University Press.

BonJour, L. 2001. "Toward a Defense of Empirical Foundationalism." In DePaul, 2001: 21–48.

Brandon, R. 1990. *Adaptation and Environment*. Princeton, NJ: Princeton University Press.

Burge, T. 1997. "Interlocution, Perception, and Memory." *Philosophical Studies* 86: 21–47.

Cassam, Q. 2009. "Can the Concept of Knowledge be Analyzed?" In Greenbough and Pritchard, 2009: 12–30.

Casullo, A. 2003. *A Priori Justification*. New York: Oxford University Press.

Chalmers, D. 1996. *The Conscious Mind: In Search of a Fundamental Theory*. New York: Oxford University Press.

Chisholm, R. 1966. *Theory of Knowledge*, 1st edn. Upper Saddle River, NJ: Prentice Hall.

Christensen, D. 2007. "Epistemology of Disagreement: The Good News." *Philosophical Review* 116: 187–217.

Chuard, P. and Southwood, N. 2009. "Epistemic Norms without Voluntary Control." *Noûs* 43: 599–632.

Churchland, Patricia. 1987. "Epistemology in the Age of Neuroscience." *Journal of Philosophy* 84: 544–53.

Churchland, Paul. 2009. "Is Evolutionary Naturalism Epistemically Self-Defeating?" *Philo* 12: 135–41.

Clifford, W. K. 1947. *The Ethics of Belief and Other Essays*. London: Watts and Co.

Cling, A. 2004. "The Trouble with Infinitism." *Synthese* 138: 101–24.

Coady, C. A. J. 1992. *Testimony: A Philosophical Study*. Oxford: Clarendon Press.

Cobb-Stevens, R. ed. 2000. *Epistemology: Proceedings of the Twentieth World Congress in Philosophy.* Bowling Green, OH: Philosophy Documentation Center. vol. 5.

Cohen, S. 1984. "Justification and Truth." *Philosophical Studies* 46.3: 279–95.

Cohen, S. 1988. "How to be a Fallibilist." *Philosophical Perspectives* 2: 91–123.

Cohen, S. 1999. "Contextualism, Skepticism, and the Structure of Reasons." *Philosophical Perspectives* 13: 58–89.

Cohen, S. 2002. "Basic Knowledge and the Problem of Easy Knowledge." *Philosophy and Phenomenological Research* 65: 309–29.

Cohen, S. 2004. "Knowledge, Assertion, and Practical Reasoning." *Philosophical Issues* 14: 482–91.

Cohen, S. 2005. "Why Basic Knowledge is Easy Knowledge." *Philosophy and Phenomenological Research* 70/2: 417–30.

Cohen, S. 2010. "Bootstrapping, Defeasible Reasoning, and *a Priori* Justification." *Philosophical Perspectives* 24: 141–59.

Comesaña, J. 2010. "Evidentialist Reliabilism." *Noûs* 44: 571–600.

Conee, E. and Feldman, R. 1998. "The Generality Problem for Reliabilism." *Philosophical Studies* 89: 1–29.

Conee, E. and Feldman, R. 2004, eds. *Evidentialism: Essays in Epistemology.* New York: Oxford University Press.

Cosmides, L. and Tooby, J. 1997. "Evolutionary Psychology: A Primer." At: <http://www.psych.ucsb.edu/research/cep/primer.html>.

Darwin, C. 1881. Letter to William Graham, Down, July 3, 1881. In Francis Darwin, ed., *The Life and Letters of Charles Darwin including an Autobiographical Chapter.* London: John Murray, Albermarle Street, 1887, 1: 315–16.

Dennett, D. l. 1987. *The Intentional Stance.* Cambridge, MA: MIT Press.

DePaul, M. R. 2001. *Resurrecting Old-Fashioned Foundationalism.* Lanham, MD: Rowman and Littlefield.

DePaul, M. R. and Zagzebski, L. T., eds. 2003. *Intellectual Virtue: Perspectives from Ethics and Epistemology.* Oxford: Oxford University Press.

DeRose, K. 1992. "Contextualism and Knowledge Attributions." *Philosophy and Phenomenological Research* 52: 913–29.

DeRose, K. 1995. "Solving the Skeptical Problem." *The Philosophical Review* 194: 1–52.

DeRose, K. 2005. "The Ordinary Language Basis for Contextualism, and the New Invariantism." *The Philosophical Quarterly* 55: 172–98.

DeRose, K. 2006. "Bamboozled by Our Own Words." *Philosophy and Phenomenological Research* 73: 316–38.

DeRose K. and Warfield T. A., eds. 1992. *Skepticism: A Contemporary Reader*. Oxford: Oxford University Press.

Descartes, R. 1931 [1641]. *Meditations on First Philosophy*. In E. S. Haldane and G. R. T. Ross, eds and trans., *The Philosophical Works of Descartes*. New York: Dover Publications.

Downes, S. M. 2000. "Truth, Selection, and Scientific Inquiry." *Biology and Philosophy* 15: 425–42.

Dretske, F. 1970. "Epistemic Operators." *Journal of Philosophy* 67: 1007–23.

Dretske, F. 1981. *Knowledge and the Flow of Information*. Cambridge, MA: MIT Press. Republished in 1999, Stanford, CA: CSLI Publications.

Dretske, F. 1991. "Two Conceptions of Knowledge: Rational vs. Reliable Belief." *Grazer Philosophische Studien* 40: 15–35.

Elga, A. 2007. "Reflection and Disagreement." *Noûs* 41: 478–502.

Elga, A. 2010 "How to Disagree About How to Disagree." In Feldman and Warfield, 2010: 175–86.

Engel, P., ed. 2000. *Believing and Accepting*. Dordrecht: Kluwer Academic Publishers.

Evans, I. Forthcoming. "The Problem of the Basing Relation."

Fales, E. 2002. "Darwin's Doubt, Calvin's Calvary." In Bielby, 2002, 43–58.

Fantl, J. 2003. "Modest Infinitism." *Canadian Journal of Philosophy* 33: 537–62.

Fantl, J. and McGrath, M. 2002. "Evidence, Pragmatics, and Justification." *The Philosophical Review* 111: 67–94.

Fantl, J. and McGrath, M. 2007. "On Pragmatic Encroachment in Epistemology." *Philosophy and Phenomenological Research* 75: 558–89.

Fantl, J. and McGrath, M. 2009. *Knowledge in an Uncertain World*. New York: Oxford University Press.

Feldman, R. 2001. "Voluntary Belief and Epistemic Evaluation." In Steup, 2001: 77–92.

Feldman, R. 2003. *Epistemology*. Upper Saddle River, NJ: Prentice-Hall.

Feldman, R. 2006. "Epistemological Puzzles About Disagreement." in Hetherington 2006: 216–36.

Feldman, R. and Conee, E. 1985. "Evidentialism." *Philosophical Studies* 48: 15–34.

Feldman, R. and Warfield, T. A. 2010. *Disagreement*. Oxford: Oxford University Press.

Fodor, J. 1981. "Three Cheers for Propositional Attitudes." In J. Fodor, *Representations*. Cambridge, MA: MIT Press. 100–23.

Fodor, J. 1998. "The Trouble with Psychological Darwinism." *London Review of Books* 20.2 22, January 1998: 11–13.

Fodor, J. 2007. "Why Pigs Don't Have Wings." *London Review of Books* 29/20, 18 (October): 19–22.

Foley, R. 1987. *The Theory of Epistemic Rationality*. Cambridge, MA: Harvard University Press.

Foley, R. 1994. "Egoism in Epistemology." In Schmitt 1994: 53–74.

Foote, A. L. and Crystal, J. D. 2007. "Metacognition in the Rat." *Current Biology* 17: 551–5.

Fricker, E. 1994. "Against Gullibility." In Matilal and Chakrabarti 1994: 125–61.

Fumerton, R. 1995. *Metaepistemology and Skepticism*. Lanham, MD: Rowman and Littlefield.

Gettier, E. 1963. "Is Justified True Belief Knowledge?" *Analysis* 23: 121–3.

Ginet, C. 2001. "Deciding to Believe." In Steup 2001: 63–76.

Ginet, C. 2005. "Infinitism Is Not the Solution to the Regress Problem." In Steup and Sosa 2005: 277–91.

Goldberg, S. ed. 2007. *Internalism and Externalism in Semantics and Epistemology*. New York: Oxford University Press.

Goldman, A. I. 1978. "Discrimination and Perceptual Knowledge." In Pappas and Swain 1978: 120–45. Reprinted from the *Journal of Philosophy* 73 (1976): 771–91.

Goldman, A. I. 1979. "What is Justified Belief?" In Pappas 1979: 1–23.

Goldman, A. I. and Whitcomb, D. eds. 2010. *Social Epistemology: Essential Readings*. New York: Oxford University Press.

Goode, R and Griffiths, P. E. 1995. "The Misuse of Sober's Selection of/Selection for Distinction." *Biology and Philosophy* 10: 99–108.

Gopnik, A. and Melzoff, A. 1997. *Words, Thoughts and Theories*. Cambridge, MA: MIT Press.

Graham, P. J. Forthcoming. "Epistemic Entitlement." *Noûs* 46: forthcoming.

Greco, J. 2003. "Knowledge as Credit for True Belief." In DePaul and Zagzebski 2003, 111–34.

Greco, J. 2007. "The Nature of Ability and the Purpose of Knowledge." *Philosophical Issues* 17: 57–69.

Greco, J. 2010. *Achieving Knowledge*. Cambridge: Cambridge University Press.

Greco, J. and Sosa, E. eds. 1999. *The Blackwell Guide to Epistemology*. Oxford: Blackwell.

Greenbough, P. and Pritchard, D. 2009. *Williamson on Knowledge*. Oxford: Oxford University Press.

Griffiths, P E. and Wilkins, J. S. 2010. "When Do Evolutionary Explanations of Belief Debunk Belief?" *PhilSci-Archive*. At: <http://philsci-archive.pitt.edu/archive/00005314/>.

Gutting, G. 1982. *Religious Belief and Religious Skepticism*. Notre Dame, IN: University of Notre Dame Press.

Haacke, S. 2001. "'The Ethics of Belief' Reconsidered." In Steup 2001: 21–33.

Haldane, E. S. and Ross, G. R. T., 1931. eds. and trans., *The Philosophical Works of Descartes*. New York: Dover Publications.

Harman, G. 1973. *Thought*. Princeton, NJ: Princeton University Press.

Hasan, A. 2011. "Classical Foundationalism and Bergmann's Dilemma." *Journal of Philosophical Research* 36: 391–410.

Hawthorne, J. 2004. *Knowledge and Lotteries*. Oxford: Oxford University Press.

Hawthorne, J. and Gendler, T. eds. 2005. *Oxford Studies in Epistemology, Volume 1*. Oxford: Oxford University Press.

Heil, J. 1983. "Doxastic Agency." *Philosophical Studies*. 43: 355–64.

Henderson, D. and Horgan, T. 2007. "Some Ins and Outs of Transglobal Reliabilism." In Goldberg 2007: 100–30.

Hess, M. P. 2010. *Is Truth the Primary Epistemic Goal?* Frankfurt: Ontos Verlag.

Hetherington, S. ed. 2006. *Epistemology Futures*. Oxford: Oxford University Press

Huemer, M. 2005. "Logical Properties of Warrant." *Philosophical Studies* 122: 171–82.

Hume, D. 1748 (2006). *An Enquiry Concerning Human Understanding*, ed. Tom Beauchamp. Oxford: Clarendon Press.

Hurley, S. and Nudds, M., eds. 2006. *Rational Animals?* New York: Oxford University Press.

Jordan, J. and Howard-Snyder, D. eds. 1996. *Faith, Freedom, and Rationality*. Lanham, MD: Rowman and Littlefield.

Kahneman, D. and Tversky, A. 1984. "Choices, Values, and Frames." *American Psychologist* 39: 341–50.

Kelly, T. 2003. "Epistemic Rationality as Instrumental Rationality: A Critique." *Philosophy and Phenomenological Research* 66: 612–40.

Kelly, T. 2005. "The Epistemic Significance of Disagreement." In Hawthorne and Gendler 2005: 167–96.

Kelly, T. 2010. "Peer Disagreement and Higher Order Evidence." In Goldman and Whitcomb 2010: 111–74.

Kim, J. 1988. "What is Naturalized Epistemology?" In Tomberlin 1988: 381–405.

Klein, P. 1971 "A Proposed Definition of Propositional Knowledge." *Journal of Philosophy*. 67: 471–82.

Klein, P. 1999. "Human Knowledge and the Infinite Regress of Reasons." *Philosophical Perspectives* 13: 297–325.

Klein, P. 2000. "Why Not Infinitism?" In Cobb-Stevens 2000: 199–208.

Klein, P. 2005a. "Infinitism is the Solution to the Regress Problem." In Steup and Sosa 2005: 257–76.

Klein, P. 2005b. "Reply to Ginet." In Steup and Sosa 2005: 149–52.

Klein, P. 2007a. "Human Knowledge and the Infinite Progress of Reasoning." *Philosophical Studies* 134: 1–17.

Klein, P. 2007b. "How to Be an Infinitist about Doxastic Justification." *Philosophical Studies* 134: 25–9.

Klein, P. 2010. "Infinitism." In Bernecker and Pritchard 2010: 45–56.

Korcz, K. A. 1997. "Recent Work on the Basing Relation." *American Philosophical Quarterly* 34: 171–91.

Kornblith, H. 1999. "Knowledge in Humans and Other Animals." *Philosophical Perspectives* 13: 327–46.

Kornblith, H. 2002. *Knowledge and Its Place in Nature*. Oxford: Oxford University Press.

Kornblith, H. 2009. "A Reliabilist Solution to the Problem of Promiscuous Bootstrapping." *Analysis* 690: 263–7.

Kornblith, H. 2010. "Belief in the Face of Controversy." In Feldman and Warfield 2010: 29–52.

Korcz, K. A. 1997. "Recent Work on the Basing Relation." *American Philosophical Quarterly* 34: 171–91.

Lackey, J. 2007. "Why We Don't Deserve Credit for Everything We Know." *Synthese* 158: 345–61.

Lackey, J. 2009. "Knowledge and Credit." *Philosophical Studies* 142: 27–42.

Lasonen-Aarnio, M. 2008. "Single-Premise Deduction and Risk." *Philosophical Studies* 141: 157–73.

Lehrer, K. 1971. "How Reasons Give Us Knowledge, or the Case of the Gypsy Lawyer." *The Journal of Philosophy* 68: 311–13.

Lehrer, K. 1991. "Reply to Dretske." *Grazer Philosophische Studien* 40: 31–5.

Lehrer, K. 2000a. *Theory of Knowledge*. Boulder, CO: Westview Press.

Lehrer, K. 2000b. "Acceptance and Belief Revisited." In Engel 2000: 209–20.

Lehrer, K. 2003. "Coherence, Circularity, and Consistency: Lehrer Replies." In Olsson 2003: 309–56.

Lehrer, K. and Paxson, T. 1969. "Knowledge: Undefeated Justified True Belief." *Journal of Philosophy* 66: 225–37.

Leite, A. 2005. "A Localist Solution to the Regress of Epistemic Justification." *Australasian Journal of Philosophy* 83: 395–421.

Leite, A. 2007. "Epistemic Instrumentalism and Reasons for Belief: A Response to Kelly's 'Epistemic Rationality as Instrumental Rationality: A Critique.'" *Philosophy and Phenomenological Research* 75: 456–64.

Lewis, C. I. 1929. *Mind and the World Order: Outline of a Theory of Knowledge.* New York: Charles Scribners.

Lewis, C. I. 1946. *An Analysis of Knowledge and Valuation.* Chicago, IL: Open Court.

Lewis, D. K. 1973. *Counterfactuals.* Oxford: Blackwell.

Luper, S. 2003. *The Skeptics: Contemporary Essays.* Aldershot: Ashgate Publishing Company.

Lyons, J. 1997. "Testimony, Induction and Folk Psychology." *Australasian Journal of Philosophy* 75: 163–78.

McCain, K. Forthcoming. "The Interventionist Account of Causation and the Basing Relation." *Philosophical Studies.*

MacFarlane, J. 2005. "The Assessment Sensitivity of Knowledge Attributions." *Oxford Studies in Epistemology* 1: 197–233.

MacFarlane, J. 2010. "Relativism and Knowledge Attributions." In Bernecker and Pritchard 2010: 536–44.

McKay, R. T. and Dennett, D. C. 2009. "The Evolution of Misbelief." *Behavioral and Brain Sciences* 32: 493–561.

Markie, P. J. 2005. "Easy Knowledge." *Philosophy and Phenomenological Research* 70: 406–16.

Markie, P. J. 2009 "Justification and Awareness." *Philosophical Studies* 146: 361–77.

Matilal, B. K. and Chakrabarti, A., eds. 1994. *Knowing from Words: Western and Indian Philosophical Analysis of Understanding and Testimony.* Dordrecht: Kluwer Academic Publishers.

Millar, A. 2010. Review of Hess 2010. *Notre Dame Philosophical Reviews.* At: <http://ndpr.nd.edu/review.cfm?id=20047>; accessed June 23, 2010.

Moser, P. ed. 2002. *The Oxford Handbook of Epistemology.* Oxford: Oxford University Press.

Mourenza, A, and Smith, N. D. Forthcoming. "Knowledge is Sexy." *Philo.*

Neta, R. and Rohrbaugh, G. 2004. "Luminosity and the Safety of Knowledge." *Pacific Philosophical Quarterly* 85: 396–406.

Norman, A. 1997. "Regress and the Doctrine of Epistemic Original Sin." *Philosophical Quarterly* 47: 477–94.

Nozick, R. 1981. *Philosophical Explanations.* Cambridge, MA: Harvard University Press.

Olsson, E. ed. 2003. *The Epistemology of Keith Lehrer.* Dordrecht: Kluwer Academic Publishers.

Pappas, G. S. ed. 1979. *Justification and Knowledge.* Dordrecht: D. Reidel.

Pappas G. S. and Swain, M. eds. 1978. *Essays on Knowledge and Justification.* Ithaca, NY: Cornell University Press.

Penhollow, T. M. and Young, M. 2008. "Predictors of Sexual Satisfaction: The Role of Body Image and Fitness." *Electronic*

Journal of Human Sexuality 11. At: <http://www.ejhs.org/volume11/Penhollow.htm>.

Plantinga, A. 1993a. *Warrant: The Current Debate*. New York: Oxford University Press.

Plantinga, A. 1993b. *Warrant and Proper Function*. New York: Oxford University Press.

Pollock, J. L. 1974. *Knowledge and Justification*. Princeton, NJ: Princeton University Press.

Pollock, J. L. 1984. "Reliability and Justified Belief." *Canadian Journal of Philosophy* 14: 103–14.

Pollock, J. L. and Cruz, J. 1999. *Contemporary Theories of Knowledge* 2nd edn. Lanham, MD: Rowman and Littlefield.

Popper, K. 1972. *Objective Knowledge*. Oxford: Oxford University Press.

Pritchard, D. H. 2005. *Epistemic Luck*. Oxford: Oxford University Press.

Pritchard, D. H. 2007. "Anti-Luck Epistemology." *Synthese* 158: 277–97.

Pritchard, D. H. 2010. "Knowledge and Understanding." In Pritchard, Millar, and Haddock 2010: 3–88.

Pritchard, D. H., Millar, A., and Haddock, A. 2010. *The Nature and Value of Knowledge: Three Investigations*. Oxford: Oxford University Press.

Pryor, J. 2000. "The Skeptic and the Dogmatist." *Noûs*, 34: 517–49.

Pryor, J. 2001. "Highlights of Recent Epistemology." *British Journal for the Philosophy of Science* 52: 95–124.

Pryor, J. 2004. "What's Wrong with Moore's Argument?" *Philosophical Issues* 14: 349–78.

Putnam, H. 1992. "Brains in a Vat." In DeRose and Warfield 1992: 27–42.

Quine, W. V. O. 1969a. *Ontological Relativity and other Essays*. New York: Columbia University Press.

Quine, W. V. O. 1969b. "Epistemology Naturalized." In Quine 1969a, 69–90.

Quine, W. V. O. 1969c. "Natural Kinds." In Quine 1969a: 57–75.

Quine, W. V. O. 1986. "Reply to White." In *Theories and Things*. Cambridge, MA: Belknap Press, 1–21.

Radford, C. 1966. "Knowledge – By Examples." *Analysis* 27: 1–11.

Rakoczy, H. 2008. "Pretence as Individual and Collective Intentionality." *Mind and Language* 23: 499–517.

Ramsey, F. P. 1990 [1929]. "Knowledge." In D. H. Mellor, ed., *F. P. Ramsey: Philosophical Papers*. Cambridge: Cambridge University Press. 110–11.

Ramsey, W. 2002. "Naturalism Defended." In Beilby 2002: 15–29.

Reebs, S. 2009. "Spider Builds Body Double to Catch Prey." *Natural History Magazine.* November 30, 2009. At: <http://www.livescience.com/animals/091130-orb-spider.html>.

Reid, T. 1997 [1764]. *An Inquiry into the Human Mind on the Principles of Common Sense.* Transl. and ed., D. R. Brookes. Pennsylvania, PA: Pennsylvania State University Press.

Riggs, W. D. 2002. "Reliability and the Value of Knowledge." *Philosophy and Phenomenological Research* 64: 79–96.

Ristau, C. ed. 1991a. *Cognitive Ethology: The Minds of Other Animals.* Mahwah, NJ: Lawrence Erlbaum Associates.

Ristau, C. 1991b. "Aspects of the Cognitive Ethology of an Injury-Feigning Bird, the Piping Plover." In Ristau 1991a: 91–126.

Rogers, J. and Matheson, J. Forthcoming. "Bergmann's Dilemma: Exit Strategies for Internalists." *Philosophical Studies.*

Ruse, M. 1986. *Taking Darwin Seriously.* Oxford: Blackwell.

Russell, Bertrand. 1929. *Our Knowledge of the Empirical World.* New York: W. W. Norton and Co.

Russell, Bruce. 2001. "Epistemic and Moral Duty." In Steup 2001: 22–32.

Ryle, G. 1932. "Systematically Misleading Expressions." *Proceedings of the Aristotelian Society* 32: 139–70.

Schaffer, J. 2005. "Contrastive Knowledge." In Hawthorne and Gendler 2005: 235–71.

Schaffer, J. and Szabo, Z. G. Forthcoming. "Epistemic Comparativism: A Contextualist Semantics for Knowledge Ascriptions." At: <http://www.jonathanschaffer.org/comparativism.pdf>.

Schechter, J. Forthcoming. "Rational Self-Doubt and the Failure of Closure." *Philosophical Studies.*

Schiffer, S. 1996. "Contextualist Solutions to Skepticism," *Proceedings of the Aristotelian Society* 96: 317–33.

Schmitt, F. ed. 1994. *Socializing Epistemology.* Lanham, MD: Rowman and Littlefield.

Schusterman, R. J., Southall, B. L., Kastak, D., and Kastak, C. R. 2001. "Pinniped Vocal Communication: Form and Function." *Proceedings of the 17th International Congress on Acoustics Proceedings.* Rome. 1–2.

Setiya, K. 2008. "Believing at Will." *Midwest Studies in Philosophy* 32: 36–52.

Seyfarth, R. M., Cheney, D. L., and Marler, P. 1980. "Monkey Responses to Three Different Alarm Calls: Evidence of Predator Classification and Semantic Communication." *Science* NS 210/4471: 801–3.

Shah, N. and Velleman, D. 2005. "Doxastic Deliberation." *Philosophical Review* 114: 497–534.

Shuker, K. P. N. 2001. *The Hidden Powers of Animals: Uncovering the Secrets of Nature*. London: Marshall Editions Ltd.

Smith, N. D. 2002. "Generic Knowledge." *American Philosophical Quarterly* 39: 343–57.

Sosa, E. 1997. "Reflective Knowledge in the Best Circles." *Journal of Philosophy* 94: 410–30.

Sosa, E. 2007. *A Virtue Epistemology: Apt Belief and Reflective Knowledge, Volume 1*. New York: Oxford University Press.

Sosa, E. 2009. "Timothy Williamson's *Knowledge and Its Limits*." In Greenbough and Pritchard 2009: 203–16.

Stanley, J. 2004. "On the Linguistic Basis for Contextualism." *Philosophical Studies* 119: 119–46.

Stanley, J. 2005. *Knowledge and Practical Interests*. Oxford: Oxford University Press.

Stanley, J. and Williamson, T. 2001 "Knowing How." *Journal of Philosophy*, 98: 411–44.

Steup, M. 1988. "The Deontic Conception of Epistemic Justification." *Philosophical Studies* 58: 65–84.

Steup, M. 2000. "Doxastic Voluntarism and Epistemic Deontology." *Acta Analytica* 15: 25–56.

Steup, M, ed. 2001. *Knowledge, Truth, and Duty: Essays on Epistemic Justification, Responsibility, and Virtue*. New York: Oxford University Press.

Steup, M. and Sosa, E., eds. 2005. *Contemporary Debates in Epistemology*. Oxford: Blackwell.

Stich, S. 1990. *The Fragmentation of Reason*. Cambridge, MA: MIT Press.

Tierney, H. and Smith, N. D. Forthcoming. "Lehrer on the Basing Relation." Special issue of *Philosophical Studies* dedicated to the Philosophy of Keith Lehrer. M. Fürst and G. Melchior, guest editors.

Tomberlin, J. E., ed. 1988. *Philosophical Perspectives 2: Epistemology*. Atascadero, CA: Ridgeview Publishing Co.

Triplett, T. 1990. "Recent Work on Foundationalism." *American Philosophical Quarterly* 27: 93–116.

Turri, J. 2011. "Believing for a Reason." *Erkenntnis* 74: 383–97.

Unger, P. 1979. *Ignorance*. Oxford: Oxford University Press.

Van Cleve, J. 2003. "Is Knowledge Easy – or Impossible? Externalism as the Only Alternative to Skepticism." In Luper 2003: 45–59.

Van Inwagen, P. 1996. "It is Wrong, Always, Everywhere, and for Anyone, to Believe Anything, Upon Insufficient Evidence." In Jordan and Howard-Snyder 1996: 137–54.

Velleman, D. 2000. "On the Aim of Belief." In D. Velleman, ed., *The Possibility of Practical Reason*. Oxford: Oxford University Press.

Vogel, J. 1999. "The New Relevant Alternatives Theory." *Philosophical Perspectives* 13: 155–80.

Vogel J. 2007. "Subjunctivitis." *Philosophical Studies* 134: 73–88.

Watanabe, S. and Huber, L. 2006. "Animal Logics: Decisions in the Absence of Human Language." *Animal Cognition* 9: 235–45.

White, R. 2005. "Epistemic Permissiveness." *Philosophical Perspectives* 19: 445–59.

Williamson, T. 2000. *Knowledge and Its Limits*. Oxford: Oxford University Press.

Williamson, T. 2005. "Contextualism, Subject-Sensitive Invariantism, and Knowledge of Knowledge." *The Philosophical Quarterly* 55: 213–35.

Wright, C. 2001. "On Basic Logical Knowledge." *Philosophical Studies* 106: 41–85.

Zagzebski, L. T. 1994. "The Inescapability of Gettier Problems." *Philosophical Quarterly* 44: 65–73.

Zagzebski, L. T. 1996. *Virtues of the Mind: An Inquiry into the Nature of Virtue and the Ethical Foundations of Knowledge*. Cambridge: Cambridge University Press.

Zagzebski, L. T. 1999. "What is Knowledge?" In Greco and Sosa 1999: 92–116.

Zagzebski, L. T. 2003. "Intellectual Motivation and the Good of Truth." In DePaul and Zagzebski 2003: 134–54.

Index